An Alternative Textbook in Special Education

An Alternative Textbook in Special Education

People, Schools and Other Institutions

Edited by
Burton Blatt, Douglas Biklen and Robert Bogdan
The Center on Human Policy, Syracuse University

LOVE PUBLISHING COMPANY
Denver, Colorado 80222

Copyright © 1977 Love Publishing Company
Printed in the U.S.A.
ISBN 0-89108-073-2
Library of Congress Catalog Card Number 77-77698
10 9 8 7 6 5 4 3 2 1

CONTENTS

PREFACE vii

PART ONE   TRADITIONAL CONCEPTS
AND SETTINGS: THE PROBLEM 1

1   Issues and Values, *Burton Blatt* 3
2   The Politics of Institutions, *Douglas Biklen* 29
3   Attendants' Perspectives and Programming on
    Wards in State Schools, *Robert Bogdan, Steven
    Taylor, Bernard de Grandpre, and Sondra Haynes* 85
4   The Public Schools, *Steven Apter* 105
5   The Integration-Segregation Issue: Some
    Questions, Assumptions, and Facts, *Burton Blatt* 127
6   Exclusion, *Douglas Biklen* 135
7   Surplus Children, *Douglas Biklen* 153
8   Missing Agendas in Social Policy: Head Start
    and the Handicapped, *Robert Bogdan and
    Douglas Biklen* 167

PART TWO   ALTERNATIVE CONCEPTS AND
SETTINGS: THE PROMISE 183

9   Research Orientations in Special Education,
    Burton Blatt 185
10 A Phenomenological Approach to "Mental
    Retardation," *Steven Taylor and Robert Bogdan* 193
11 Handicapism in America, *Douglas Biklen and
    Robert Bogdan* 205
12 The Judged, Not the Judges
    An Insider's View of Mental Retardation, *Robert
    Bogdan and Steven Taylor* 217

13 Translating Psychological Concepts into Action,
    *Seymour Sarason, Murray Levine, I. Ira Goldenberg,
    Dennis Cherlin, and Edward Bennett* 233

14 What Teachers Need to Know, *Frank Garfunkel
    and Burton Blatt* 263

15 Psycho-Educational Assessment, Curriculum
    Development, and Clinical Research with the
    "Different" Child, *Burton Blatt and Frank Garfunkel* 277

16 Resistance to Change, *Douglas Biklen* 295

17 The Principle of Normalization, *Wolf Wolfensberger* 305

18 Normalizing Activation for the Profoundly
    Retarded and/or Multiply Handicapped, *Wolf
    Wolfensberger* 329

19 Legal Change for the Handicapped through
    Litigation, *Alan Abeson* 351

20 Advocacy Comes of Age, *Douglas Biklen* 391

Preface

The three editors are colleagues at Syracuse University. During the past four years we have engaged ourselves with the usual many trials and the usual few accomplishments encountered during the creation of our Center on Human Policy. From those experiences, we began to better comprehend that special education may be connected more with ideological than pedagogical issues. Yet most, if not all, of the standard texts in the field deal with the latter almost exclusively. This we view as unfortunate, misleading in the extreme. And this is what we hope to rectify with the volume before you. For example, examine the current rage in education — individualized instruction. One can hardly pick up a contemporary book on teaching or teachers without reading something about this subject. In fact, implicit in the continuing search for better methods, better curricula, and better administrative design of schools is the conviction that methodology and, to a much lesser extent, process are everything.

We do not dismiss or hold less valuable those expositions of special education dealing with pedagogical and psychological matters. Rather, we attempt here to raise other equally compelling issues — those dealing with goals more than means, values more than competencies, power more than authority, process more than method. To illustrate, let us focus on the prepotent difficulty shared by most so-called handicapped children in the public schools. It is not that their instruction has been insufficiently individualized or inadequately attended to, or that too little time or consideration has been given to their learning needs. These are not the essential problems, although they may be present. The pervasive difficulty faced by the so-called handicapped is that *expectations* for them have not been individualized. We individualize instruction but expect people to meet stipulated criteria eventually. Those who do not are relegated to the segregated special class, excluded from school, or institutionalized. If goals for people were individualized to the degree that instruction is, we would not need or want as many institutions or other segregated programs as now flourish in our society.

Why then, we have asked ourselves, are we so loath to individualize goals — better, to give people the freedom to individualize their own goals, the right to shape their own lives? We have struggled with this question and have collected a great deal of data relating to it. The product of our thinking is this book.

We discuss the original promise of generic "special education" and "mental health" for the future, and the monolith they have become. The central issue embedded in every chapter, not far from the surface of every argument, is that single block of ideological stone — that massive, solid, uniform, no-option, no-alternative monolithic system. At the core of this book is the argument that we must maximize variance in society and thus enrich us all; that we must maximize opportunities and options for all and thus permit each person a truly equal opportunity to develop. We must create human settings where people are not victimized and need no longer be the victimizers.

We also attempt throughout the book, especially in the first chapter, to illuminate the hypothesis that development is a function of practice and training; i.e., that intelligence is educable. However, our society has organized programs for children with special needs and has set priorities for those children in such ways as to illustrate that people do not change, that alternatives to segregated settings are not necessary, that segregated classes and institutions serve us well. We have tried to elaborate on the "nature-nurture" question; although there is little scientific evidence to permit definitive answers, there is considerable clinical observation to indicate that human beings *can* change, that intelligence *is* educable. As teachers, our essential task is to help learning and intellectual growth rather than to make determinations as to whether someone can or cannot change.

We have attempted to reinforce the idea, enunciated since the beginning of civilized society, that as human beings all people are valuable. We hope that one day humankind will take this concept more seriously than it does now. We also have tried to deal with the myth of terms such as "mental retardation" and "emotional disturbance." Witness the recent nomenclature change in the field of mental retardation, in which a decision to redefine "psychometric retardation" as at least two standard deviations, rather than one, on the wrong side of the mean reduced the theoretic eligibility from 16 percent to 2 percent. Obviously, "mental retardation," like other so-called disabilities, is more an administrative than a scientific term.

We have attempted to reinforce the conception that the child in school knows what is good for him, or at least knows something about what is good for him, and that curricula should be designed and implemented around that notion. Similarly, we have tried to encourage the idea that teachers know what is best for teachers. Lastly, we have tried to describe reasons why we must return some responsibility to the consumers of services. It is not that professionals are less able or less trustworthy than consumers; but they are different, with different agendas and priorities.

And what about priorities? In this culture we revere life, as well we should, and we seek to demonstrate in every way possible our intention to protect it, even in those most disabled. We house the state school resident and create segregated schools for the so-called trainable mentally retarded because we are fearful that these children may otherwise be hurt. Yet in our zeal to protect, in our reverence for life, we have forgotten another concept — the concept of freedom. We revere life while we prohibit freedom for those who must be protected "for their own good," in spite of their wishes, because the state or other agency knows what is best for them. This book deals with our personal priorities and the belief that freedom is more important than protection, that one's humanity is more significant than one's competence.

In view of the seeming flood of conventional books published in recent years, the editors invited the participation of colleagues not always associated with the field of special education. However, all have considerable experience with children. The editors themselves are examples of diverse interests, training, and experience.

Each of the contributors was invited to prepare a chapter, setting down as plainly and as simply as he could what he had learned about children with special needs during his years of work. We did not require that authors bring either heavy documentation or a traditionally academic format to their assignments. Rather, we encouraged them to offer challenging questions and suggestions, presenting issues in ways that might be unique and might hold promise for new solutions to old problems. Obviously, we could not expect each presentation to be a necessary and coordinated part of a single philosophical fabric; but as editors, we grouped chapters in a logical sequence, bringing to the volume a degree of unification and meaning. Our intention was to prepare a book that would stimulate fruitful thinking and behavior on behalf of children with special needs, and to give further expression to a growing national trend that has as its goal the normalization of all people.

A word about labels: In our culture, to be able to label something permits a claim to understanding it. Thus, with issues so complex as these with which we are dealing here, some of us attempt to hide behind such traditional labels as mental retardation, emotional disturbance, learning disability, or cultural deprivation. But despite our disdain for their inappropriate usage, and despite the problems such terms create, we do not wish to develop a new professional jargon which might distort serious issues (adding to the cumulative substantive ignorance in our field) or to contribute to the general illiteracy. Therefore, the editors compromised — we have used the traditional terms only when we felt they were necessary, and we have permitted our collaborators a free choice.

Deliberately, we have *not* included chapters dealing with disability categories; by this decision, we hope to make an important point: We do not want to contribute in any way to the further locking in of children to these categories and, thus, to stigmatized life styles. The influence of special categories and labels has been pervasive. Not only have they separated children with special needs into narrow and stigmatized groupings, but also they have lent credence to the notion that each category represents and delineates uniform needs of all those who fall within its boundaries. Further, when society categorizes individuals in this manner, it creates images of personal deficit rather than of potential.

Related to labeling is the popular belief that children with special needs are best served in special placements; that they are limited essentially by their own inadequacies or problems; and that the best way to remove the disability is to treat the child. This notion is overwhelmingly disputed in the literature. We hope this book will reveal how educators and others might benefit from an analysis of the child's total environment, in and out of school, and how the process of interaction between children and others is often more explanatory than individual children's disabilities or behaviors.

BB
DB
RB

PART ONE

TRADITIONAL CONCEPTS AND SETTINGS:

the Problem

1

Issues and Values

Burton Blatt

Soon after I began teaching in 1949, I embarked upon a career with the so-called "mentally retarded." During the subsequent years, I reached the basic conclusions that:

1. People traditionally underestimate their potential for changing or — to use a more common term — for learning.
2. Pessimism concerning the conditions of change becomes a self-fulfilling prophecy. People do not learn when they become convinced that they cannot or should not learn.
3. Under proper conditions, it can be demonstrated that intelligence is plastic; i.e., intelligence is a function of practice and training. That we have not been able to accomplish widespread change in people is, I believe,

The author is grateful to Frank Garfunkel, Richard Hungerford, Seymour Sarason, and Thomas Szasz, whose generosity contributed greatly to development of the ideas embedded in this chapter, originally published in much lengthened form as, "A Basic Kit to Confront the Human Disposal Authority, Department of Subnormal Affairs of the Monolith, in This Land of Opportunity," *Journal of Education*, 1974, *156*, 70-104.

less a defect of this hypothesis than it is of our practice.

As I remarked in an address before the Massachusetts legislature in 1970, there is a dark side of every mirror, a side beyond inspection (Blatt, 1970). While our optimism and pride as a people in the Declaration of Independence and Constitution are reflected by the gains made in civil rights, and some achievements in the area of mental retardation, surely a dark side in the evolution of our civilization in this mid-twentieth century must be noted for the deeply unremitting, unrewarding lives of drudgery and pain we inflict upon the institutionalized and all others who are needlessly segregated.

I said to the legislature — and believe even more firmly today — that no resident of a state school needs to live in a denuded condition, needs to be a head banger, or needs to be locked in solitary confinement. Almost every resident of a state school can be taught to eat meals independently and to live among others without the use of physical restraints. All building odors can be eliminated without the need for even more repugnant chemical treatments or electronic gadgetry that mask the sources of these odors but do not eliminate the causes: filth and neglect. If intelligence is educable and people can change and learn, the concept applies to the retarded, to those who minister to their needs — to all of us. We can change our view of human potential and thus promote change in others. Ultimately, we can create a society that does not need closed institutions. The lives of Anne Sullivan and Helen Keller speak volumes about this concept.

The term "monolith" is central to some of the ideas in this chapter. I use it in a special way — to mean a closed, no-option system, as the monolith of mental health or the monolith of the educational establishment. The education monolith involves a network of seemingly open, but actually closed, systems that are integral parts of a larger whole. A monolith is created and sustains itself because of an absence of alternatives. The problem is not with officialdom's good intentions, but with a limited vision of human potential and what the world may become.

What are the consequences of such unitary approaches? What price must society pay for a contemporary system that has a fragile optimism and too little vision, where the only hope is to expect a future that is little more than a larger portion of the past? In that culture, to know one's direction would require merely to look back in anguish. One could not learn from history; one would relive it and relive it again. It may be that such a culture is required not only to produce but also to sustain policies supposedly on behalf of children with special needs, which in reality deprive those children of basic developmental opportunities. Perhaps in this age we are products of that culture.

The areas of special education and mental health have certain striking affinities: They deal with similar populations and have similar values and objectives. Yet, those responsible for special education know little about institutional caretakers and vice versa. Obviously, the grossly horrifying institutions you read about, and some of us have seen, are different from most conventional schools. In several basic ways, however, the caretaker or the client are no different from any other human being — each is a victim and each ultimately a victimizer. In the institution and in the conventional school, sufficient options are not available for families, for children with special needs, and — of equal importance — for teachers and other staff. The disdain of one generation becomes the enthusiasm of another, because institutions and schools, more than open environments, are vulnerable to fashions of the moment which dupe us into believing that, when we follow the fashion, we are the height of chic and enlightenment. Possibly, had it not been for the monolith, special education would have led to something grander than the creation of the largest and most pervasive segregated special class and institutional system known to civilized people.

The promise of special education was not a special curriculum, or special methods, or even special teachers. It was to demonstrate that each person can contribute to the larger society; that all people are valuable; that a human being is entitled to developmental opportunities; and that development is plastic. The gifts that this movement was to bestow were optimism and belief in the human ethos, charity and love for our brothers, and the conviction that our work is not to judge who can or cannot change, but rather to fulfill the hope that all people can change; each person can learn. For the promise to be kept, for these things to occur beyond wish or fantasy, one must begin with oneself. Before I ask the world to change, *I* must change.

THE PERSPECTIVE

With admonitions from the past and the present, too many scholars appear afraid of being wrong or wronged, seem intimidated by critics, colleagues, their shadows, and other ghosts. There is a joylessness in our literature, and it is suffocating us while advancing neither science nor mankind. How many ideas change a person, and possibly change others because of him? Can we name a handful of human beings whose ideas so profoundly influenced us that our own works would otherwise have been different? There have been few. Yet this has not been a completely barren time. We have had our share of unique human beings whose influence will remain long after their words and books are forgotten. Therefore, admonitions notwithstanding, one who has participated in this period might feel obligated to document it, both for those who were not present and for those who were there but missed the excitement.

I want to list some of the ideas and a few of the people and movements that still influence our lives. I want to analyze what we have become, what we have accomplished for people, and what the world is about for the disabled, the sick, the different, the frail — anyone in jeopardy. This chapter is for those who seek to do battle with the monolith. It may prepare you to think differently about people, their natures, their capacities to change and contribute and rise to new heights. It is less about the so-called "handicapped" and what we can do for them than it is about people and what we must do for each other. The day may come when I will feel that I am entitled not only to an equal educational opportunity, but also to the right to live in an educated society. Thus, I am franchised only when you are franchised.

The trick is to both guarantee such entitlements and deliberately maximize human variance. The objective is to offer each human being opportunities to live in peaceful surroundings and engage in his work and interests within a community included, not hidden away, in a land where no longer will there be special institutions to cage a human spirit.

SINS OF THE PROPHETS:
A SHORT PREJUDICED HISTORY

In the beginning, humans were created, and then humans created the criteria for being human. In the beginning, such criteria were simple: The mere emergence from a woman's belly made one human. When no person had language, humans needed no language. When no person had tools, humans needed no tools.

Subsequent discoveries led to the invention of laws, books, print, civilization, science, and attempts to control the environment. Humans sought new understandings of themselves, their relationships with others, and with a higher being. All the while, new criteria were invented and stipulated, first to classify, then to separate and set aside, and eventually to defile, to dehumanize, to murder.

People with special characteristics — the blind, the deaf, the retarded, the special for a particular time period, or the special irrespective of time or culture — became consistent targets for those who would separate one human being from another. With each separation, prophets would announce that

7

solutions to problems were at hand; the light at the end of the tunnel would now shine brightly. The ancients had their solutions, not humane but honest and without sham: Go, mother, take your sick child to the mountaintop; there the gods will decide who should live, who should die, who will be inscribed in the Book of Life or the Book of Final Decree. So they went, some to the mountains, and the Hansels and Gretels to the forests.

But our priests told us that God was not pleased: Go not to the mountains and the forests. Thou shalt not kill. We, the State, will take your child in our asylums. We will care for the sick, the mad, the idiot child that you have spawned and let loose in this cruel and hard world. Certain dissenting prophets told the people that the god-state was not pleased with that solution: We must design new homes, small homes, regional homes, halfway homes, group homes, normalized homes, unit homes, extended-care homes; but we must keep separate those who belong with us from those who do not. We must guarantee to families who have a child with special needs that the family will be here and the child will be there. This is a Great American Dream.

Consequently, it was almost universally agreed that special homes for mental defectives should be created. The doctors believed that such homes would be healthier for eligible patients than the precariousness of community existence. The psychologists believed that such homes would prove more therapeutic than other arrangements. The educators believed that such homes would provide greater developmental opportunities than would public community facilities. The economists believed that such homes would be less expensive. Public safety officials believed that such homes would be more protective of both the general society and the defectives. The politicians believed that such homes were what the people wanted. The parents thought they should be grateful for whatever was allocated to relieve their problems. The defectives, not expected to think, were never asked to comment on the matter.

HISTORIES, VANITIES, AND DELUSIONS

Research

History can be a strength of society or its anchor. We can learn from it or not. In the field we call "special education," history has not served us well because we have not learned from it. Note the discrepancy between the research and the practice in special education for the mentally retarded; note, too, that research in the broader social sciences has neither prohibited poor practice nor stimulated good practice. Is research little more than something for scholars to do, with the major value being in the process of doing it rather than in the results, or even the implementation?

Since the early 1930s, hundreds of researchers, involving millions of dollars, millions of hours, and thousands of children and their teachers, have attempted to study the effectiveness of curricula, methods, administrative designs, and other factors that contribute to variance among special education programs for disabled children. Using the field of mental retardation as one example, the dollars and the hours essentially have been wasted, and the products are generally useless. It is not that the research has been dishonest or even "untrue"; it has been merely trivial or irrelevant. For example, research on the efficacy of special classes for the so-called mentally retarded fails to indicate the superiority of special classes over more conventional classroom settings, although it should be noted that neither are the regular grades as they now exist proper placements for the mentally retarded.

The earliest studies comparing mildly mentally retarded children in regular and special classes found that special class children did poorly in physical, personality, and academic areas when compared with children in regular classes (Bennett, 1932; Pertsch, 1936). Research by this writer (Blatt, 1956) was the first postwar study roughly analogous to the Bennett and Pertsch studies. I, too, found that special class placements did not appear to enhance the development of these so-called

9

mentally retarded children. Cassidy and Stanton (1959) and Johnson (1961), among many others, also conducted projects that were basically isomorphic with the aforementioned studies, reporting similar results; i.e., it has yet to be demonstrated that placement of mildly mentally retarded children in conventional special classes meets their needs in ways that regular class placement cannot. Studies concerned with so-called "trainable mentally retarded" (TMR) children have been no more successful in demonstrating the superiority of special class placements (Cain & Levine, 1961; Dunn & Hottel, 1958).

A more recent review (Blatt & Garfunkel, 1973) confirmed the continued popularity of these efficacy studies, as well as the continued profusion of research on curriculum and teaching methods. In one way, the abundance of research of this type is disconcerting and frustrating. However, we have learned important lessons from these efficacy and methodology studies — if we remember those lessons well enough to take them seriously. The accumulation of evidence vis-a-vis special classes, special curricula, and special methodologies leads to a *clear rejection* of the special class-regular class dichotomy, special-nonspecial curricula, and special-nonspecial methodology as defensible independent research variables. Although there may be rare exceptions to this conclusion, the regularity of data findings suggests strongly that children's experiences are not systematically different if they are, for example, in one or another class. A child can have individual attention, warmth, support, friends, and an exciting program in either class. Furthermore, his home varies independently of the kind of class he is in; it contributes so potently to variance that the home may well drown out the effects of any differences connected with education programming (Blatt & Garfunkel, 1969; Coleman et al., 1966).

Why is there a plethora of research activity dealing with the effectiveness of curricula and methods and, on the other hand, a virtual absence of studies concerned with the effects of the home and community on learning and achievement? In view of the enormous support to compensatory education and subsequent documentation during the past decade of a persistent and pervasive relationship between socioeconomic class and educational achievement (Coleman et al., 1966; Hurley, 1969), it should be apparent that families and communities have a great deal of influence on the education and development of young children. Not only is the dearth of research dealing specifically with the home and community discouraging, but when such variables are employed as part of an intervention design, they are usually trivial in nature; i.e., they do not have particular meaning or importance, nor are they expected to contribute much to the researcher's general understanding of the problems. Asking parents of Head Start children questions about how they feel toward their children, toward Head Start, or toward their community does not deliver revealing data. It amounts to using a teaspoon to do the work of a steam shovel. Similarly, attention to socioeconomic status does not, in itself, attend to the relationship between poverty and the ways that poor families, or families with mentally retarded children, or any families deal with schools.

Why the disinterest in family-community studies and — in spite of a discouraging history of neither research payoffs nor program development — why the continued adherence to experimental and quasi-experimental efficacy-curricula-methods studies? An answer may lie in the widely held belief that when one diverges into other than traditional research methodologies, many months of observation usually are required. Secondly, most researchers are loath to use the less well-established instruments, which have uncertain reliabilities, and the long and difficult data collection procedures that characterize family-community studies. Probably, researchers take satisfaction in doing relatively "clean" research, even if it has neither meaning nor relevancy. Researchers, like other people, have needs to conceptualize and pursue problems in management terms. A covert factor may be related to whatever biases researchers have concerning the concept of change itself. To discover that others can change implies that

11

the researcher too can change. He could be somebody other than who he is. Expectations for change are tied up with the lives of the expectors as much as with those for whom they have greater or lesser expectations. Designs, variables, procedures, and analyses certainly are influenced by these expectations.

Although all of the above are reasonable explanations for the continued interest exhibited by researchers in traditional attempts to study the effects of stipulated interventions, it is doubtful that those explanations, even collectively, could continue to persuade intelligent and educated professionals to devote themselves to an endeavor that fails to reinforce either the researchers or the public at large that sponsors them. There must be additional reasons for this pollution of feeble research on trivial problems.

During the years, and to the present time, many well-reasoned theories and methods have been presented to both explain behavior and describe ways to modify it efficiently and beneficially. We may label and discuss these developments either in terms of methodological pronouncements or in their fuller contexts — the application of method derived from theory. For the sake of simplicity, I will refer to, for example, the Montessori method or Moore's responsive-environments method, knowing that they have rich and exciting theoretical histories that deserve discussion in their own rights.

An examination of the more spectacular methods that have been developed in pedagogy and psychology has led me to the following observation; it is based on a review of the lives and works of such early greats as Itard, Seguin, Sullivan, Freud, and Montessori, as well as the study of contemporary methodologists including Skinner, Frostig, Omar Moore, and others who have developed reading, mathematics, and special and general methodological approaches to teaching children: Each significant methodological contribution begins with an individual who is interacting with a child or a group of children in such a way as to promote extraordinary change. This change is noted and causes astonishment and excitement. Why are the children doing so well? Why are they learning to read so quickly? Why is mathematics no longer a horrendous puzzlement? Why is the sick person getting better?

Closer attention is given to the interaction between the teacher (or therapist, or experimentor, or psychologist) and the child. A careful description of the interaction is reported. From this inductive approach, a recording of the educational or therapeutic presentation is prepared; a new "method" unfolds. The teacher is teaching in a certain way, using a certain style, and promoting certain desired responses. Various people develop collaborations with the methodologist, around the method. They study it in its original natural setting. They experiment with it. They refine and modify it. They become infatuated with the notion that the gains they observe are dependent on the order, style, and materials of the presentation. They learn a good deal about this method, the responses it ordinarily generates, its frailties, its problems and how to overcome them, and its most efficient utilization. They train others to use the method. They write books about it and develop elaborate ways to present, test, and relate it to a host of other methods, treatments, and conditions. Hence, we have literally thousands of studies on how almost infinite varieties of individuals behave — for example, in psychoanalytic settings, what the behaviors mean in innumerable circumstances, what responses should be presumed to be pathological and what responses are healthy.

Several things strike me about individuals who have been responsible for the development of spectacular methods. From an examination of the literature and from my own observations of the current scene, each appeared to be a gifted teacher and interactor. Each appeared to have a powerfully charismatic personality that brought droves of disciples into the fold. An analysis of the research relating to spectacular methodologies produces other interesting conditions about which to speculate. From the sensationalist method of Itard and Seguin to the present works of Doman and Delacato,

Omar Moore, Bereiter and Engelmann, the new math, and the special reading programs, verification studies of special methodologies find less conclusive, less promising, less significant results than those found by the method's originator(s). For example, Omar Moore has demonstrated a good deal more with automated or nonautomated typewriters than have those who replicated his work. The most significant changes observed in children using the Doman-Delacato methodology can be observed at their Institute for the Development of Human Potential.

If a method has an integrity of its own, if it is not almost singularly dependent on the skill and interactive ability of the applicator and the social-psychological setting of its application, it should work when properly applied by other capable people. One would suppose that psychoanalysis, for example, after more than a half century of the analytic model, would have advanced, on methodological refinements alone, beyond its current place in the psychological scheme of things. There is no doubt that some methods work well. There is no doubt that some methods work better for some people than do other methods. Further, there is no doubt that some methods are more logically conceived, implemented, and utilized than others. There is a great deal of doubt, however, that any method is far removed from those who employ it, understand it, have faith in it, and experiment with it. There is only assurance that great teachers have great methods and poor teachers have poor methods — irrespective of the methods the teachers employ, and of the fact that, regularly, great teachers and poor teachers utilize similar methods in contiguous settings.

Yet, the vanity and delusion are sustained — the vanity that we have effective curricula and methods, and the delusion that these contribute most to change in children. History teaches us that there are no especially superior theories and methods of studying and dealing with behavior, that there are only teachers and psychologists whose endeavors yield low productivity. Precision and vigorous controls are not available in the study of natural settings. We should have learned by now that only extreme changes in placement, procedure, or opportunity can possibly produce measurable effects on individuals. One hour each day for "enrichment," a summer Head Start program, even a special class, much less a special method or curriculum, will be as effective as any trivial intrusion into an enormously complicated human totality.

What research should be done then — and why? Let us set aside, for the moment, most educational research, which has used traditional designs such as efficacy studies, follow-up studies of children in special and regular classes, and studies of different methodological and curriculum approaches. There may be more appropriate ways to study teaching-learning environments. These ways utilize research perspectives that may be characterized as "process" and focus on human interactive concerns rather than methodological concerns. As methods do not exist outside unique psychological-educational settings, only a naive or cynical researcher could conclude that the superiority of his method has direct and specific transferability to other educational settings. Our strategy recommends the study of children and adults in different educational environments, generalizing about their interactions rather than the procedures utilized to promote their interactions. We believe that independent variation in the classroom obtains more from interaction effects (what we now usually try to neutralize or ignore in most experiments) than from methodological or curricula effects (what we now usually design as "independent variables").

As unpopular as this idea may be, the history of research in the social sciences suggests that its primary value is for those who do the research. If it is helpful to the greater society, or disabled children, or the child you teach, all to the good, but the payoff to the larger community results as those researchers and their various colleagues, and *their* colleagues, influence us.

The above considerations cause me to recommend that we should not promote studies that examine the effects of a

15

special curriculum (or talking typewriters or open classrooms) on the intellectual development of mentally retarded children. Studies of this kind are doomed to demonstrate little, and — more seriously — will scarcely influence even the researchers. Rather, we might study a group of children, their teachers, their schools, their families, and their community: how the effects of our intervention changed the "traffic patterns" of parents vis-à-vis the school than how the intervention stimulated IQ changes in the children; how the intervention influenced the community, the city leaders, and the media in directions related to issues such as equal educational opportunities, advocacy, options for people, and consumer rights and responsibilities. As long as we continue to study children developmentally, utilizing single-variable approaches, we will continue to exaggerate group differences as we attempt to minimize individual differences; we will continue to reinforce the position of those who claim that you can't make a silk purse out of a sow's ear, that dull children must always remain dull, that nothing is curable and hardly anything preventable. The dominant research strategy in our culture virtually guarantees the triviality of our research.

Teaching

The preparation of teachers in special education, regular education, you-name-it education, has not suffered from a lack of discussion. However, the preparation of teachers remains essentially an unstudied problem in education (Sarason, Davidson, & Blatt, 1962); unstudied for the same reasons that research activities in our field are of little consequence. As researchers seek better methods and general solutions to pedagogical problems, professors in our teachers' colleges teach "best" methods and "best" curricula, hoping to fortify students with enough techniques for them to teach well and, so it turns out, to teach without having to think independently. The relationship between educational research and teacher preparation is so direct as to hardly permit the separation of one from the other, each activity mobilized in search of universal, happy, and simple solutions to complex problems and issues.

Those who prepare teachers make the extraordinarily puzzling extraordinarily simple in their quest for ways to educate the child. In their distrust of the unknown, they return to some simple life of order and design, of cherished theory and trusted method. The pattern continues in the same way that young children maintain fantasy lives for long periods of time, and in the same way that escapist adults believe that by ignoring a problem, it will go away. We continue to grind out teachers whose teaching reflects the conception that education is primarily what one puts into children rather than what one can get out of them, teachers who at best can claim they are good technicians and im-plementors. Our competency-based efforts, our technologies, our new certifications or noncertifications are making matters worse rather than better. There is a difference between the competent teacher and the teacher who can demonstrate stipulated competencies.

Further, the educational enterprise endures its problems and critics with stiff-necked forbearance; hardly anything changes. Given the circumstances of our teachers and their training, given the world as it is and what it was, the future portends yesterday. The educational enterprise is a monolith, no more capable of dealing with revisionism than any other monolith. Although the possibilities for flexibility and change are embedded in a monolith (or it crumbles), the only actual freedom is contained within the confines of rigidly enforced rules, regulations, customs, and values. This rigidity is found in children's classrooms because their teachers found it in their classrooms, because their teachers' teachers found it in theirs.

Sameness of mind is the mortar that binds and strengthens the monolith. In the elementary classroom, a child who remembers well scores well. In the education col-lege, the student who consumes and implements is preparing

17

for the "Teacher of the Year" award. We train technicians in our colleges who, from the beginning and to the present, seek technical competency. We train for technical skills as we train people to live apart from those who have lesser skills, or who appear different, or who think different, or whose metaphors are different. Essentially, our technical consumer education promotes an invariance of life and spirit, both by the influence of the technology on us and by our subsequent behavior as consuming experience-bound beings.

Consequently, there is an apparent — and in a sense, real — flexibility and innovation to be found in our schools: We advertise segregated schools, open schools, free schools, and ungraded schools in the educational supermarket for the same reasons others advertise Chevrolets, Keds, and popsicles; we believe we have the best product or, at the least, we wish to convince the consumer that our products offer the most value. As a result, our schools virtually have become franchised — duplicative in the same way General Motors and Howard Johnson are duplicative — strengthened by our teachers' colleges, who have always been educational supermarkets: "See all the goodies we offer; choose within this wide array, and consume to your satiation level. Buy, but do not create. Do not struggle to understand the process from the product. Do not go beyond the boundaries of the marketplace. Be different, but do not be different from any of the rest of us. Be a part of this wonderful educational slot-machine world." The franchised school and the educational supermarket are the enemies of those who would seek an education for themselves — not because of any deliberate wickedness, but because they represent a limited view of human potential.

What does humanity receive for its educational investment? Without doubt, most children learn to read and write; some progress far beyond their teachers' hopes, some far beyond their teachers. It is not that a consumer orientation prevents learning; it merely interferes with it. To the degree that teachers do not discourage abstract behavior and classroom variance, learning (changing) is more likely to occur. To the degree that teachers — elementary and university teachers alike — impose a standard curriculum, method, school organization, even content (perhaps *especially* content), the educational monolith will thrive.

We need more child and teacher independence (thus, fostering their interdependence), learning toward greater generalizations, inductive models, options, and the maximization of heterogeneous groupings of people. I am suggesting that educational fields should be studied from historical rather than prescriptive perspectives: Curricula, methods, media, and school organizations might be understood best in the context of what is accomplished rather than what must be attempted. This strategy seems less restrictive and promises greater discovery and illumination than the traditional prescriptive "best method" strategy. The literature on pedagogy and psychology confirms this position; i.e., there is no consistent significant source of independent (treatment) variation obtaining from special methods, curricula strategies, or administrative organizations. Further, I believe that the process of creating educational environments contributes more to independent variation than the environments themselves, especially when these are artificially contrived from educational supermarkets.

Educability

During the years, my work has dealt with several recurring themes, such inevitably anchored to the hypothesis of mankind's educability. The first such theme deals with the nature-nurture question. Although there is little hard scientific evidence to permit definitive answers to this age-old issue, I have concluded that there is considerable clinical observation to suggest that people can change. The work of Itard, the autobiography of Helen Keller, the works of Mae Seagoe, Harold Skeels, Samuel Kirk, Seymour Sarason, and my own experiences and research lend support to the educability hypothesis. This hypothesis is our only defensible one, for reasons concerning the historic responsibility of those in the helping professions.

The philosophical underpinnings of my research and other activities are strengthened by the belief that, as human beings, all people are equally valuable. Bengt Nirje enunciated this concept through the "normalization theory." However, the religious and ethical teachings of countless others since the beginning of our civilization provide us with varied expressions of this idea.

Unfortunately, human beings have a penchant to segregate, to separate, to stigmatize, to make pariahs of other human beings. On the other hand, people today seem to want to discuss these issues. At last, the myth of such terms as "mental retardation" appears to be partially appreciated. The efficacy studies, the nomenclature changes,[1] the black revolution, and other scientific and social movements have led us to a better comprehension that "mental retardation" is no more than an administrative term. The words "mental retardation" have little, if any, scientific integrity. We had to appreciate that idea before we could take seriously the concept of educability. Or, maybe, it is the other way around; before we were able to learn that mental retardation is a contrived administrative label, referring to a current functional condition, we had to admit to a notion of human educability.

We are learning. More than that, learning — changing — need not necessarily proceed at an invariant rate. Even more

---

[1]The most recent, little appreciated but astonishing, revision of the American Association on Mental Deficiency definition of mental retardation to include theoretical eligibility — i.e., psychometric retardation — to from one to two standard deviations on the "wrong" side of the mean literally revolutionized the incidence, prevalence, and concept of mental retardation, all with the simple stroke of Herbert Grossman's pen (1973). We cannot redefine measles, or cancer, or pregnancy with so easy and such external procedures. The Grossman Committee, sitting around a conference table, reduced enormously the incidence of psychometric mental retardation, never having to "see," or "dose," or deal with a client, only having to say that, hereinafter, mental retardation is such and such, rather than this or that. What, then, is mental retardation?

importantly, educability need not refer only to children, but to their teachers, and their teachers' teachers, to all people. Most importantly, learning and knowing are not enough. People are essentially what they do, not what they think or hope. Not only should we consider the possibility that people can change but, if we want to give that hypothesis a chance to prove itself, we must behave as if people *can* change. Hence, my preoccupation with the hypothesis of educability of intelligence. Literature relevant to the research in this area is vast, partly because it deals with problems as old as man, and partly because the questions asked and the answers given remain, to this day, far from clear. The evidence is ambiguous. The jury is out — Jensen notwithstanding, Blatt notwithstanding.

By "educating intelligence," I refer to procedures and conditions that elicit capacities for changing, both in rate and complexity, a person's learning performance in school-related and other problem-solving tasks (Blatt & Garfunkel, 1969). Change may be measured through the use of standardized and informal tests. On the behavioral level, change is reflected in the ability to handle with increasing skill the variety of problems confronting a person as a student and as a human being. It is our assumption that change becomes both significant and possible when the individual: a) needs to change, b) aspires to change, and c) is optimistic about the possibility for change. Educating intelligence refers to more than hypothetical mental faculties or abilities. It also refers to attitudes about self, learning, and abilities, without which the phenomenon of change cannot be comprehended.

Alfred Binet, whose concepts provided much of the inspiration for our research on educability, was unable to create an environment to promote intellectual development. Neither Binet's "Mental Orthopedics," Omar Moore's "Responsive Environments," our Early Education Program, nor any other known to us has been able to demonstrate convincingly that capability is educable. However, we still have much to learn about the nature-nurture interaction, the most efficient period

21

to begin intervention, the varieties of intervention models, better ways to study groups of children interacting with teachers, and how these interactions affect families, communities, and cultures.

Epidemiology

Epidemiological research aims to define and describe conditions associated with specific disorders. It analyzes the incidence, characteristics, and distributions of such disorders, attempting to relate demographic variables to etiological factors. Epidemiological study of the handicapped places even greater burdens on the researcher. Review of our own study, *Mental Retardation in Southeastern Connecticut* (Blatt, 1973), or any of the other serious investigations of the incidence, prevalence, distribution, and antecedents of disability (Tarjan, Wright, Eyman, & Keeran, 1973) reveals why there are relatively few comprehensive epidemiological reports in our literature. However, there is a sufficient body of work available for us to have learned that the incidence and prevalence of mental retardation depend almost precisely on such influences as definition and criteria, age, program supports, community resiliency, broad cultural values, and social class.

To describe mental retardation merely as a condition which affects 2% or 3% (or, since the Grossman *Manual* [1973] 1%) of the total population is to camouflage reality. After several years of intense involvement in our aforementioned study of the incidence and prevalence of retardation, we are persuaded that we are dealing with no more than 1%, and possibly no more than .75%, of the total population, who at any one time needs (or was known to have needed) special services because of mental retardation. Although it is quite apparent that 3% of our population are psychometrically retarded (the test construction guarantees this in the exact manner it guarantees that 50% of our population have an IQ below 100), no more than 1% of our population are in need of special services because of mental retardation. Further, one-half of that 1% are either in public school special programs for the mentally retarded or do not need any special services at the present time. Further still, given an adequate community-based program of alternatives for families, there should never be a need for more than .1% of the total general population to require residential placements because of some situation associated with retardation; and such residential placements need never be in arrangements that include populations greater than eight.

Our large, traditional institutions should be evacuated as speedily as possible. They neither help people, nor are they necessary; they persist only because they serve magnificently those in our society who are responsible for the creation and maintenance of human slot fillers, wherever and for whomever they are.

For purposes of program planning and service delivery, it is important to understand the difference between psychometric and administrative mental retardation, a concept that unfortunately has not reached most of our textbooks in the field. On one hand, we have psychometric mental retardation (essentially IQ less than 75) comprising approximately 3% of our total population. On the other hand, we find the incidence of known (i.e., administrative) retardation to be approximately 1%. Further, prevalence among preschool and adult populations is somewhat less than 1%, while it is somewhat more than 1% among school-aged children. From group to group — depending on age, socioeconomic status, community values, etc. — prevalences of mental retardation range from much less than 1% to much more than 1%; nevertheless, 3% of the total population are psychometrically (but not necessarily mentally i.e., administratively) retarded, and no more than 1% are mentally (i.e., administratively) retarded.

This problem, concerning the incidence and prevalence of a particular condition, exists across all disability groups; consequently, estimates of the various categorical handicaps vary from study to study, from culture to culture, and from time to time. The most relevant definition of a disability must include reference to the fact that it is essentially administratively determined.

Developing incidence estimates, predictions of program needs, and cost-benefit analyses are extraordinarily hazardous when dealing with these diverse populations. For example, in one state, attempts are made to integrate so-called educable mentally retarded (EMR) children in regular grades; in another state, such youngsters already are in regular grades and are not considered mentally retarded; in yet another state, every effort is made to place as many children as possible with IQs less than 75 in special classes for the mentally retarded. As many as 30% or 40% of the public school population in one community may be psychometrically retarded; in another community within the same city or region, psychometric retardation may be as low as .5% of a school population. Similarly, estimating the incidence of behavioral disturbances is difficult. Surprisingly, even estimates of such apparently objective disabilities as blindness, deafness, and physical handicap do not provide the clear-cut data some might expect (*Fleischmann Report on the Quality, Cost and Financing of Elementary and Secondary Education in New York State*, 1972).

After all is counted and analyzed, the prepotent lesson one learns is that there is a difference — a political, pragmatic, legal, and scientific difference — yet hardly understood, between psychometric and administrative mental retardation.

THE PROMISE

Since the early 1950s, when I began the study of public school special education programs, a great many attempts have been made to evaluate the effectiveness of those programs. Although state schools, being more secluded and more segregated, have been subjected to fewer formal evaluations in contrast with special classes and the numerous efficacy studies, the former now are regularly examined.

Research on the effectiveness of special classes for handicapped children, as mentioned earlier, has not grown to impressively large and depressingly hollow proportions, with the conclusion that very little research encourages the expansion of special classes as we now know them. As to the state school, there is consistent confirmation, from Dorothea Dix to Kraepelin, to the more recent observations of Wolfensberger, Klaber, Menolascino, Dybwad, and others, that this institution, by its very nature, is infinitely less able to offer its residents humane care and that it is completely incompetent to provide them opportunities to contribute to society and live dignified and purposeful lives. Yet, in total disregard of the few but powerful reports of institutional life and the scientifically questionable but numerous reports of special class life, and our inability to demonstrate either the efficacy or moral rectitude in continuing (much less encouraging) these segregated programs, we continue to utilize more and more institutions and pass more and more mandatory, rather than permissive, special class (not education) laws. Little wonder that we have lost sight of the distinction between human privileges and human rights.

Why this discrepancy between what we know and what we do? Why do we, in the United States, know more about and do less for disabled people than other Western cultures? Although we enact child-labor laws and public education laws and support treatment services for handicapped children, there is more violence, more frustration, more alienated youth in our culture than ever before. Consequently, we seriously must consider the notion of a child-centered society, that we use this term in an unexamined way. On the evidence of too many reports, I am forced to consider the possibility that we never had a child-centered society. We are for children to the degree that children are for us; but in this adult-centered society, each person is first, and sometimes only for himself. One would be hard put to find sufficient evidence to reject this characterization of ourselves.

What must we become, and what must we do now? The answer is as plain as it is complicated. We must create a union of consumers, professionals, attendants, students, their professors, great people, ordinary people — each concerned with monoliths, with departments of mental health and education, with the inner city, with institutions and public schools, with the legislature; united on behalf of all who have asked or wondered what we have become. We must join together in support of the inmates of the state schools and hospitals, the ghetto children, and — finally — on behalf of each of us living through these difficult times.

We must seek a society that will be free of dehumanizing and debilitating state-sponsored domiciles, a society that will evacuate human beings from any facility that abuses or enslaves. We must create a society that has compassion.

We must create an organization that earlier reformers, were they here today, would join. We must unite, not about specific task orientations but about powerful ideologies, not about special means but about a consensus of humanistic ends. We must convince others (and ourselves) that the state does not own people, that freedom is more important than life itself. We must illuminate the irony of a state that is permitted by law to take or reduce my life while I, who should be the owner, may not take my own life or cause myself bodily harm, under penalty of fine, imprisonment, or institutionalization. The state may, with (or sometimes without) provocation, kill me, institutionalize me, seclude me, shock me, drug me, dirty me, animalize me; but I, who should be the owner, may not kill myself, scandalize myself, drug myself, dirty myself, or dehumanize myself. The state — as it substitutes pills for straitjackets and therapeutic isolation for solitary cells — does not change in the truly important dimensions, as it demands that each of us bend and twist and pay homage. Long live the state, and to hell with people.

Therefore, we must band together, as each makes his special commitment to change. We must become a new people, no longer underestimating the potentials we have for changing, no longer pessimistic concerning the conditions of change.

REFERENCES

Bennett, A. A comparative study of sub-normal children in the elementary grades. *Teachers College Contributions to Education.* New York: Columbia University, 1932.

Blatt, B. *The physical, personality, and academic status of children who are mentally retarded attending special classes as compared with children who are mentally retarded attending regular classes.* Ann Arbor, MI: University Microfilms, 1956.

Blatt, B. *Exodus from pandemonium: Human abuse and a reformation of public policy.* Boston: Allyn & Bacon, 1970.

Blatt, B. (principal research consultant and project writer). *Mental retardation in southeastern Connecticut.* Waterford, CT: Seaside Regional Center, 1970.

Blatt, B., & Garfunkel, F. *The educability of intelligence.* Washington, DC: Council for Exceptional Children, 1969.

Blatt, B., & Garfunkel, F. Teaching the mentally retarded. In N. L. Gage (Ed.), Handbook of research on teaching (2nd ed.). Chicago: Rand McNally, 1973.

Cain, L. F., Levine, S., and others. *A study of the effects of community and institutional school classes for trainable mentally retarded children.* San Francisco: San Francisco State College, 1961.

Cassidy, V. M., & Stanton, J. *An investigation of factors involved in the educational placement of mentally retarded children.* Columbus, OH: Ohio State University Press, 1959.

Coleman, J. S., Campbell, E. Q., Hobson, C. J., McPartland, J., Mood, A. M., Weinfeld, F. B., & York, R. L. *Equality of educational opportunity.* Washington, DC: United States Government Printing Office, 1966.

Dunn, L. M., & Hottel, J. V. *The effectiveness of special day class training programs for severely (trainable) mentally retarded children.* Nashville: George Peabody College for Teachers, 1958.

Fleischmann report on the quality, cost and financing of elementary and secondary education in New York state, Vol. 1. New York: Viking Press, 1972, 494 pp.

Grossman, H. J. (Ed.). *Manual on terminology and classification in mental retardation.* Washington, DC: American Association on Mental Deficiency, 1973.

Hurley, R. *Poverty and mental retardation: A causal relationship.* New York: Random House, 1969.

Johnson, G. O. *A comparative study of the personal and social adjustment of mentally handicapped children placed in special classes with mentally handicapped children who remain in regular classes.* Syracuse, NY: Syracuse University Research Institute, 1961.

Pertsch, C. F. A comparative study of the progress of subnormal pupils in the grades and in special classes. *Teachers College Contributions to Education.* New York: Columbia University, 1936.

Sarason, S. B., Davidson, K. S., & Blatt, B. *Teacher preparation: An unstudied problem in education.* New York: Wiley, 1962.

Tarjan, G., Wright, S. U. Eyman, R. R., & Keeran, C. U. National history of mental retardation: Some aspects of epidemiology. *American Journal of Mental Deficiency,* 1973, 77, 369-379.

2

The Politics of Institutions

Douglas Biklen

> *If you want the happiness of the people, let them speak out and tell what kind of happiness they want and what kind they don't want.*
> Albert Camus

> *I want to be free. I want to do what I want to do.*
> Inmate, Southern State School

EVALUATION OF INSTITUTIONS

This chapter describes and discusses the nature of life in state schools and state mental hospitals, and evaluates these settings as educational, social, and residential milieus. In designing our research, we decided to look not only at programs and activities, but also at overall life patterns within institutions; we decided to look not just at children, but we also wanted to

---

This study is based upon observations in six state schools and five state hospitals. We originally requested permission to observe in 26 such state institutions, as part of the 1970 and 1971 Workshops on Human Abuse, Protection and Public Policy at Syracuse University, but were accepted by only these 11, which may suggest that they are among the better ones in the state. We purposely have disguised all names of institutions and people to protect those who permitted us to observe, and to avoid giving the impression that conditions described exist only in the facilities visited.

meet people who have spent their lifetimes in state schools and state hospitals, in order to understand and appreciate the impact of long-term institutionalization.

Most of our observers are special educators and supervisors of programs for handicapped children. We trained them briefly in certain aspects of participant observation, but did not provide them with interview schedules or specific research aids. We thought we could best describe and evaluate milieus as large and complex as closed institutions by observing and recording, as specifically and intensely as we could, the ward scenes, staff conversations and meetings, picnics, recreation programs, dinnertimes in the cafeteria, and the many other scenes that are part of the entire setting. We knew it would be impossible to observe or describe everything, but we hoped to communicate a sense of these settings by providing a series of concrete descriptions of scenes, practices, interviews, and conversations.

In preparing for this study, the observers discussed their concerns with people who had great experience with institutions, by viewing relevant films and slides, and by spending two three-day periods living in and observing mental hospitals and state schools. Our purpose was to sensitize ourselves and others to the nature of institutional life. Each observer was asked to record observational notes of conversations, incidents, architectural descriptions and programs. They prepared their notes privately, out of the view of institutional staff and inmates, in order to not upset or alter the settings wherein they observed. We cannot be certain of the reliability of the notes, except that the observers reported strikingly similar experiences. Further, our informal discussions with former inmates of state institutions and our familiarity with literature on the subject of institutional life all confirm our belief that, despite the brevity of our visits, the more than 2,800 pages of field notes seem to describe mental hospitals and state schools accurately and in considerable depth. My own visits to a variety of institutions during the past several years, including extensive, in-depth observation of life on a locked ward of a mental hospital, have added to my confidence in the reliability of this analysis.

Before visiting the mental health facilities and schools for the retarded, we were warned about the smell of feces and urine, the havoc at feeding time, isolation cells, locked doors, endless boredom, drab dayrooms, understaffing, and sadistic attendants — almost to the point where we thought only the worst hell could compare with the horrible conditions we would find. As it turned out, *nothing* could have prepared us for what we experienced.

One observer at the Southern State School wrote in his field notes, after only a few hours of observation, "I feel like I've spent the longest five hours of my life." He had seen 20 "severely retarded" boys, clothed in short gray pants or naked, locked in a large, barren room with nothing to do. Another observer, at the Central State Mental Hospital, witnessed a man batter his head against the locked steel doors of a ward. She visited a locked ward where 60 elderly women, under the supervision of one or two attendants, day after day received no stimulation. She saw one young girl "who ate everything she could get her hands on, from shoestrings to her own excrement." For two hours, the attendants locked up the ward and went away for coffee. In their absence this young girl ate a shoelace and a television knob. In the evening, after leaving the premises, the observer noted, "I almost felt as though I was escaping illegally. I can honestly say that I have never felt what the word 'freedom' meant until those moments when I drove off the grounds."

Nearly all the observers felt their bodies react in horror to what they saw and experienced: Their mouths went dry, and suddenly nothing tasted good; sometimes the smell of urine stuck in their nostrils. For others, there was just a general sickness at seeing people treated as objects or as animals.

In spite of our practical working experiences and familiarity with problems in the fields of mental retardation and emotional disturbance, we were shocked, upset, and even nauseated by the sight of young children locked in isolation

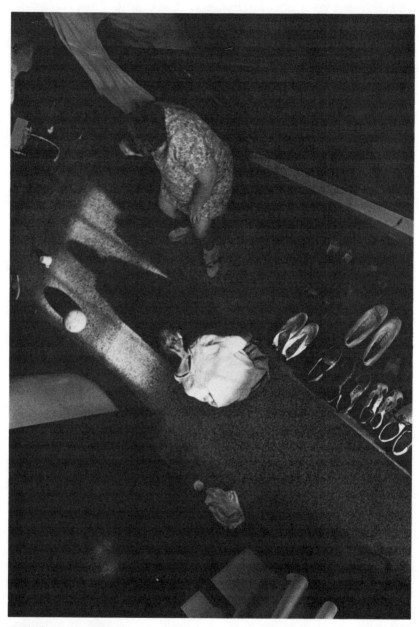

Photo by Derrick TePaske

cells, old women tied to benches, and young men labeled as "vegetables" or "low grades." Practices and conditions which all too often were considered part of the institutions' normal operating procedures were, to us, blatant abuses.

We feel compelled to answer the silent pleas of those old and younger human beings who sit in locked wards, staring into space or at television sets (both on and off). We cannot ignore the message of the man who batters his head against a steel door, of a girl eating shoelaces, of a woman picking at open ulcers on her leg, of a young boy jabbing at his naked companion, of attendants who no longer speak with residents except to spit out orders, and of patients incarcerated behind thick wooden doors and barred windows. We must answer the pleas of those who cry out:

I want to go home. They should burn the place down.
(Inmate, Central State Hospital)

I don't want to stay here all my life.
(Inmate, Southern State Hospital)

We're coming to the age of Aquarius. Then things will be different, man.
(Inmate, Central State Hospital)

For three hot days in July, I personally visited a state school for the mentally retarded, and met a middle-aged man named Joseph. An inmate[1] of the school, Joseph walked from ward to ward, along the wooden-floored corridors of this rambling, former military installation. One day I ran into him in the hallway. Joseph has white curly hair and wears glasses. He told me he was blind in one eye and that doctors had removed a cataract from his other eye about five years ago. He was wearing khaki pants and a white shirt with bulging pockets. (During this visit, I became accustomed to the inmates' bulging pockets, where they stored their pipe tobacco and other items they were afraid might be stolen.)

---

[1]We use the term "inmate" rather than "patient" or "resident" because we feel this term best describes the role of those incarcerated in institutions.

Joseph was one of 800 adult inmates at Lakeside State School[2] who were being moved to other state institutions as a result of budget cuts that were forcing the closing of this school. I asked Joseph if he was pleased about being moved. "No, sir, I do not want to move." Like many other inmates at Lakeside, this was just another move Joseph had come to expect as a career resident in the state school system. As Joseph repeated over and over again that he was not pleased about the impending move, I could not help but think about the apparent ease with which policy makers in the State Department of Mental Hygiene could move Joseph from one place to another without even meeting him or asking his opinion on the matter. The decision to close the institution had been made in the state capitol, and the inmates, as well as most of the staff, heard about it through the news media and the grapevine. For us, Joseph's predicament characterized much of institutional life; we could see that he had been denied opportunities to make choices and take responsibility for matters (such as where he would live) that affected the most basic elements of his existence.

Though the initial reaction to institutional life was overwhelmingly and intensely personal for all of the observers who joined together to research institutional conditions, we do not wish to overpersonalize what should be regarded as an essentially political-social situation. Joseph is not being pushed about and treated as human baggage simply because someone does not like him. His problems are not essentially personal difficulties. Rather, he is one of the millions in this society who have been marked as "mentally retarded" or "mentally ill," terms used to identify deviants who are, by the society's standards, unfit to share a normal existence with the rest of us.

One cannot examine institutional life without exploring the concept of deviance; closed institutions such as prisons,

---

[2]Lakeside State School, a pseudonym, was one of two facilities operated by the State Department of Mental Hygiene ordered closed as a result of budget cuts.

mental hospitals and state schools exist to "serve" people whom society judges to be deviant. It is important to study the history and needs of institutionalized people at a personal level to determine what has happened to them in the past and to formulate a prescription for how we can interact with them as fellow human beings in the future. However, it is even more crucial to examine the position of institutionalized people as a whole, rather than as individuals, to understand the social implications and origin of their plight. Our analysis of institutions, then, proceeds with an eye toward understanding deviance and social control.

We belabor the importance of maintaining a political and social, as opposed to a personal or private, perspective of institutional life because we feel that reports such as ours which rely heavily on descriptions of people and settings in vivid detail can easily spawn simplistic solutions. Unless we examine the broader issues of deviance and social control, for example, people may conclude that the conditions described can be altered or eradicated by making several changes in personnel, physical structure, and funding. There is always the danger that, when presented with concrete data, one will tend to seek specific and immediate answers without considering more global issues. It would be easy to recommend that a dirty ward room be cleaned or that shabby clothes be replaced by new and stylish clothing, but such changes would not expunge those forces which create dirty wards and ill-clothed inmates.

Our concerns reflect our belief that institutions are products primarily of society, not of individuals, and that the effects of institutionalization can best be understood as originating from social rather than individual forces. Although we were profoundly upset and in some cases repulsed when we saw inmates given depressant shots when they were "too active," and saw others left in day rooms all day with little or no recreation, programming, or employment to occupy them, and saw infants who were fed entire meals in a minute and a half, these acts are less the products of individual staff members than they are of the society that creates the institutional structures where such scenes become commonplace. We also must note that many of the programs we viewed reflected great efforts by staff members to counteract the usual deadening effects of institutions and that many of these activities were carried on in spite of formidable pressures against them. It would be easy to lay the blame for wrongdoing with the attendants who manage these wards, but that would be rather like prosecuting the soldier for firing his gun after sending him to do battle. While individuals occasionally may make institutional life intolerable, institutions are primarily the products of societies, not individuals.

Many of the scenes described below may arouse anger or admiration for individuals without providing hints as to how these scenes can be changed or replicated. Responsibility lies with the attendant and with the teacher, but it also lies with all of us — professionals and laypeople, legislators and taxpayers, who have had a hand, however remote, in creating the structure, policies, and atmosphere that permit such suffering. We are all the benefactors of public institutions, and it is our continued cooperation with them, through our payment of taxes and through our silence, that enables institutions to continue in whatever fashion they choose.

Most of us rarely meet a person labeled "mentally retarded" or "mentally ill," since we have excluded them from typical community settings and have forced them into special classes, special schools, sheltered workshops, and institutions, to be guarded by institutional staff. In fact, those who work in institutions that we visited consistently expressed their concern, and in some cases their resentment, that society will not make an effort to help people labeled as "retarded" or "ill" to live in the community. The Chief of Community Services at Western State School remarked:

> It just makes me sick. Doctors tell their patients to put their kids in an institution. There is no reason why some of these kids couldn't be kept home for much longer periods and then let the community offer

services to the family directly. But no. Hospitals, doctors, well-meaning friends, all tell the parents to put their child in an institution.

Another hindrance to the integration of the "mentally retarded" or "ill" into community life is the total lack of resources available to them. As one director put it:

> We try our best to convince them (parents) to keep their people at home, but there aren't too many community services available. We're trying to establish a day-care center, so that these people can benefit from an institution without being institutionalized.

The absence of resources increases the burden that individual families feel when they try to cope with special requirements. Institutional staff members cited instance after instance where families simply found they could not deal with the person's needs. In the cases cited to us, the staff was critical of the parents, yet we could not help feeling that the position of the parents, like the position of attendants and other institutional staff, reflects the social structure and values. A young social worker at one state school gave an example of a young woman who was having her five-year-old boy admitted:

> His father died a couple of years ago, leaving adequate means for his support. Now the mother, who is young and quite good-looking, wants to have the child admitted because she can't find a baby sitter for him between the hours of four and five o'clock Monday through Friday. Can you imagine! Wanting your child institutionalized for such petty reasons. Well, believe it or not, she got on the good side of a couple of our staff members, one of whom is a social worker, and the child was admitted. I think it's a shame. But mine is simply one voice crying in the wilderness. She probably wants to remarry and doesn't want the boy to present a problem.

When we combine the pressures of society for people to work, to remain independent, and to live at a breakneck pace, with the absence of community services (even one hour baby sitting service per day) for children who have special needs, parents are placed in an awkward and sometimes impossible dilemma. Families all too often must institutionalize a loved one as a result of the burden created by the service void.

As a society, we are frightened by what we consider abnormal; we have created rigid standards of normality and fear all that lies outside those bounds. We have created myths about people whom we consider to be abnormal. As the children grow older, society becomes even more frightened of their existence. One doctor in a hospital said:

> We do have many problems, but society creates many of them. We have children who should and could be placed outside, but there are few places for them. It is difficult to place them in jobs and foster homes.

One of the major difficulties lies not in the lack of funds but in outright fear. We all deserve responsibility for such fears because we are part of the society that incarcerates deviants and creates a climate for myths to abound. We have so isolated ourselves from people who have special needs that we have come to view them as people from another world, to be feared. This attitude holds especially for people who have been labeled "mentally ill."

The purpose of raising the issue of social attitudes is not to exonerate institutions or institutional staff from responsibility but to say that when we uncover institutional conditions which appear abusive, we must remember that these conditions exist and are fostered by a social prejudice against people with extraordinary needs. If children with special needs were accepted into public schools instead of being excluded, if they were allowed in day-care centers instead of being rejected, if all people could participate in all of the activities and programs that are open to people whose needs are more typical, institutions would probably never have been built and there would have been no context for abuse.

We will attempt to convey the nature of life within mental hospitals and state schools by focusing on several key issues that consistently emerged from our observations. Naturally, our attention was drawn to those events and practices that offended our sensibilities, but we have collated these experiences into a variety of hypotheses and conclusions which it is hoped will explain, as well as describe, what the observers saw.

MEANS OF CONTROL

> I've been here five years. I don't like it. If they don't let me out this summer, I'll run away.
> (Inmate, Metropolitan State School)

> What's it like on the outside? Remember, I knew you on the outside. What's it like?
> (Inmate speaking to an observer who did know her on the "outside," Metropolitan State School)

> Sure, kids get beat up. When we are noisy in bed, some attendants will come over and slap us. They slap real hard on the back.
> (Inmate, Metropolitan State School)

> I can't do anything without being put in seclusion and given a shot.
> (Inmate, Central State Hospital)

Whenever researchers examine organizational settings, they inadvertently, though sometimes purposely and explicitly, impose their own definitions and ideologies on what they observe. Psychiatrists acting as observers may view state schools and hospitals through a clinical paradigm. Sociologists tend to view them as elements in complex social systems. Certainly we hope that our presentation reflects more about what we observed than about how we interpret it. Yet we also recognize that, like all observers, we have our special concerns. Through a sociological framework, we have focused on the issue of dehumanization and its correlate, humanization.

Isolation

At one level of analysis, isolation can be viewed as a means of cutting off individuals from potential allies. Many of the institutions we observed have been built far off in the countryside or behind high walls and fences, away from population centers. Inmates have lost contact with their

39

families and with other potential allies who could help promote a certain level of services and conditions on the "inside." Without such outside contacts, inmates are powerless against institutional abuses. Inmates' communication with outside allies is further impeded by censorship policies, unavailability of telephones, policies which restrict them to the institutional grounds, and limitation on visiting hours. Newspaper reporters and photographers are usually prohibited from entering large, closed institutions as reporters or photographers, since they could easily become allies of inmates by publishing reports of conditions.

All but one of the state schools we visited was located far out in the countryside, away from large cities, set off in the woods or perched on a mountaintop. One had formerly served as a military installation and another as a tuberculosis center; all were isolated from neighboring communities.

At each institution, whether mental hospital or state school, the architecture and location bore witness to the notion that society regards the inmates as deviants who must be segregated from the larger community. The institutional settings were awesome in their ability to create barriers between the inmates and the outside world. One group of observers reported on the appearance of Central State Hospital, which is typically imposing:

> The institution sits alone, out in the countryside. Approaching from the north, one first encounters a high, ornate iron fence stretching along for thousands of feet directly in front of the state hospital. On the grounds, you see an immense layout of brick buildings with heavily-barred windows.

Similarly, at the Metropolitan State School an observer noted an almost identical setting, except that this was the one school located in an urban environment. The image of isolation was nevertheless intensely projected. Whether through police security systems, high walls, or pastoral location, isolation has become a theme common to state schools and state hospitals.

Isolation, however, reaches far deeper than the physical setting. As a person enters institutional life, the first state of personal isolation is the commitment procedure. Through this process, one is effectively cut off from the outside and becomes an "official" inmate. Formal commitment marks the beginning of a long, often intricate process of isolation from normal community life.

When a person enters a state school or hospital, he is usually placed in quarantine or under observation. While such policies are considered standard procedure for new inmates, similar policies are not employed on new staff members. One administrator defended quarantine procedures on the basis that they guard against diseases from the outside community, though hundreds of staff members come from the community to the institution every day without passing through a quarantine. Thus, the quarantine period, rather than serving any medical or therapeutic purpose, creates a physical barrier, a stripping process that effectively communicates to inmates that when they move into institutions, they are indeed leaving one world and entering a new one.

In several institutions official policy limited visiting hours for friends and relatives of the residents to a few hours a day. In at least one of those institutions, the policy stated that parents could not visit the day room or ward where their child spent nearly all of his life. In some instances parents were not permitted to see the bed where the child slept. In one institution the staff had inmates don dress clothing before meeting their friends or family in a special meeting area. In another state school the better wards were kept open to visitors, while back wards remained locked and off limits to outsiders.

Other factors contribute to the pervasive isolation. Inmates' mail, for example, is censored as it moves to and from the institution, thus cutting off open communication between inside and outside. Institutions often require that phone calls to the outside be approved by the staff. Similarly, they often demand that visits with friends and relatives be approved, or that such visits be coordinated within official visiting times,

41

which are invariably restrictive. Inmates may not vote in public elections. Thus, in a variety of ways inmates are captives of policies and practices that cage them in and prohibit them from the normal channels of interaction with society.

Inmates of state schools and mental hospitals also are isolated from areas and people within the institution. Males are separated from females, so-called "low-grades" are separated from "high-grades," "chronic" patients from "acute" patients, and so forth. The ultimate extent of institutional isolation cannot be appreciated fully without observing the isolation cell or makeshift detention areas. Many wards and day rooms might be seen as isolation rooms, since they are securely locked and therefore restrict passage in and out by inmates. However, the actual isolation cells that exist in a large number of institutions represent a more intense form of segregation and imprisonment. The following is a description of an isolation cell area in the Southern State School:

> We walked out into the hall of the ward. There were about seven small rooms on either side of the long hall. At the far end of the hall, there was a bed with a girl in it, under a restraining sheet. The restraining sheet was almost as long as the bed and covered the inmate from neck to foot; it was fastened to the bed so the girl was kept relatively immobile.
>
> The isolation rooms on the right were used as "reward" rooms for those residents who behaved well. Each room had a regular bed and a dresser. These rooms were formerly used as punishment rooms.
>
> The isolation rooms on the left were still used for punishment and restraint. The doors were made of heavy metal, with one 3" x 4" peephole in each. Inside was a gray mat about three inches thick, placed on the terrazzo floor. Except for the mats, the rooms were completely barren. All of the isolation cells were empty except two. In one was a nude girl curled up on the mat so I could not see her face. In another was the girl under the restraining sheet. . . . The attendant said the girl under the sheet was in the isolation room because she had just been given a "hypo" and . . . needed a place to "quiet down."

It is impossible to generalize about the use of isolation cells, especially since many institutions seem to be phasing them out or, perhaps more accurately, replacing them with behavior modification drugs; i.e., depressants. At several institutions there were no isolation cells, while others used them frequently.

Inmates generally regard isolation cells, or "special treatment" areas, as instruments of cruelty and are quick to express their feelings, often in a rather articulate fashion for people who are supposed to be retarded, deficient, or disturbed. They see their time spent in isolation as punishment for a crime or even punishment for their existence. Not every inmate resists; some sit in lonely day rooms all day, staring into space, shuffling from one chair to another, waiting for lunch and dinner. But those who speak out do so venomously:

> I hate this place. It's like a prison. When you run away, they put you in isolation. Then, when the doctor talks to you and you tell him that this place is terrible, he just shrugs off your complaints and says you shouldn't run away. I've run away a few times. I don't like the isolation rooms. The doctors don't understand us. They just don't listen.
> (Inmate, Metropolitan State School)

> I hate it around here. There is nothing to do. I tried to run away from here but they caught me. My brother-in-law says he's going to get me out of this place.
> (Inmate, Metropolitan State School)

> I love my teacher. I call her my grandmother. She's kind to me. I don't like the attendants. They're mean to me. They put me in the Special Treatment Area (isolation).
> (Inmate, Metropolitan State School)

> When I grow up, I'm going to be an attendant. And I'll be a nice attendant. I'll never send anyone to S.T.A. (isolation).
> (Inmate, Metropolitan State School)

The Central State Hospital, a typically large institution with many locked wards, has no special isolation wards to incarcerate recalcitrants. However, our observers noted frequent use of a "side room" as a temporary isolation cell for children as young as five years old. In one instance an observer saw a young boy locked in a bathroom.

43

The isolation ward, lock-up, sweat box, side room, or locked bathroom represent a threat within the institution to those who would run away or disobey the rules. The isolation unit is a prison inside a prison. All institutional residents are inmates in the sense that they have been forcefully incarcerated by society, but the residents of isolation units are prisoners two times over; they have been judged deviant in the institution as well as in society.

Administrators defend isolation cells by saying that inmates need them to "cool off." However, one cannot help feeling that isolation cells exist to curb all activities by inmates that mar the efficient institutional operation and to keep the "disease" (as the medical model would have it) of recalcitrance or resistance from spreading.

While isolation units can accommodate inmates of all ages, the observers found that most of those in isolation were under 30 years old, and some were under 10. Several observers saw young children placed in restraining jackets (camisole or straitjacket) as well, while they were in isolation.

Restraints

In all of the state schools and mental hospitals, a much more common practice than forced isolation is the use of individual restraints. These are additional mechanisms by which institutions control inmates and deny individual responsibility and freedom. Among the milder and more informal restraints are denial of vacation privileges, forced labor in an undesirable job, and requirement to wear pajamas during the day. Observers met one girl who had been denied the right to sleep in bed. Instead, she had been strapped down to a mat. Apparently, she reacted so strongly to this form of restraint that she broke her arm in the process of trying to free herself. An observer at the Central State Hospital encountered a situation in which the attendant used a camisole to restrain a young boy:

> The rain had slackened off to a slight drizzle as an administrator and I walked over to Building B. We walked to the third floor, the adoles-

cent ward. A boy was walking around in a straitjacket. The administrator asked, "What did he do?" The attendant answered quickly, "Last night he started to tear up his clothes, tear at his face, break things, and *he even hit me.*" The administrator asked, "When are you going to take it off?" The attendant answered, "As soon as he can behave himself."

A teenage girl at the Metropolitan State School, described by staff as particularly aggressive, receives a combination of drugs, restraining jacket, and isolation, as noted by an observer:

> We saw a teenage girl wearing a camisole being led into an isolation room where there was only a mat on the floor. The room was barren. One attendant spoke to another, "We took her over to the hospital this morning to give her an enema. We had to put the camisole on her in order to do it." The girl remained expressionless. I asked why she needed an enema. The attendant told me, "Well, she's on such heavy doses of tranquilizers, it's necessary."

It hardly need be said that restraining devices, drugging, and isolation actually conflict with the stated goals and objectives of most institutions. At Southern State School a 1969 "Descriptive Brochure" prepared by the state school staff makes no mention of restraining measures and shows no pictures of wards where restraints are in use. In fact, a radically different image is presented:

> The goals which we are striving for at our institution are to provide shelter, food, security, sympathetic care and understanding for each retarded individual entrusted to us. In this connection, we offer opportunities for the retardate to develop physically, mentally, emotionally, socially, and spiritually to the full limits of his potential.
>
> For none is it a dungeon of oblivion and neglect, walled up against the rest of the world. Rather it is a place of devotion and dedication which draws upon the good will, resources and services of society and, in turn, contributes to the benefit and welfare of that same society.

At this same institution an observer experienced the following conditions:

> We walked over to the women's infirmary. Here I saw women tied down in chairs, women tied to chairs that were tied to the walls. I

45

heard moaning as I walked through the day room, and the stench was overwhelming. We went upstairs into other day rooms. I saw a woman tied under a restraining sheet. "How long has she been there?" I inquired. The attendant answered, "A long time." I asked, "Do you get her out every so often?" The attendant smiled, "Yes, we have to rub her down every two hours. That's the law." I asked another question: "How long will she be under that sheet?" Our guide responded, "For the rest of her life." "Why?" I asked. "She's a head banger," he said.

Does this example typify Southern State School's attempts to provide "sympathetic care and understanding" and "opportunities for the retardate to develop physically, mentally, emotionally, socially, and spiritually to the full limits of his potential"? Can we honestly say that this woman does not live in a "dungeon of oblivion and neglect"?

We found that head bangers at another state school were either segregated or placed in cotton restraining shirts that covered their heads. One young boy had weights placed on his arms so that he would use them less. If there were not enough staff to supervise the ward, the children were tied to restraining chairs. Only once or twice did the observers see the attendants respond to headbanging or biting by providing activities, programs, or attention for the person in question. The usual policy for dealing with "self mutilation" was to restrain or isolate the inmate. One attendant said he knew that isolation and restraint were inadequate answers to inmates who showed that they needed something to do or that they were so bored they "acted out" their frustration, but he lamented that there was no alternative besides isolation and restraints.

As one tries to assess institutional policies for isolation and restraints, it becomes obvious that they vary considerably. Whereas isolation cells and restraining sheets are used on inmates for days and even years at a time in several institutions, others employ such measures rarely. Several of the institutions do not have isolation cells, and many refuse to use restraining sheets or camisoles. In each institution measures

Photo by Derrick TePaske

are taken against inmates considered troublesome but, overall, there is no uniformity in policy or practice.

One might expect that the schools and hospitals would follow consistent patterns of restraint and seclusion, especially in view of the fact that in the state where we made our observations, the Department of Mental Hygiene had issued the following rules on the use of protective restraint and seclusion:

a. Protective restraint or seclusion is to be employed only for satisfactory surgical or medical reasons, or to prevent a patient from injuring himself or others.
b. Protective restraint or seclusion shall be employed only on the order of a physician, setting forth the reasons for its use. A full record of restraint and seclusion, including the signed order of the physician giving reasons, shall be kept from day to day and shall be subject to inspection by authorized persons.
c. Protective restraint consists of any apparatus that interferes with the free movement of the patient and which he is unable to remove easily. The only forms of protective restraint permissible are the camisole and the restraining sheet.
d. The maximum period in the daytime during which a patient may be continuously kept in protective restraint shall be two hours. Such patient shall be visited as frequently as indicated. At night the patient shall be removed from restraint every two hours, except when asleep.
e. A patient shall be considered in seclusion, either in the daytime or at night, when in a room alone with closed door which it is not possible for the patient to open from the inside.
f. The maximum period of continuous seclusion shall not exceed three hours in the daytime and the patient shall be visited every hour, day and night.
g. Dry packs shall not be used in the treatment of patients.
h. Wet packs shall be used only as therapeutic agents and shall be regarded as such.
i. Safety vests or similar garments of light material as approved by the Department for the protection and nursing care of suitable geriatric or pediatric patients are not to be considered as restraint but their use shall be prescribed by the physician.

The main reason why institutions sometimes ignore these rules and why some use restraints and isolation cells more than others is the lack of regulation of the schools and hospitals. A public school or medical hospital usually has a group of outsiders, such as parents or taxpayers, who take an interest in regulating those service organizations. Most state institutions have visiting boards, but these groups historically have ignored the conditions described here. State schools and hospitals discourage outsiders from interfering with their activities. As long as family and friends are kept from visiting inmates in the ward or from viewing the isolation cell in practice, they cannot formulate complaints; they cannot evaluate institutional programs. Thus institutions operate freely, according to their own rules, without community interference.

An aspect of institutional practice that is even less policed and more complicated — and perhaps more debilitating to the inmates — is the use of drugs as restraints to control behavior. Since many inmates of state schools and hospitals have seizures, a rather large number receive daily medication. However, we also found that the staffs administer drugs frequently and regularly to nearly all inmates, including those who do not have seizures. The staffs apply drugs to restrain inmates, to combat "hyperactivity," to help the "disturbed" stay on an "even keel," to punish the recalcitrant, to replace the isolation ward or restraining sheet, and to substitute for programs which might interest a person enough to alleviate his frustrations. Most doctors and attendants at the institutions favor drugs as a simpler and safer mechanism for controlling the inmates.

As with restraints and seclusion, the state officials mandated that drugs be prescribed only by institutional physicians and that their use be reviewed periodically. Practice, however, varied. In some institutions inmates were heavily drugged, while in others, which served basically the same population in terms of types of disabilities, drugs were imposed on very few inmates. One observer reported that implementation of policies governing drugs was so lax that "I saw an empty prescription blank already signed by the doctor, sitting on a ward desk." In this particular state school, she was told by a staff person that a child might be drugged "not because he

Photo by Derrick TePaske

was bad or anything" but because "he was just too lively." Many attendants regard drugs as the modern equivalent of isolation wards. One attendant agreed that drugs are replacing "less humane" restraining techniques. The observer found, however, that patients on drugs may go days, perhaps months, without seeing a doctor and without discussion of their cases.

Staff members often told the observers that drugs served to counteract "hyperactivity." What surprised the observers was the frequency of "hyperactivity." In some institutions it was said to afflict nearly all the inmates. An observer at Western State School saw a child receive Thorazine because he was running around, jumping from bed to bed.

An observer reported a conversation with a nurse about behavior modification drugs for a child's "hyperactivity":

> When the nurse came into the ward, I asked her what her duties were and she replied, "I administer all medication." Since I had seen many attendants administering drugs too, I inquired about the institutional policy. She said that although attendants dispensed drugs on the wards, "when you're dealing with children, you have to be more careful with drugs, but even on the other wards, I don't feel that medication should be given out by attendants; they just don't know enough. But there aren't enough nurses here, only 60 nurses in a staff of over 900."

In the Western State School, an observer experienced almost the identical situation, but in this case the child who was being given drugs resisted:

> I saw the nurse come over to a three-year-old boy who was sitting quietly in his crib. She was going to give him a cup of liquid tranquilizer. The boy fought her off, but then lost the fight and was forced to drink the medicine. Before she had arrived, he had been sitting quietly. As she walked away from the crib, he was crying loudly. When I asked why he was given the medication, she told me that he would get too "hyper" without it.

The observer was unable to verify this explanation because she never saw the child when he was not under medication. In fact, she reported that most of the inmates, from infants to the aged, were tranquilized daily.

51

The pharmacist at a state hospital told observers that he sometimes has to tell the doctors when they prescribe more than the manufacturer's suggested limit, but that even with his warnings, inmates occasionally receive more than the limit. Attendants in several of the institutions disclosed that many inmates who receive drugs regularly, over a period of years or even throughout a lifetime, become immune to the effects. They become so accustomed to high dosages that they "don't feel it," according to some attendants. However, where drugs were applied regularly and heavily, it usually was apparent to the observers that the inmates were dazed, quiet, and inactive.

Some interesting programs currently are operating in institutions, and some inmates apparently receive no drugs; yet one cannot help notice the extent of boredom and inactivity that pervades most wards and day rooms and the relative freedom with which drugs are dispensed to inmates who are considered overactive or bothersome. We cannot prove that staffs substitute drugs for programs, either frequently or infrequently; this certainly would require a study of staff motives, at the least. Our purpose is to describe what we saw and attempt to bring some understanding to these observations. In this context we can say unequivocally that drugs serve to pacify inmates and, coincidentally, that institutions provide fewer outlets in which inmates may expend their energies or realize their interests than are provided by the larger society for so-called "normal" people.

Architecture

It is easy to become indignant at these starkly dehumanizing institutions. It is more important, though perhaps more difficult, to understand that institutions not only cause a few human beings to suffer in such obviously dehumanizing ways, but also actually ensure suffering and dehumanization throughout, by their very design. These institutions do not require malicious staff or medical tortures to produce cruelty. By their physical environment, institutions guarantee human suffering and degradation.

Most of the institutions in this study were traditional brick buildings, but one was a more modern, sprawling school, much like a new college campus. However, all of the institutions, regardless of their outside appearance, were quite similar on the inside. Again, some were more modern than others, but all projected an aura of institutionalism; they were barred windows, barren walls, high ceilings, toilets without toilet seats or stall doors, and metal doors with huge locks. Others were more modern but retained the hard floors, un-padded furniture, thick doors, metal beds, and similar institutional markings. To be sure, the newer state schools had fewer all-metal doors, wire mesh, or barred windows, but they were hardly homelike. Most contained large dormitory-style rooms, hard cement or cinderblock walls, television sets placed high up on the walls (out of the inmates' reach), locked doors, and tile floors.

Although many of the ward rooms were spotlessly clean and neat, they were, on the whole, starkly impersonal, devoid of warmth and comfort. The institutional trappings indicated that those who designed these settings might have viewed the occupants as wild, destructive, unruly, undisciplined, or, more plausibly, as people who were not to have basic luxuries. The architecture and furnishings that we observed were cold, dull, or unimaginative and indestructible.

A few of the institutions had several individual bedrooms and small, homelike livingroom arrangements for teenagers and adults, but these facilities were available only as rewards for the "brighter" and "better behaved" inmates; they were not available to all. Staff persons repeatedly explained that the average inmate would not know what to do with warm, pleasant furnishings. We observed one state school where two day rooms were set up as "independent living units." While

Photo by Derrick TePaske

these day rooms were homelike, and indeed represented a step forward in institutional living accommodations, they portrayed the prevailing attitude toward furnishings; the staff used such furnishings as rewards for good behavior or as special learning environments for inmates who were preparing to move into the community.

Not all the day rooms were as barren as those described for the majority of inmates. A few had games and toys for the children or recreational materials for adults and were decorated with draperies, pictures, crepe paper, and mobiles. Typically, though, the pictures were placed high on the walls, far above the children's line of vision and (more importantly from the standpoint of the staff), out of the children's reach. One observer described a day room with large pictures of Mickey Mouse, Donald Duck, Popeye, the Three Little Pigs, and some other cartoon figures high up on the walls, almost touching the ceiling.

Our visits to many institutional settings, both for this study and for others, reveal radically different behavior exhibited by inmates who have been locked up in cold, hard environments compared with those who live in more homelike environments and who have more freedom to define their own life styles. In some institutions there are no locked wards and almost no head banging, wall pounding, or chair throwing. In other institutions, serving the same basic population in terms of observable disabilities of needs, we saw people locked up behind thick steel doors, throwing chairs, biting ears, punching out windows, and pounding on walls. The lesson seems quite simple: If you lock a person in a barren room and give him nothing to do day after day, it is likely that he will act out by banging his head against the walls or by swearing at attendants and occasionally hitting them.

Surely there are experts who will argue that this reasoning is too simplistic. Yet, after many visits to a dozen state schools and mental hospitals, we conclude that if people are allowed to live in homelike environments, if they have things to do, classes to attend, programs in which to participate, if they are allowed responsibility, and if they are free to interact with friends and teachers, they are much less likely to act destructively. Even if only a few of these positive conditions are sustained, inmates will probably exhibit less frustration.

THE INSTITUTIONALIZED: HOW AND WHY THEY COME TO BE INCARCERATED

We don't have normal people.
(Doctor, Southern State School)

Just people here you can't reach. People with IQs 0 to 5. What kind of recreation can you do with them?
(Attendant, Southern State School)

Did you think we are retarded? The sign outside says so, but we're not.
(A young boy, inmate, Metropolitan State School)

What does "handicapped" mean?
(A 43-year-old resident, Metropolitan State School)

If isolation cells, drugs, restraining jackets, shock treatment, and institutional architecture comprise an extensive system of control to which inmates are committed involuntarily, should we conclude that the sole or primary purpose of mental hospitals and state schools is to control the inmates? In other words, do these institutions serve a purpose roughly similar to prisons?

Such questions strike at the heart of institutional service, for they question the prevailing rationale for therapeutic institutions — that they exist to serve people who have special needs. One way of approaching this problem is to examine institutions from the outside by asking why and how people are sent to institutions. (Are they committed for service or for control? When society institutionalizes a person, what is the identifiable problem, and how is the institution expected to deal with that problem?)

Based on prevailing images of institutions as service centers, one might expect to find that the determining factors in institutionalization are test scores (IQ) and other indices of physical and mental ability. In state schools one would expect to find children with low IQ scores, brain damage or other professionally recognized indicators of "mental deficiency." Inmates of mental hospitals might be expected to have records of bizarre behavior that correspond to various psychiatric classifications. Instead, we found that these measures, while prominent in the records of institutionalized people, were not the initial presenting evidence at the time of admission. Such tests and descriptions were used to confirm or further justify institutionalization, but inmates seem to have been placed for other reasons. Most institutional staff members readily admit that if other criteria are strong, people with IQs above the mark of 70 or 80 could be, and are, permanently committed to state schools. Similarly, many inmates of mental hospitals have been committed by court order as a result of drug possession, alcoholism, disturbing the peace, and other legal infractions, rather than for psychiatric disorders.

Many of the people whom we interviewed did not know why they had been placed in state schools, but those who claimed to know said that in some way they had been troublesome or bothersome to others. One child reported that he had been sent by the court because he had disrupted a school classroom:

> I got into trouble in school — throwing chairs around, hitting people, knocking a teacher over the head with a chair, stuff like that . . . I had a choice. I could either come here or go to Auburn or some prison. I came here.

Another child, a girl at the same state school, said that she had been institutionalized because her parents had moved around from place to place and that she was unable to move with them because all the traveling hurt her back. She also said:

> You see, my mother was hurt when she was going to have me. Well, I have two parts of my brain missing. I can't remember things as well as other people. I have trouble remembering.

Another boy, institutionalized at the same institution for two years, told one of the observers why he had been sent to the state school:

> Got into trouble . . . messing up a cemetery, so they sent me here, the courts.

At the Metropolitan State School, articulate people are among those who have been committed. Several observers inquired about this. One observer reported her conversation with a social worker on the subject:

> She agreed that not all of the residents were retarded, but "the way things are," she said, "the disturbed get better psychological help at Metropolitan School than at other institutions."

I queried the staff psychologist about the same problem and was told that the IQ test was responsible for such misplacements. He explained that the IQ test is divided into school-related parts (e.g., arithmetic and comprehension) and nonschool-related parts such as digital memory. Thus, the doctor explained, "It's possible for a bright person to get a low IQ score if he has had no schooling or bad school experiences, even though he may not be congenitally retarded." He said some patients were born with low IQs but others were simply dumped by their parents or the courts. I asked him if he thought many of the inmates could work "outside." He said he had been instrumental in getting four "patients" out. When asked if he thought some of the inmates had been committed improperly, he replied, "As I think of the total population now, I can think of only one borderline case."

Our own discussions with inmates revealed that the primary reason for their institutionalization was rarely a low IQ score. The case history of one boy at Southern State School shows how people become candidates for institutionalization more because of social or living problems than as a result of their disabilities. The history in his records reports the following:

Both parents apparently are of "subnormal intelligence" and one brother of the mother is mentally retarded. He, the patient, was a premature baby, weighing only 3 pounds at birth and was hospitalized after birth for about eight months because of a collapsed lung and asthma. He was totally rejected by his mother and already as a baby was placed in a foster home. His development was very slow; he started to walk at the age of three years, but he never learned to talk, apparently because of his deafness. Except for moderate mental retardation, patient's somatic growth is quite defective due to hormonal deficiency (growth hormone).

Later reports indicate that the boy "learns to lip read a specific word quickly once he understands the basic concept." The key reason for his commitment to institutions relates not to his disability but rather to rejection by his family. Intimations that his relatives are retarded and that his disabilities are severe do not explain why the child was institutionalized.

Based on our observations and conversations with residents and staffs of state schools, it appears that inmates are placed in institutions for either one of two reasons: First, the court or parents and relatives consider them "troublesome" or difficult to care for or to live with. Second, the inmates' families experience some difficulties (the reason cited by many inmates). The children report, for example, that the parents did not have room at home; that the parents had to work during the day; that the children required 24-hour attention, or had nowhere else to go. One 19-year-old state school inmate who had been incarcerated for five years said, "My mother was sick and couldn't take care of me." Like most inmates, he spoke incessantly of going home, of his desire to return to his community, especially to his relatives.

According to the director of Easton Mountain State School, when community agencies refuse to serve the person who has special needs, the institution becomes a family's sole alternative. He cited an example of a child who was first excluded from a public school special class and then was referred to the State School. Of course, we heard from many staff members that people are institutionalized because the "institution is the best place for them" or because "they can't survive in the community." One doctor told an observer that "all this talk about community (placement) is nonsense." However, a much more prevalent attitude among staff members is indignation at state officials and leading experts who have spoken at length of the need for community programs but have not provided for such services. They complain that community professionals have not found it in their interest to include people with special needs in regular programs and services offered to those who have more typical needs. Thus, most staff persons seem to agree that the primary reason people end up in institutions is that they have not been served in the community.

"Right to treatment" lawsuits have highlighted the obvious connection between the absence of adequate community facilities and programs and the institutionalization of large numbers of children. A federal judge decreed in the now-famous Partlow case in Alabama (*Wyatt* v. *Stickney,* 1972) that no person was to be institutionalized in Partlow State School unless it could be shown that the institution was the least restrictive environment in which the person could be served. That test of "least restrictive environment" could have the effect of forcing states to create a full range of community services, provided the judge's language can be implemented. Our own experience in advocacy work through the Center on Human Policy, Syracuse University, would tend to support the hypothesis that community services can serve all disabled persons and that if we fail to develop necessary community services, we will, in effect, condemn parents and disabled people to the no-option monolith that has already become our heritage.

Nonetheless, children and adults do not enter institutions to find services. The institutional role as service agency pales in the shadow of the much more obvious role — custodial care. Even before one examines an institutional environment, it is possible to sense the hidden controlling aspect: policies of labeling, segregating, and denying. The practice of labeling inmates, be it to denigrate or legitimately indicate need, further reveals the tendency of institutions to objectify inmates. Each institution has its own idiosyncracies, but they all share an intricate and dehumanizing system of labeling. They categorize people according to IQ test scores or by psychiatric condition. The professional jargon used by institutional staffs to label residents includes words such as "deficient," "abnormal," "exceptional," "retarded," "special," "low grade" and other euphemisms for "deviant." On the wards observers encountered less polite labels such as "basket case" and "vegetable." Official records include more technical labels such as "schizophrenia," "dementia praecox," "simple," and "paranoid."

Systems of labeling and ranking inmates probably vary from school to school and hospital to hospital, but the effects seem rather consistent. The labels become self-fulfilling prophesies. Once a person is labeled as "low grade," he usually is viewed as someone who cannot develop beyond a certain level or cut-off point. Much institutional labeling reflects common social attitudes toward people who have special needs or who exhibit behavior that others consider abnormal. One attendant said that on his ward he had "everything from smart to one vegetable." The word "vegetable" usually refers to people who have difficulty caring for their most basic needs, such as toileting and eating, though it is also used to denigrate people who are considered unintelligent. One doctor, who perhaps was not representative of all doctors in state institutions, said,

> What does a mongoloid person know about personalism? Nothing! Because they have no brains to know. Do you think they have feelings? Do you think they know what is good for them? Blah. What do they know?

Even in institutions where an effort was made to communicate distrust of labels to the observers, it was clear that children and adults usually were labeled and placed into wards according to their levels of "retardation" — mild, moderate, severe, and profound. Those who were judged to be mildly or moderately retarded usually were considered more "normal." Some comments which were heard frequently from attendants include: He is real cute — he doesn't look retarded. He's a possibility for foster parents. He's trainable, so he can learn something.

An inevitable effect of labeling, whether intended to be degrading or not, is that those who use labels come to treat inmates as nonpersons. Several observers realized this when taken on "etiological tours" of wards. Attendants would lead the observer through the ward or day room and point out people and conditions almost as if the people being observed were objects with no feelings. Scenes such as the following were fairly common:

> As we sat talking, the attendant put his arm behind me and pointed to a man seated in a high chair. He said, "Now that one there is a vegetable. We have a few who are capable, but most of them can't do much." He took me outside of the ward and pointed to individual inmates saying, "Now this one can't do anything. He's got an IQ of about 4. And this one's blind. He's pretty smart. Sometimes he's trouble, but usually he's nice. This one's deaf, but he's a kleptomaniac."

So it went. The attendant walked among the inmates, pointing out their problems or disabilities as one might point out different kinds of plants to botany students during a nature walk. For him, the inmates had become objects to be differentiated by their etiology.

Labeling by disability or intelligence quotients has led to the creation of ranking systems for the institutionalized. Usually, the more intelligent receive more respect from the staff. However, one staff person said, "The smarter they are, the more problems they are." Thus, while each institution possesses means of ranking inmates, such ranking systems may vary from ward to ward or from institution to institution, and interpretations of the labels also vary.

One labeling custom that pervaded every institution we visited was the habit of calling all inmates "boys" and "girls" or "kids," regardless of age. The observers rarely heard staff

62

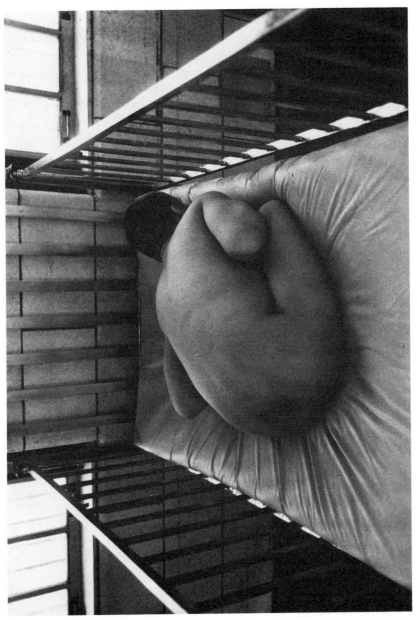

Photo by Derrick TePaske

persons refer to adult inmates as "women" or "men" — never "Mr." "Miss" or "Mrs." The distinction between inmates and staff was constantly emphasized. Many staff people wore uniforms, name plates, keys or other markers to indicate their difference from inmates. One youthful attendant compensated for not carrying any of these identifying markers by saying, "I'm an attendant" when he introduced himself to several observers at the Metropolitan State School.

Perhaps it is because inmates are considered to have childlike behavior patterns that they are treated as children or nonpersons. Institutional staffs generally do not view teenage or adult inmates as their equals; rather, they treat them as objects. The following scene portrays this practice:

> We attended the evening dance at the state school. As soon as we arrived, a tall, blond man asked me to dance. Just as we got to the floor, however, a male attendant in street clothes came up to us and, after looking at my partner, whose name I did not know, shouted, "I'll give you two minutes to go change your pants and get a decent pair of shoes on. No more than two minutes, boy!" The man left me standing there and went out of the hall as ordered. I later learned that the attendant was in his 20s and the "boy" was 42 years old.

The word "boy" is used above much as white society has used the word to denigrate black men. Referring to older inmates in terms appropriate to children reflects directly on the overall nature of labeling. Essentially, labeling is a means of objectifying inmates, of creating an impression that they cannot mature or learn beyond certain levels or be responsible for themselves.

Institutional labeling, which characterizes adults as children and children as "low grades" and "hyperactives," represents only a small aspect of an entire system of controlling those who because of living problems, social prejudices, or disabilities have been judged deviant. Perhaps the best indication that therapeutic institutions exist primarily to hold or control individuals rather than to serve them is the volume of complaints from inmates about their plight. They speak of rights being denied and of indignities suffered, all without recourse. We met inmates who complained many times that they were neither "sick" nor "retarded." We met people who obviously had disabilities but who could not understand why these should justify their being excluded from society. For virtually all of these inmates, their relationship with a controlling institution was unwanted.

INSTITUTIONAL SERVICE AND SOCIALIZATION

The realization that most inmates come to institutions involuntarily and that they are forcibly "treated" against their will must inevitably taint our perception of these "therapeutic" settings as service centers. Drugs, isolation cells, and routinized institutional life may be considered therapeutic by those who administer them, but inmates perceive them as punishment. Despite any good intentions, those who endure the treatment are best able to understand the cruelty.

Our observers quickly, though somewhat painfully, found that the institutional helping relationship is very much a subordinate-superordinate one, ripe with paternalism. Underneath the euphemisms about therapy and rehabilitation lie institutional practices that confirm the inmate's position as a deviant in the society.

Recreational, therapy, and educational programs within institutions vary tremendously, not only from one institution to another but also from ward to ward. The observers found that some programs were well equipped with staff and materials, while others were drastically understaffed and had no resources at all; some were ongoing, and other appeared defunct; some seemed to interest the inmates, and others did not. There were, however, a few commonalities that emerged in the observers' notes.

Several classroom situations resembled scenes one might expect to find in any good school. One observer reported on such a class:

> I sat on a small chair against the wall. . . . The classroom did not differ sharply from the "average" classroom, except there were only nine or

ten desks in the room. There was a record player on a table near the blackboard, and several children were huddled around it. An easel was in the corner near the desks, which were grouped in a semi-circle. Miss Olsen mentioned that the class was usually "disorganized" for the first 30 minutes. As I looked around, I noticed a girl . . . sitting at her desk, her ankles crossed, and her hand supporting her head . . . the only child out of nine who was not occupied. Jimmy, Tommy, and Billy were gathered around the record player; Donna was coloring in a numbers book; Candy was working on a jigsaw puzzle; Betsy was thumbing through a book; Ginny was looking very hard for a book. Miss Olsen divided her time among the children.

While classrooms like this one were not altogether unusual for the institutions, many settings appeared much less stimulating.

In each of the institutions, and in many wards and classrooms, shortage of staff or lack of interest and training among particular staff persons led to an absence of programming. Frequently, staff shortages were so great that when attendants bathed and dressed some children, other were left unattended. An observer noted the following scene in a state school:

There were two playpens side by side in the corner by the door. One girl was standing in one of them, crying loudly. Across the floor there was a tire and a child lying on the cold cement floor next to it. There was a practice set of stairs at the far end of the room. No one was using them. A spring board was off to one side. A little boy, crouched up in a "ball," was sitting on it. Several children were sprawled on the floor, some sleeping, some just lying there. . . . Some were just running around screaming.

The only interaction between the children and the two attendants was in the form of commands: "Stop that." "Let go." "Get off there."

Admittedly, these descriptions of ward scenes emphasize the plight of inmates and underplay the difficulties staff persons encounter. They do so primarily because we view inmates as unwilling victims of incarceration; they cannot leave. Staff members, on the other hand, may go home each day; or they are free to quit. Nevertheless, we do recognize that the role of staff, and especially the role of attendants, is difficult.

Attendants are caught in the inevitable institutional context. It was as if they too had been institutionalized.

In ward after ward, observers found attendants seated together at a corner table, or in their offices. One observer sat in a ward full of inmates for almost two hours while the two attendants remained in their office. Some wards with 70 inmates had only one attendant on duty. Even when there were six attendants for 40 inmates, the attendants seemed worn out and incapable of extended interaction with inmates. One observer summarized a typical scene:

> The attendants would usually sit together at their corner table. The children felt free to come up to them, sit on their laps, play with their hands, or interrupt the conversation. The attendants seemed worn out from the drudgery of their job. I never observed attendants reading to the children or playing games, but they did not withdraw from the children or push them away either.

Most of the observers became visibly angered at the way attendants treated the inmates, but they recognized that institutions force attendants to act in unfortunate ways. Can attendants play games, read to inmates, and otherwise interact "normally" in a locked ward with 50 or 70 inmates, each of whom has extreme personal needs? Can attendants bring warmth to a cold and sterile environment that has been cut off from the outside? Can attendants and other staff counteract societal pressures to dehumanize incarcerated individuals? It is unrealistic to expect attendants to deal with each inmate individually.

Institutions harbor the same notions of deviance and abnormality that have been popularized in the larger society. Thus, staff roles can reflect nothing else. A staff person told one observer that 50 percent of the children in the institution attend classes or occupational therapy — the others were such "low grades" they had to remain in the day rooms. This reflects an unwritten rule in state schools: the "brighter" children get more attention. With staff shortages, children who are strapped in restraining chairs or required to lie around continually in day rooms usually are those who have been judged less bright or less self-sufficient. One attendant in a "spastic infants" ward said, "They are too heavy for us, so we leave them in bed when we are short of help. When we have enough help, we take them out for a walk."

We heard staff complaints about resources in the day rooms. One attendant told us wryly that it takes three years to requisition a piece of tissue from the state capitol and, therefore, there were no toys or recreational materials with which to work. At one state school, therapists and attendants went into the neighboring community and persuaded local groups to contribute toys, art supplies, clothing, and other materials; but, generally speaking, staff members complained vehemently of the lack of resources. Some of the complaints were legitimate. In many instances observers saw wards with few resources; the state schools usually had only one, sometimes two, occupational therapy areas for a thousand inmates. However, in some cases supplies on hand were not being used. An observer at Southern State School reported:

> When I visited the day room for older, "less severely retarded" children, I saw many toys, all of which were out of reach of the children. The children were . . . wandering about the room, sitting on the floor and in wooden chairs, and lying on one another.

In a few cases, toys were unavailable because the staff felt that the children did not need or desire them in the way that "regular" children might. One attendant saw her job as essentially custodial; her prime duty was to simply stand or sit and watch the inmates. Some therapy and recreational areas were well equipped but little used. One large gymnastic area was equipped with basketball facilities and other games, but it could not be used between Wednesday and Sunday because the custodian found it convenient to set up chairs on Wednesday for Sunday church services.

The overall pattern of institutional life, at least in those institutions we observed, assumes that the inmates, both adults and children, are not only "unreachable" but also incompetent and therefore unable to make decisions for themselves. Inmates are not allowed to act independently or to assume responsibility for their actions, except in the most mundane areas of their lives. Most inmates do not even have the choice of how much toilet paper they may use, when they can eat, or when they can go outside.

In some state schools, inmates may walk freely from one end of the facility to the other, unhindered by locked doors, but this "open door" policy is considered such an anomaly within the state system that it receives wide attention and praise. Even the modern institutions that we visited exhibited highly structured activities and daily schedules. Inmates rarely were allowed to have snacks between meals; they were "fed" at prescribed hours and then were led to the toilets. Everyone, regardless of age, was expected to be in bed by 9:00 p.m. or earlier.

Routinization

Inmates learn at a very early age that the best way to get along in an institutional setting, be it a state school or a state hospital, is to take orders and to wait for commands. A doctoral student at Syracuse University who studied language stimulation in state schools found that children actually engage in dialogue with attendants about three or four minutes a week (Giles, 1971). Attendants often speak to inmates, but rarely do they speak in such a way that the person is encouraged to answer. Most of the attendants' words are commands or orders.

The amount of time inmates spend "waiting" is extraordinary. In ward after ward, observers saw children and adults waiting for the next meal or waiting for recreation. Many of us felt that perhaps the awaited activities rarely occurred. Usually the amount of time spent waiting for an activity far exceeded the amount of time spent in the actual program. Two observers placed in two similar state schools, one old and the other

Photo by Derrick TePaske

newer, reported seeing children who were forced to sit in their day rooms and wait for up to an hour for the next meal, even though staff persons on duty knew quite well that the dinners would not arrive until a preappointed time. One observer in a state school found children waiting 45 minutes before meals. Attendants would dress them in bibs and tell them to wait; this was their "activity." At one state school an observer questioned the lack of purposeful activity in the institution:

> I asked the attendant, "What do the children do all day?" She responded, "Right now we're in the waiting period." "What's the waiting period?" I interrupted. "It's the hour before meals when they wait for their food," she replied. I was curious by now, and so I inquired, "What do they do when they're not waiting for meals?" To this she responded, "Mostly sit around, look at each other and sleep."

Although the observers witnessed some personal and homelike dinner scenes, the vast majority reflected some of the worst qualities of institutions. When the meal period finally arrived, it was not a time for socializing or quiet enjoyment. Usually it was chaotic, hardly any more directed or purposeful than the hours that children spent lying around on day room floors, waiting for something to happen.

The following scene typifies institutional "feeding time" even though it occurred at a new institution, one that has been called a "showcase" by its director:

> We arrived at the dining room for lunch, and the girls were in line out in the hallway, waiting to receive their food. . . .

> When the attendant in the kitchen gave the word, the girls began to file into the dining area. After they had gone through the line and been given their food, they sat down at the tables.

> Each girl ate her own meal while the attendants stood in front of the room, chatting to each other.

> Most of the children ate with tablespoons. They ate as if the spoons were shovels. I never saw an attendant come to these girls and show them how to use the other silverware. One girl at another table had her tray taken away from her and was told to sit in a high chair along

71

the wall of the dining room, because she had tried to use a plastic glass as a spoon.

In institutions many children and adults never see a fork simply because someone thinks it is too much trouble to teach them to use forks, or that they "could never learn anyway," or that they would misuse them in a dangerous fashion. The issue of the fork and the spoon is not a trivial one. If a person is not allowed to use ordinary eating utensils, if he is not allowed to sit quietly at a dinner table and to eat slowly, he will not be allowed to live in the community outside the institution. As long as we fail to teach inmates to eat as we do, we help to prohibit their ever leaving the institution, for this society will not tolerate people who do not eat in the accepted fashion. As long as dinner is regarded as just one more routine that the staff must "get through" each day, inmates will remain deviants.

In one institution, observers witnessed forced feeding. The attendant concluded that the child would not eat unless her nose were held and the food forced down her throat when she tried to breathe through her mouth. The attendant apologized for this practice, saying, "It's the only time they can get some food. You'd think they'd be starved." An attendant in another state school complained that "it takes time, you have to shovel it down fast." Indeed, each institution tended to optimize speed and efficiency in "feeding." Is it surprising that children resist eating in an environment where they receive little attention, let alone warmth and affection?

One observer encountered a 19-year-old girl in a state school who ate from a bottle; she had never learned to eat solid food. The attendants claimed they did not have time to teach her.

The final lesson we learned from observing dinnertime was that this activity, like other institutional activities, is one in which inmates are given no individual responsibility. The attendant does not ask a person if he wants an ice cream cone; he gives it to him. In one institution, everyone was required to finish completely his or her meal. At each of the state schools, inmates were forced to line up and march to the dining room in single file or in pairs. There was little informality, few opportunities to do what one wanted, or to sit where one wanted. At every turn, even in the few institutions where people are allowed to walk around freely and where doors are left unlocked, there is a high degree of routinization.

In many institutions the routinization extends even to the process of toileting. It is more efficient, simpler, and less trouble for the staff to line up inmates and run them through the bathrooms at regular intervals than to take the time to teach the inmates how to use the facilities or to perceive them as fellow human beings who can take responsibility for themselves. In some bathrooms the toilets have no seats because seats are considered "dangerous" (like knives and forks) and difficult to clean. Some toilet stalls have no doors so that inmates cannot hide in the toilets and "play with themselves." One group of observers found three of four toilets on one ward marked "out of order" so that the attendant would have to clean only the fourth. In the same institution toilet paper was rationed, three pieces at a time, so that inmates would not clog the plumbing.

In a modern, campus-like state school considered a model by many experts, an observer found that the inmates' bathrooms were locked. However, the children were toileted on a regular schedule, the observer was told, and a child could request permission to use the toilet at an unscheduled time. To be denied toilet paper, stall doors, and toilet seats is an indication to an inmate that he is not to be trusted, that he is a prisoner in his institutional home. Institutionalized people are rarely trusted, unless it is considered in the interest of staff (such as when inmates become "workerboys" and "workergirls"). At an older institution it was found that inmates were prohibited even from controlling the temperature of their shower water. Attendants regulated the shower controls outside of the stalls. Inmates may shower only when told to do so; the frequency varies with the institution.

73

Photo by Derrick TePaske

In one ward, routinization reached such "sophistication" that the attendant would call the roll to find out how many bowel movements each person had that day. Laxatives were administered when the number was considered inadequate.

"Shut up and say your prayers"

One observer noted an attendant at the Metropolitan State School tell 41 middle-aged women to kneel on the day room floor and recite a prayer. The attendant stood over the women and yelled at those who were slow to chime in. The women mumbled the words in a droning monotone. On another ward, an attendant told 20 young boys to say the Lord's Prayer; he continued to speak aloud to the observer as they recited the words.

Attendants generally make no effort to create a religious atmosphere. Rather, they use the prayer as another means of exerting authority. They shout out directions for the prayer in the same way they bark out orders for inmates to make the beds and line up for dinner. The following account of prayer time at the Southern State School projects this tone:

> I heard an attendant's voice boom out in the other room. She yelled, "Get in line; shut up!" I heard flesh being hit with flesh. The attendant continued to scream, "I said get in line. Be quiet, I said. Just shut up. Shut up and say your prayers."

Another attendant at the same state school was overheard saying,

> That was terrible. You girls can say a prayer better than that. Now the next time we say a prayer, you do it right.

In many instances we found that staff denied the inmates certain privileges as a means of maintaining control. An attendant at the Metropolitan State School was heard saying,

> Don't you ever walk away when I call you again. I told you to stop. Look at me when I call you again. I told you to stop. Look at me when

75

> I'm talking to you. Do you want to go to the lock-up? Look at me. You lose two weeks free time for this. Don't ever try that again. Every day from now on you will wait, in your seat, at the table, until I say that you may leave. Is that understood? Say yes when I ask you a question. Is that understood?

It could be said that even in private homes, parents threaten to cancel an outing or to send children to their rooms when they are "bad." But there is a difference between home and the institution, a difference between loving parents rearing their children and paid attendants performing a job. Observers met staff persons who are fond of the inmates; yet, the prevailing theme in each institution is management and control. In this milieu, convenience of the staff supersedes any affection and understanding they might feel for the inmates. As for those few attendants and staff members who object to these authoritarian practices and attitudes, institutional traditions continue to hold sway. The prevailing philosophy is that affection, understanding, and compassion invite chaos. Three staff persons at three different institutions articulated this disciplinarian philosophy in strikingly similar terms. A supervising attendant at the Metropolitan State School said,

> You can trust a couple of the kids, but not all of them. You can't love them too much or they'll turn against you. They like discipline. They get too much freedom now.

Through a system of routinization and punishment, relieved only rarely by activities or attitudes that inmates desire or respect, institutions tend to transmit social ideologies toward the "retarded" and "mentally ill" which intensify the inmate's status as a deviant.

COLONIZATION

> If they'd pay 50 cents an hour I could really make some dough.
> (An inmate at the Seaway State Hospital)

> I don't have enough money for coffee.
> (An inmate at the Metropolitan State School)

I don't get paid on the laundry truck, so I just sit around now.
(An inmate at the Central State Hospital)

Even though inmates in state schools and mental hospitals are denied certain freedoms and responsibilities altogether, they live within hierarchies of freedom and responsibility. Some inmates are clearly better off than others. Each institution has its status systems by which inmates are differentiated.

Reward systems are common to most societies, certainly to our own, but what sets an institutional hierarchy apart from similar patterns of organization and reward in the broader society is that inmates have been colonized. Inmates have been captured and incarcerated in much the same way that a country is conquered and colonized. Administrators and staff define the rewards (usually cigarettes, small amounts of change, points, extra privileges), as well as the acceptable ways of achieving those rewards. They are the colonizers. Inmates have only two possible responses. They can reject the system and languish in drab, locked day rooms and isolation cells or they can play the game of seeking out the rewards, and thus perpetuate a system that is designed to keep them satisfied but that manipulates and uses them as pawns.

Status systems in institutions are elaborate mechanisms for coopting inmates into maintaining institutional life. With the promise of a cup of coffee or a cigarette, inmates will scrub floors and dishes for hours, often performing the same tasks as attendants and other personnel. In fact, inmates contribute so much toward institutional maintenance that some staff members consider the inmates' maintenance role indispensable. One nurse at the Southern State School said, "I don't know what we'd do without our workerboys."

Colonization is made complete by the practice of denying inmates the means of achieving in socially accepted or legitimate ways. Inmates are taught the values of the dominant culture with regard to money, hard work, sexual responsibility, neatness, cleanliness, and so forth, but then are denied the socially accepted ways of exhibiting those values. Residents cannot earn a minimum wage; instead they are expected to work all day for a single cigarette. Normal sexual relations are forbidden. Hard work is encouraged, but inmates are denied access to formal job roles in the society. Cleanliness and neatness are prescribed, yet inmates are not allowed to bathe when they desire and often are provided with drab, loosely fitting clothes. Most of the activities and rewards which typical citizens in the society take for granted are to the inmate extraordinary privileges.

Some inmates, such as the child who said he wanted to become an attendant when he grows up, may aspire to the same life style and consequent rewards as their colonizers. Unfortunately, they live in an atmosphere of denial, where dreams go unfulfilled and where the best one can hope for are modest amenities to relieve the emptiness.

One way of determining which people in institutions receive the greatest amounts of attention and concern from the staff and the most freedom to do what others are not allowed is to examine their clothing. We found that if a person was dressed better than most in the institution, it was usually because she was favored by the staff. If an inmate had nice clothes, she often was considered to be one of the "brighter" or "acute" inmates; she was given more freedom than others.

A group of observers reviewed the method of dispensing clothes in one state school. The following observations are excerpted:

> The woman who was giving us a tour of the building opened another locked door that led into a large room lined with attractive looking clothing. There were brightly colored dresses and racks of suits. As she opened the door, the attendant explained, "When one of them has company, we get some of these clothes for them. Each girl has a few dresses; they are all marked here. Most of these are private clothes. Or, in case one of them dies, we have to have something for them to wear." The attendant also explained that if a person received too many dresses from her parents, someone else who had no dresses would be given her old ones.
>
> On the next floor, near the day room, our guide showed us another room full of clothes. The clothes were on racks and folded neatly in

boxes. She began explaining that one rack of brightly colored dresses was supplied by the state and the dresses were used for "entertainment; like when they go to a dance or the movies, we pick a dress from here for them." We were told that state dresses are for anyone to use. They are not owned by individuals.

After we had looked at the "entertainment" clothing, I asked which clothes were used for everyday life on the ward. She picked up one of the laundry bags . . . "Now, night shift makes up bundles of clothes for each girl every day. These dresses are bright dresses," she said as she pointed to colorful dresses that had been allocated for the "brighter" girls on the ward, "and those over there are low-grade dresses". . . . The dresses provided for inmates who were considered to be less bright or "low grade" were dull, faded, and loosely styled. The woman explained to us that, "Each girl gets a dress, underwear, and socks. Then, in the morning the names are called out and the bundles are passed out in the day room."

According to this account, clothes reward "intelligence." In several of the institutions it was the "workerboys" or "workergirls" who received the nicest clothing. A person considered "low grade" did not need nice clothing because she did not "know the difference anyway." Clothing was also a way of maintaining the institution's status image with the outside community.

Status systems based on clothing were part of a broader status system in each of the institutions. We found that institutionalized people sought the same kinds of commodities that most citizens in American society seek. The difference was that, in institutions, the interest seemed so much more intense. We had not even opened the door of our car at a state school before we saw a young man in his late teens or early twenties sauntering toward us to ask for a cigarette. We met countless inmates who were beggars for candy, cigarettes, clothes, and other items.

Staffs use money as a carrot to entice the young and adult inmates to maintain the institutions. This practice has been formalized at one institution, where inmates' "good" behavior is rewarded with gifts of money, cigarettes, and candy. The money comes from the inmates' own funds which the institution controls (i.e., the reward money that inmates receive is legally already theirs). At another state school we found a similar program where the staff rewarded inmates' "good behavior" (which includes working) with points. The points could be exchanged for a cup of coffee or a trip to the canteen. Each institution had some form of reward system, whether it was completely informal, with attendants dispensing cigarettes or candy for good behavior, or part of a formal program designed to modify inmate behavior. Most state schools and state hospitals arrange to give each person one dollar a week or five dollars a month to be spent in the institutional store. However, we found after long and tedious staff interviews that some inmates who have no parents' gifts or government aid were given no money at all. Usually, staff members were reluctant to admit this.

One observer reported on his conversations with a number of inmates who were not paid for their work. He states:

> I was sitting in a waiting room, talking with a male resident who worked in the school laundry. I asked, "Do you get paid?" "Of course not," he said. "Why do you work in the laundry if you don't get paid?" I inquired. He said, "I need a job." "What do you need a job for?" I asked. He explained further, "If I get a good record in the laundry, they will get me a job in the workshop."

Unfortunately, even if an inmate proves his worth in a job, there is no guarantee that he will ever get a better job or that he will be allowed to leave the institution and return to the community. Recently, advocacy lawyers have characterized such dead-end, no-pay work conditions as institutional peonage (Mental Health Law Project, 1973).

Inmates continue to work under these conditions to keep busy, to earn small amounts of money, and most of all to achieve a position of prestige on the status hierarchy. The system can lead inmates to work against each other in attempts to "get in good" with the staff. By accepting the status arrangement that the staff encourages, "workerboys" and "workergirls" attain advantageous prestige positions, while other inmates receive drab clothing, few cigarettes, and little attention.

Staff persons pointed to the opportunities for inmates to become "workerboys" and "workergirls" as examples of how inmates could learn to live meaningful and productive lives. However, inmates perceive the worker system differently. Even those considered to be excellent workers were critical of their low pay and were anxious for more recognition. Others were cynical; they saw themselves being manipulated. A boy who worked in a local high school each day was typical of those considered responsible enough to work but not responsible enough to handle their own money. A woman who had terminal cancer, and was therefore not paid, felt ill-used by the supervisor of the sheltered workshop. Further, these inmates considered themselves powerless to alter their plight; they knew that if they complained or refused to work, they would be left in the day rooms to stare at the walls. Thus, the work system and the status system continue, with only muffled protests. Inmates, like colonized people, are expected to maintain the system that subjugates them.

TRANSFORMATION

The problem of institutional change centers on the method of altering the setting without inadvertently compounding the cruelty. In the past, many innovations — tranquilizing drugs, seclusion cells, technical labeling systems, restraining clothes, rehabilitation programs, occupational therapy, and behavior modification — have been introduced with the stated intent of improving the inmates' lives. However, such "reforms" almost invariably have increased the level and sophistication of institutional cruelty and, from the inmates' perspective, have compounded suffering.

There is a danger, too, in viewing the problem of change as a problem of resources. While some institutions have spent less than others, and inmates often are given miserable food and little or no clothing, the history of closed institutions is

Photo by Derrick TePaske

marked by massive financial and manpower commitments. Undoubtedly some of these efforts result in a few exciting programs, but the overall effect of increased commitments to closed therapeutic institutions has been an expansion of these institutions and a consequent expansion in institutionally based abuse.

We probably should abandon all hope of reforming institutions from within. To assume that one can instigate reform from within is to assume that closed institutions exist primarily to serve inmates and that dehumanization is an aberrant condition in an otherwise acceptable system. As this chapter demonstrates, institutions emphasize other, less charitable ends. With this knowledge we should frame our reforms.

An obvious solution to the problem might be the abolition of total institutions. Such institutions will not cease to dehumanize people until the people incarcerated have opportunities to interact with the larger society and until the society decides to live with its so-called "problems" rather than isolating them. I suggest, therefore, that any proposal for transforming institutions be accompanied by a detailed plan to evacuate these settings altogether.

The process of arriving at this decision has been a long and often trying one, propelled by the cruelty we observed. When we began our examination of institutions, many observers were reluctant to condemn a system they already had come to accept professionally. At first, none of us wanted to admit that so fantastically expensive and elaborate an arrangement could be so basically wrong. But once we had been trained to observe carefully and systematically, we quickly realized that closed institutions are, by their very design, abusive.

Even this conclusion, however, emanates from a larger and more profound realization that we must alter our concepts of mental retardation and mental illness. As long as we regard certain groups of people as incompetent or pitiable, as less than human, as ineducable, as troublesome and therefore expendable, we perpetuate the justifications for institutionalization. One cannot arrive at any useful blueprint for transforming institutions without first realizing that the most important element of future planning is our basic conceptualization of other people, including those with special needs.

The observers for this study were Margy Bartlett, Douglas Biklen, Jim Brasington, Sandy Chaput, T. Mark Costello, Lee Cummings, Bernie deGrandpre, Jim Denton, Emilie George, Nancy Glusker, Robert Goguen, Elizabeth Hammond, John F. Kearney, Fred McCurry, Bernice Millman, David Musselman, Roger Parent, Arnold Rehman, Ted Riggen, Audrey Sayles, Susan Shotland, Sonja Sorkin, Dean Stickles, Bob Swanson, Kinsley Swinyer, Kathy Wajda, Goldie Welikovitch, Otha Lee Wooden, Tim Andriano, Marcia Beneville, William Beneville, Mary Benton, Stefan Berg, Mark Blazey, Rhonda Buckner, Digna Chafaris, Carol Cohen, JoAnn Cullen, Susan Gannon, Robert Goodrich, Harvey Greenstein, Betsy Helfrich, Lawrence A. Hoefler, Carol Hooper, William Hughes, R. Steven Jonas, Laverdia Roach, Susan P. Minor, JoAnn Ottman, Fred Pfeifer, John Rafter, Jerry Rispoli, Bruce Shenker, Judi Silver, Dennis W. Tuttle, Marie Vitagliano, and Lucinda Young.

REFERENCES

Mental Health Law Project. *Basic rights of the mentally handicapped.* Washington, DC (1751 N. St., N.W.): Author, 1973.
Wolfensberger, Wolf. *The origin and nature of our institutional models.* Syracuse, NY: Human Policy Press, 1974.
Wyatt v. Stickney, et al. 325 Federal Supplement 781 (M.D. Alabama 1971).

3

Attendants' Perspectives and Programming on Wards in State Schools

Robert Bogdan, Steven Taylor, Bernard de Grandpre, and Sondra Haynes

Those who attempt to introduce therapeutic programs at "total institutions" (Goffman, 1961) often fail to take into account the invariable effects of the ward setting (Scheff, 1961). New programs are planned and implemented without a sufficient understanding of the context into which they are being introduced. Many of those interested in change subscribe to a system of definitions and beliefs which they assume are shared by those in the setting they are attempting to change. Those within the setting, however, may act from totally different perspectives. The result is a poor interface between the change agent and the setting — a factor which inevitably circumscribes the potential effectiveness of the change.

Reprinted from *Journal of Health & Social Behavior*, June 1974, *15*(2), 141-151; by permission.

Here, we present specific aspects of attendants' perspectives on their supervisors, their jobs, and residents and show how these relate to the implementation of "innovative" programs designed by supervisory and professional staffs to serve the needs of the residents on the attendants' wards. Our discussion deals with a specific type of total institution that is relatively unknown to social scientists: state schools for the "mentally retarded."[1]

In the United States, between 200,000 and 250,000 people reside in the often massive facilities which physically and administratively resemble state mental hospitals. They generally operate through a rigid hierarchy and are dominated by the medical model.

Although criteria for admission to state schools vary, an IQ of 75 or below makes one eligible in most states, and "maladaptive" behavior combined with the social contingencies of poverty, family crisis, or lack of community services completes the formula. "State School" is, in the institutions we have studied, a euphemism for the most barren kind of custodial care offered to any category of "client" in our society. Straitjackets, isolation cells, beatings, nudity, herding, medical neglect (e.g., skin burns from lying in urine), massive drugging, and unsanitary conditions (e.g., drinking from toilets) are characteristic of what has been termed the "back wards" of these facilties, but more subtle forms of dehumanization characterize the best of the wards. They chronically suffer from poor patient-to-staff ratios and other impediments to providing even decent custodial care.[2]

---

[1]Writings can be found in professional mental retardation literature (see the *American Journal of Mental Deficiency and Mental Retardation*). For studies in the social science literature, see Braginsky and Braginsky (1971); Morris (1969);Edgerton(1967); Tizard (1970); Klaber (1971).

[2]For descriptions of the conditions in these institutions, see the work of Burton Blatt (Blatt & Kaplan, 1966; Blatt, 1970, 1973) and the proceedings of the recent lawsuits involving Willowbrook State School in New York, Belchertown State School in Massachusetts and Partlow State School in Alabama.

The study reported here is based on data collected through intensive observation on three different wards in three different institutions, as well as supporting data from more casual field work in other wards in the same facilities and in eight other institutions. All of these institutions are located within the northeastern United States. The primary field work was conducted by three of the authors. Supporting data collection was carried out by others over a three-year period. The three authors who conducted the field work each spent a minimum of one year of at least weekly observations in one of the three wards. One lived at the institution for five months in addition to conducting prior and post observations. The observers, in participant observation style (Bogdan, 1972), spent much time with the attendants in the natural setting, interacting with them as they went about their normal activities. They presented themselves as university students[3] who were interested in mental retardation and were successful in developing a rapport characterized by trust and candor (as the quotations cited throughout this paper will suggest). The observers collected thousands of pages of field notes from which the quotations have been drawn to illustrate our points.

The three institutions on which this study concentrates are located on the edge of a middle-sized city and in rural communities. One institution houses 400 residents, another 2,500, and the third 3,000. The wards were an infant/children's ward, a ward for adolescent girls of rather high ability, and a ward for the "severely and profoundly retarded aggressive young adult males" (age range 14 through 44) — to which we shall refer as the "back ward." The wards, as one can imagine from their brief introduction, vary in the kind of residents and the nature of the environment and services provided. We have attempted to draw from our data the commonalities in

---

[3]The three observers were all graduate students interested in the field of mental retardation during the time they collected data (de Grandpre, 1973; Taylor, 1973; Haynes, 1973).

attendants' perspectives that are directly related to understanding the implementation of programs. While we do not maintain that the material we present represents the views of all attendants, we do take the position that it characterizes their dominant views.

PERSPECTIVES ON SUPERIORS: "THEY DON'T KNOW WHAT IT'S REALLY LIKE"

Attendants share the view that their superiors, be they administrators, line professionals, or supervisors, misunderstand the needs of the residents and the nature of life and work on the wards. It is their belief that their own proximity to the residents, and time spent on the ward, provide them with a knowledge of ward life which is inaccessible to others. As an attendant from the back ward described his superiors:

> They just sit in the office and tell us what to do, but they're not here. They don't know what we know.

An attendant on the infant/children ward expressed a similar point of view in reference to staff meetings at which decisions are made about residents' placements and from which attendants are excluded:

> We're the ones who spend most of the time with the children. We know what they can do and what they can't do. At the last meeting they had a teacher come who doesn't hardly have anything to do with any of the children. Somebody from O.T. (Occupational Therapy) — they have very little to do with the children. And then Dr. Erthardman[4] who doesn't even know the children. She might make a decision that a child needs another IQ test to see what he can do since the last test. I could tell her what they can do and what they can't do.

As this quotation begins to suggest, the perspective that attendants "know best" is based on a skepticism of profes-

---

[4]This, as all proper names in this paper, is a pseudonym.

sionals and the procedures and approaches they employ. The attendants, many of whom have not completed high school, believe in direct observation and the application of "common sense," and tend to regard with tongue-in-cheek, test scores, esoteric vocabularies and explanations, and the general approach some professionals use in treating "patients" (as the residents are often termed). For example, attendants on the back ward, as well as those on the adolescent ward, hold a dubious view of the advice of the institution's professionals:

> Let me tell you, those psychiatrists are all crazy. . . . They just don't know what they are doing. They tell you to sit down with 'em and talk to them when they start going at it (fighting). Christ, if I tried that I'd get my brains kicked out.

And on all three wards attendants question the validity of IQ scores:

> That (score) can't be right. He ain't that dumb.

> I know they told us she was retarded, but after working with her a week I knew darn well she wasn't, no matter what they said.

The attendants clearly doubt the competence of the particular professionals working at the institutions. Attendants know and discuss the fact that professional work at an institution confers low status among professionals and that professional departments encounter difficulties in recruiting trained and competent personnel. Thus, the vast majority of physicians at institutions has not met state certification requirements, and more than half are foreign born and trained, which creates communication barriers. These characteristics are associated with inferiority in the attendants' minds. The following quotation illustrates their perspective:

> We have a foreign doctor and I don't think he knows what he is doing. All he does is put yellow salve on her feet and they get worse. I can't understand a word he says. We have another doctor that is even harder to understand. I think half of these kids are getting the wrong medicine. You would think they could get a better doctor.

89

Attendants offer countless examples to support their collective view that professionals at their institutions are incompetent, lazy, or lax in performing their duties. The remarks quoted below are typical of those commonly heard on the wards:

> (The professionals) read off the IQ and what the patient can do, and the stuff isn't anywhere up to date. It will say the patient is blind and you'll find the patient running around the day room.

> The care these kids get is criminal. I don't know why they can't give them decent medical care. They have to be half dead before they will do anything. I remember sending one kid up to the hospital with a 102 fever and they wouldn't do anything about it.

> I haven't seen a doctor around here all weekend. Connie (a resident) has been sick for three days and no doctor.

> I haven't seen a psychiatrist up here since I started.

As the many quotations indicate, attendants resent most professionals, supervisors, and administrators at the institutions. They believe they themselves have the "roughest" jobs, and that others are over-paid and under-worked:

> Those whose jobs require them to sit down all day get the air conditioning while we run around like sweltering pigs.

> They're always off some place to a meeting or a conference. You would think *we'd* have a conference or something.

> Dr. Lee never came in today. Boy! It must be nice to come and go like that.

The attendants' skepticism and hostility extend to high state officials and legislators who are ultimately responsible for the institutions. Legislators, according to attendants, "won't give us what we need," and state officials "don't give a darn." The attendants point to understaffing, the general ward conditions, the lack of basic supplies, and the inaccessibility of officials and legislators to buttress their view that "nobody cares." The following comment was offered by an attendant on the back ward, where the smell of feces and urine permeates the air:

You tell them they don't give us antiseptic or clothes for the patients. You tell them we can't do nothin' cause they won't give us what we need.

Another attendant summarized his own and his co-worker's feelings about the state and the institution:

It's really bad here — no programs, no nothing. We sit here and watch bodies. I've been here 27 years. The state and the doctors — they're something else. The directors get big fat salaries — they've never had experience on the wards — they don't know what's going on. After they pay them, there's no money for the people and services here. When I retire I'm gonna tell my friends in the Capitol about the way things are being run.

PERSPECTIVES ON WORK: "A JOB IS A JOB"

While attendants derive some satisfaction from the intrinsic aspects of their work (such as the companionship which other attendants offer), they define their jobs primarily in terms of the extrinsic benefits these jobs provide. Thus, they resemble unskilled workers in other settings, in their definition of their work:[5]

It's a job — nothing more, nothing less.

One attendant from the back ward related:

If I didn't need the checks so bad I'd quit.

Attendants on the back ward place an equal importance on monetary rewards and fringe benefits:

Everyone is here for one reason and one reason only — money. That's right — they're all here for the money. That's why they took this job. That's why I took this job.

---

[5]The alternative to institutional employment for most attendants is lower-level factory or construction work.

91

In keeping with this perspective, attendants see themselves not as "professionals" who are responsible for engaging the residents in programmed activities but, rather, as custodians responsible for keeping the ward clean and maintaining control and order among the residents (Taylor, 1973). An attendant on the back ward offered the following remarks:

> We're supposed to feed 'em and keep an eye on 'em and make sure they're OK. They have people in recreation — psychologists and sociologists. They're the ones who are supposed to train 'em and work with 'em — not us.

This emphasis on custodial care is so strong that the well-being of the residents often is ignored or deliberately violated (Taylor, 1973). One attendant commented:

> We have no time to keep things as they should be, let alone help the residents. We sometimes have to tie people up so that we can carry on with the work.

Another stated:

> By the time you're done with your work, you're too tired to do anything else.

Attendants develop routines to minimize their custodial work and develop methods of control to deal with "troublesome" residents. Those on the back ward use "brighter" residents ("workerboys") to do much of the custodial work and to control other residents. Attendants on all wards form work quotas and gold brick, as do factory workers (Roy, 1951). Thus, they spend much of their time "goofing off" despite the fact they they complain they never have enough time. On back wards a resident is assigned to watch out for supervisors while the attendants pitch nickels, read the newspaper, harass residents, drink, or pass the time in idle conversation. On all wards the television, which is turned to stations of the attendants' choosing, provides diversion during the long breaks. Each ward "observer" has been left single-handed to cover for the attendants while they left the wards for breaks.

Attendants resent those who disrupt their routines. They direct negative comments toward co-workers who do either too little work or who do too much, and they resent outsiders who come to help with the residents but "interfere" in other ways. The following comments were made in regard to a group of LPN trainees who were willing to help dress, feed, and bathe the children on the infant/children ward:

> They're a nuisance. Each of the girls was assigned to one of the children. They took so long bathing them that we got way behind on that. They got the laundry all mixed up.

For most attendants, then, work at the institution represents nothing more than a job, albeit a well-paying one. Some attendants are stoical in discussing their work; that is, work is not something that is to be liked or disliked — it is something which must be done. In their own words:

> My husband always asks me how I can stay on this job. Well, I figure somebody has to do it. It has to be done.

> Somebody's gotta do it. Somebody's gotta take care of the kids.

PERSPECTIVES ON RESIDENTS: "LOW GRADES," "REJECTS," AND "DELINQUENTS"

In view of the importance attendants place on the custodial aspects of their work, it is hardly surprising that they define residents in terms of either their disabilities or the amount of trouble or work they cause. Thus, attendants refer to residents with words which emphasize those characteristics: "puker," "regurgitator," "dummy," "biter," "grabber," "soiler," "headbanger," "low grade," "vegetable," "brat," "fighter."

Certain residents are sources of concern to attendants on all wards. "Hyperactive" residents and those who lack basic self-help skills are especially resented. On the infant/children ward women attendants complain about non-ambulatory children who are heavy to lift. These children are transferred from the

93

ward regardless of age, despite the fact that they are supposed to remain on the ward until they reach the age of 12 years.[6] On the back ward the population is comprised of what the attendants call "rejects" from other wards — residents who were placed there because they were too much trouble for other attendants. On the adolescent ward attendants believe that about one-third of their residents were placed there not because they are "retarded" but, rather, because they are incorrigible.

> This bunch of girls isn't retarded — they are just delinquents. They don't like school and their parents don't make them go. We get them back when the parents can't handle them.

Few attendants believe in the residents' potential to learn or to change. From their point of view, little can be done for the residents beyond what is already being done. One attendant typified this perspective in her response to a question concerning the futures of the children on her ward:

> Eventually they'll go to another building. Most of them will be this way for the rest of their lives.

Attendants on the back ward remarked that their residents are too "low grade" to learn despite the fact that some of them demonstrate competence in speech and spelling:

> I'd give anything to be able to help these kids, but you can't do it. They're too low grade.

On the adolescent ward attendants held similarly fatalistic views in regard to innate capacities of the residents they called

---

[6]This practice can have dire consequences for non-ambulatory children. Those who cannot walk by the time they leave this ward are transferred to wards for non-ambulatory adolescents or adults where they receive no training to walk. Many, therefore, never do walk.

the "poor kids" or the "really retarded." And even the "delinquents" on this ward were seen as having been morally damaged by their families to the extent that it was difficult to teach them "new tricks."

Attendants also view residents as being susceptible to being "spoiled." This view often is used by attendants to justify their own inactivity in working or playing with residents. Attendants on the infant/children ward, for example, frequently allow the children to lie in their cage-like cribs and cry rather than pick them up, with the reasoning that they have been spoiled in the past and further attention will only spoil them more. One of these attendants described the effect of the aforementioned group of LPN trainees who had spent a week on the ward and had held and fondled the children:

> It's really not fair to the children. They get used to all of this attention and then it's taken away. Some of them have been spoiled in only five days.

An attendant on the back ward revealed a similar point of view when he discussed the actions of attendants on another ward:

> These women attendants spoil these kids. They let 'em get away with anything. Jimmy used to be in that ward. He ran the place. They brought him up to us though — he was pulling out his cock and chasing women. When Jimmy came up here he was spoiled but that didn't last too long. He tried to steal food from the other kids and they let him have it. Man, he didn't pull that stuff anymore.

Another attendant from this ward stated:

> You just can't give them everything they want or you won't be able to control them.

Finally, this same "give them an inch and they'll take a mile" view was expressed by an attendant on the adolescent ward:

> If the attendants don't keep things under control, it's their own fault. They have to show them who's boss.

95

In the eyes of attendants, professionals, superiors, and state officials pose a challenge to their own "give them an inch" view. These persons, it should be remembered, "don't know what it's really like." Yet these persons also impose restrictions which attendants resent. Thus, attendants regard them as threatening and resent state rulings which allegedly affirm the rights of residents, superiors' concern with incidents of resident abuse, and new time demands and program ideas.

While attendants underline the differences between their own perspectives and those of others, the institutions' administrative and professional staffs often support attendants' perspectives. For example, physicians prescribe large dosages of tranquilizers to control residents, and the schools at the institutions provide educational services for a relatively small number of residents. Most significant in this regard, however, is the training all attendants receive in preparation for their jobs.

The focus of formal attendant training at the three institutions is on the etiology of "mental retardation" and the developmental characteristics of the "mentally retarded," as illustrated in the following quotations:

> We learn about medications, how these people are different from you and me, how to care for them, how to treat them, what to expect, things like that.

> They teach you a lot about causes and things, but you can't use that here.

Such "facts" and the concepts of "mental retardation" are reified through a series of lectures and charts which describe the limitations of the "retarded." One chart states that the "profoundly retarded" are "helpless." Attendants are trained, then, to concentrate on residents' innate limitations.

In addition to formal training sessions in which "retardation" is explained, newly employed attendants are taught first aid skills and are informed of the rules and regulations of the institution. Perhaps a more important aspect of the three-week orientation program is the experience they receive working on the wards as they are rotated from building to building. This orientation to the wards puts new attendants in contact with the "old timers" from the first day, thus exposing them to the perspectives we have been discussing early in their careers as institution employees.

THE BROTHERHOOD AT THE BOTTOM

Factors other than training give support to, intensify, and validate attendants' perspectives. While we will not discuss all of these factors at this point, an important concept to understand in this regard is what we might term "the brotherhood at the bottom." By this, we mean that attendants are both occupationally and socially isolated from supervisors, professionals, and administrators at the institution.

Attendants have little actual contact with others at the institution in the context of their work. They spend their time together on the wards and discuss the faults of this or that superior or professional and, in general, how "they don't know what it's really like." More than this, however, attendants share similar socioeconomic and geographic backgrounds and have opportunities to see each other outside of work. Thus, many attendants spend their free time together at local bars and clubs, and many are related to each other through blood or marriage. On the back ward, for example, one attendant has eight relatives who are attendants at the institution.

Attendants' perspectives are reinforced through these on-the-job and off-the-job contacts. They also develop feelings of solidarity among themselves and of alienation from others.

INNOVATIVE PROGRAMMING

It should not be difficult to imagine what happened when supervisory and professional staffs attempted to introduce "innovative" programs onto these wards.

A program that was introduced in the back ward was referred to by attendants and their supervisors as a "motivation training" program. The attendants were never quite certain of the program's intended purpose and, in fact, received their information about the program from fellow workers on other wards and shifts. In the following quotation, one "ward charge" (supervising attendant) described how he learned about the program:

> I was talking to another charge and he told me about it. You see, it's supposed to be from 6 to 8:30 every night. Then each guy will take 12 kids (age range of residents on this ward is 14 to 44) and sit around and teach 'em things — like how to take care of themselves, and dress themselves. And then every ward is getting a popcorn popper and we'll give 'em popcorn every night as a reward.

While some attendants were willing to give the program their guarded approval prior to its implementation, most viewed it with skepticism from its beginning. Some argued that they had too little time and too much other work to implement such a program:

> Now how are we supposed to motivate 'em, and clean this place and everything? We don't have enough employees.

Others believed that the intellectual capacities of the residents precluded significant "improvement":

> You see, the patients we have are all rejects and we're supposed to do something with them. You can teach them so much and that's it. They can't learn no more.

Although this ward's supervising attendant postponed the program's implementation for a period of four weeks after it was supposed to have begun, it was finally introduced with the aid of a "trained" attendant from another ward. The actual program consisted of two activities which were offered on alternative evenings: crayoning in coloring books, and listening to children's records. The sessions lasted for periods of an hour to an hour-and-a-half for the time the program was in operation.

How did the attendants view the program? Some saw it as a means of keeping the residents occupied:

> I don't think it's doing any good. It gives them something to do — that's all.

There was some truth to this statement, as this was, for the great majority of residents, the only recreation they received at the institution.

Most attendants, however, perceived the crayoning and the music as some type of "training." In spite of the tenuous (at best) connection between these activities and training, some attendants viewed the activities as the initial stage of a more comprehensive program:

> We're supposed to progress from here — start teaching them how to dress and things.

Yet the residents' performance in these simplest of activities served to further confirm the attendants' perspectives that training for the residents on this ward was futile. Their general belief in the inability of the residents to change was supported and specified. One attendant explained:

> I've been trying to teach them how to color, but it doesn't work for most of them. They don't switch colors when they're coloring, and they won't stay in the lines. I've been trying to teach them, but they just scribble.

The program was unofficially terminated six weeks after its start. One attendant related:

> It kinda fizzled out. We're not doin' it anymore.

Another stated:

> All the wards just about stopped doin' it. The whole institution was supposed to have it, but most of them stopped. I don't know — I

haven't been here that long — but I think that's the way it always goes
. . . it's too hard keeping their attention.

One attendant summed up his own and his peers' fatalism,
when he remarked:

> I bet you think we're just a bunch of lazy fat slobs here. . . . Well, we
> do sit around a lot doin' nothin'. We read the paper and watch TV.
> But actually there isn't much we could do with 'em even if we wanted
> to.

The program on the adolescent ward lasted much longer
than the program we have just reviewed and, in fact, was still
operating at last knowledge. This program was designed by
the Chief of Children's Services, Dr. Warner, who described
the program as a "behavior modification program — token
economy — designed to teach responsibility to the girls."
According to the plan, the girls were to be rewarded for doing
assigned ward jobs and for satisfactory school work by receiving points which could be redeemed for merchandise. As Dr.
Warner told one of the authors:

> This will reward them for good behavior. I really think it will make a
> difference. We need a lot more behavior modification here. It's the
> answer.

While skeptical of Dr. Warner, the attendants initially
viewed the point system as a potentially effective way for
them to control the residents' behavior and to make their
work easier. One explained:

> The girls are snapping to it and doing what they are supposed to. If
> you tell them they are going to lose some points, they pay attention to
> you now.

As this comment suggests, the program that was designed to
reward residents for "appropriate behavior" was used to
punish them for annoying behavior. Thus, attendants took
away points for insolence or vulgarity. Since residents could
receive points from personnel other than attendants, taking

away points was one of the few means by which the attendants could retain control.

In the eyes of the attendants, Dr. Warner was far too
permissive and misunderstood the girls. The attendants
claimed that the new system and other innovations would
only serve to further spoil them. Witness the following comments offered by one of the attendants:

> Have you heard Dr. Warner's last idea? He wants to let volunteers
> take the boys and girls with the most points out to dinner at some
> fancy place. These kids would probably beat up the volunteer!

Also, the precise record-keeping which the point system
entailed soon became "just a lot of trouble" for the attendants. At the end of the observation period, approximately six
months after the program's implementation, the attendants
were extremely lax in their point recording, and many of the
girls had simply forgotten about the points they had accumu-
lated.

A "range of motion" program was introduced in the
infant/children ward by the attending physician and the day
shift ward charge, a registered nurse. It lasted the shortest
period of time of the three programs we have reviewed and,
in fact, was never implemented for many of the residents. The
goal of this program was to provide children with the physical
stimulation necessary to prevent physical regression and the
development of spasticity and irreversible contractures. The
program was developed in view of the fact that these conditions had already stricken many children and that, without
some program, would strike many more.

The institution's only physical therapist (institutional
population: 2,500) visited the ward, evaluated each child, and
wrote a prescription describing the therapy each was to receive. Each child was assigned to an attendant who had been
instructed in the range of motion exercises to be employed
daily. Direct observation of the dorms revealed that few attendants ever provided their designated children with the
range of motion therapy. At one point the daytime charge,

101

who was ultimately responsible for the program's implementation, became aware of the problem and mentioned it to her supervisor in the observer's presence:

> "The attendants aren't doing anything," said Mrs. Dey, the nurse who was the daytime charge.
> "What kinds of things do you think they ought to be doing?" the observer asked.
> "I think they ought to be doing the range of motion," she responded.
> "Aren't they doing it?" asked Mrs. Dumas, the supervising nurse.
> "No," said Mrs. Dey, shaking her head, "I go into the front dorm and all they're doing is sitting around."

When they were alone with the observer, the attendants articulated the reasons for their failure to pursue the program. They maintained, among other things, that the wrong children had been selected to participate and that they themselves were neither able (trained) nor willing (sufficiently paid) to do what was expected of them.

CONCLUSION

Our primary position in this study has been that institutional programs must be examined in the context of the ward settings in which they are introduced. We have studied one aspect of that setting — the way attendants define their supervisors, their jobs, and the residents under their charge.

One might conclude, in reading a paper such as ours, that the problem of programming in total institutions lies only in attendants' attitudes and lack of training. While this is a seductive way of defining the problem — walking through these isolated, massive facilities which are filled with unwanted human beings — one must question whether the problem is not the institutional model itself. Perhaps the feeble attempts at programming which we have reported here represent the cruelest lies of this dehabilitating system. Perhaps attendants' reactions to programming are realistic adjustments to the truth of the system. To offer programming as a remedy to a system that by its very nature isolates, desocializes, and dehumanizes, reminds us of Marie Antoinette's remark when informed that her subjects were starving, that they had no bread. Her response was: "Let them eat cake."

REFERENCES

Biklen, D. *Patterns of power.* Unpublished dissertation, Syracuse University, 1973.

Blatt, B. *Exodus from pandemonium.* Boston: Allyn & Bacon, 1970.

Blatt, B. *Souls in extremis.* Boston: Allyn & Bacon, 1973.

Blatt, B., & Kaplan, F. *Christmas in purgatory.* Boston: Allyn & Bacon, 1966.

Bogdan, R. *Participant observation in organizational settings.* Syracuse, NY: Syracuse University Press, 1972.

Braginsky, D., & Braginsky, B. *Hansels and Gretels.* New York: Holt, Rinehart & Winston, 1971.

de Grandpre, B. *The culture of a state school ward.* Unpublished dissertation, Syracuse University, 1973.

Edgerton, R. *The cloak of competence.* Berkeley: University of California Press, 1967.

Goffman, E. *Asylums: Essays on the social situation of mental patients and other inmates.* Garden City, NY: Doubleday & Co., Anchor Books, 1961.

Haynes, S. *Change in a state school.* Unpublished dissertation, Syracuse University, 1973.

Klaber, M. Institutional programming and research: A vital partnership in action. In A. Baumeister and E. Butterfield (Eds.), *Residential facilities for the mentally retarded.* Chicago: Aldine, 1971, pp. 163-200.

Morris, P. *Put away.* New York: Atherton, 1969.

Roy, D. Quota restriction and goldbricking in a machine shop. *American Journal of Sociology,* March 1952, 57, 427-442.

Scheff, T. Control over policy by attendants in a mental hospital. *Journal of Health & Human Behavior,* Summer 1961, 2 93-105.

Taylor, S. *Attendants perspectives: A view from the back ward.* Unpublished paper presented at the 97th annual meeting of the American Association on Mental Deficiency, 1973.

Tizard, J. The role of social institutions in the causation, prevention, and alleviation of mental retardation. In H. Haywood (Ed.), *Social-cultural aspects of mental retardation.* New York: Appleton-Century-Crofts, 1970. pp. 281-340.

Wyatt, *Ricky* v. *Stonewall B. Stickney,* et al. Plaintiffs brief, March 2, 1972. U.S. District Court, Middle District Alabama, Northern Division, Civil Action No. 3195-N.

4

The Public Schools

Steven J. Apter

In the United States almost everyone has some understanding
of public schools. In fact, at any given time, the overwhelming majority has direct and current ties to the public schools. If
you're not a student, you probably have a child or grandchild
who is. If you don't work there, you well may have a friend
who does. And if you don't have a direct link to the public
schools today, surely you remember what it was like when
you were there, as Cindy Herbert did in her "Memories of
School" (1974):

> The room was big and smelled of chalk and old books. . . . I re-
> member the wood of the desk and chair. . . . Outside was a big oak
> tree we used to climb after school. . . . My teacher was tall and she
> wore purple dresses. . . . Once I had to stay in during recess when I
> was caught chewing gum. . . . One time I got "Needs to improve" in
> "Gets along well with others." . . . Getting chosen for the baseball
> team was an awful experience. . . . My parents expected me to make
> "A's" of course. . . .

Despite the finding that huge numbers of children — *two million* or more, according to the Children's Defense Fund (1974) — do not go to school, the fact remains that an overwhelming majority of people in America spend a significant portion of the childhood years in public schools. In one recent school year, 1969-70, the public schools enrolled more than 45 *million students* and employed well over 2 *million adults* on their instructional staffs (Silberman, 1970, p. 17). Consequently, the public school is undoubtedly the best known institution in our society. If you ask people to comment about the problems of mental hospitals or the dehumanizing conditions found in a state facility for retarded persons, you may get cursory responses or no response at all. But ask the same people about current disciplinary practices in the local elementary school or forced busing to desegregate the high schools and see what kind of responses you get!

"Public School" is such a broad and all-encompassing concept that it seems to be at the very center of life in American society. Sarason (1971) says it well:

> There are few, if any, major social problems for which explanations and solutions do not in some way involve the public school — involvement that may be direct or indirect, relevant or irrelevant, small or large. After all, the argument usually runs, the school is a reflection of our society as well as the principal vehicle by which its young are socialized or prepared for life in adult society. Therefore, it should not be surprising that discussion of any major social problem — be it violence, drug addiction, sex, illegitimacy, malnutrition, unemployability, smoking, or racial discrimination — quickly centers on what schools are and what they should be. The initial response seems to be what the federal government should or could do, and the government, in turn, usually takes action which in one way or another impinges on the school setting. Since we do not lack major social problems, and because the scope of federal responsibility has changed so dramatically, primarily as a consequence of the depression in the thirties, we are now in an era when more people spend more time than ever before planning and executing educational programs and changes. And those who neither plan nor implement spend a portion of their leisure time criticizing those who do (p. 7).

The influence of the public schools on American life is enormous. The significance of our biggest and best-known institution cannot be overestimated. The potential benefits of a public school system for the children who populate it, and ultimately for our future, are as limitless and awesome to consider as the idea of a free and mandated education for *all* children.

But there are problems in the public schools, and they are massive, significant, and can be as overwhelmingly destructive to individuals and to society as one might expect from an institution so central to our lives. What are some of these problems? How did they come about? What is their impact on children with special needs as well as on "typical" children?

CRITICISM OF PUBLIC SCHOOLS

In the early 1960's, perhaps as a result of the political climate at the time, a barrage of criticism was aimed at the public schools by many of its own employees. People like John Holt, Herbert Kohl and Jonathan Kozol have published chilling descriptions of their own work in urban classrooms. In John Holt's introduction to *How Children Fail* (1964), he says:

Most children in school fail.

For a great many, this failure is avowed and absolute. Close to 40 percent of those who begin high school drop out before they finish. For college, the figure is one in three.

Many others fail in fact if not in name. They complete their schooling only because we have agreed to push them up through the grades and out of the schools, whether they know anything or not. There are many more such children than we think. If we "raise our standards" much higher, as some would have us do, we will find out very soon just how many there are. Our classrooms will bulge with kids who can't pass the test to get into the next class.

But there is a more important sense in which almost all children fail; except for a handful, who may or may not be good students, they fail to develop more than a tiny part of the tremendous capacity for learning, understanding, and creating with which they were born and of which they made full use during the first two or three years of their lives (p. XIII).

Books like *36 Children* (Kohl, 1968) and *Death at an Early Age* (Kozol, 1967) echoed many of Holt's findings and called attention to the failure of public schools to respond to the emotional lives of so many children in America.

The range of criticisms of the public schools is wide. If Holt was concerned with children who failed to develop their capacity for learning, there have been many other critics who are more interested in the specific academic information and skills students could gain through their public school education. The impact of the Russian satellite Sputnik on public schools in America was to create a quick and vigorous new emphasis on mathematics and science in the hope that American children would progress far enough in these areas to keep our society technologically equal or superior to that of the Russians.

More recently, Howsam (1976) reminds us that average scores on achievement tests have been continuing to decline over the past few years, that 20 percent of U.S. adults are having severe difficulty functioning both in major skills (reading, writing, problem-solving and computation) and with regard to general knowledge, and that a considerably higher percentage of persons are barely functioning in these areas. The fact that suits are being filed in U.S. courts on behalf of young men and women who are graduating from high schools in our country but are unable to read as well as an average eighth grader adds to Howsam's conclusions and makes it clear that the educational effectiveness of the public schools is in serious question.

Sarason (1971) has noted the probability of every aspect of public school life being subjected to criticism at one time or another and has provided a partial list of some of those criticisms:

1. Textbooks and curricula tend to be dull and out of date.
2. Teachers are not well grounded in their subject matter.

3. Teachers do not make the learning experience stimulating and exciting.
4. Teaching is primarily a "pouring in" of knowledge rather than a "getting out" of interests, curiosity, and motivations. Put in another way, children learn for extrinsic rather than intrinsic reasons and rewards.
5. Teachers are too conforming, intellectually and personally, and resist new ideas and the need to change.
6. There are selective factors at work determining who goes into teaching. One of the consequences is that those who go into teaching tend, on the average, not to be as bright as those who go into many other professions.
7. Schools are over-organized settings, top heavy with supervisors and administrators who are barriers to the individual teacher's initiative and creativity and not responsive to the needs of individual children (p. 16).

To Sarason's list we could add:

8. Schools are too expensive. Many communities are being taxed to their limits, and still the schools need more money to operate. (For the 45 million students in school during the 1969-70 year, the tab was more than $35 billion.)
9. No matter how you define "education," there is not much evidence to indicate that public schools are doing it effectively.
10. Schools serve as the great labelers in our society, assigning names to children (mentally retarded, emotionally disturbed, etc.) that, even if they turn out to be totally inappropriate, may have severe negative implications on an individual's future.
11. Schools devalue individual differences by excluding children with special needs from regular programs.

The wave of criticism directed at the public schools in the 1960's was brought to a climax by Charles Silberman's *Crisis in the Classroom* (1970). In that report Silberman went straight to the heart of the problem in public schools:

> Most of all, however, I am indignant at the failures of the public schools themselves. "The most deadly of all possible sins," Erik Erickson suggests, "is the mutilation of a child's spirit." It is not possible to spend any prolonged period visiting public school classrooms without being appalled by the mutilation visible everywhere, mutilation of spontaneity, of joy in learning, of pleasure in creating, of sense of self. The public schools — those "killers of the dream," to appropriate a phrase of Lillian Smith's — are the kind of institution one cannot really dislike until one gets to know them well. Because adults take the schools so much for granted, they fail to appreciate what grim, joyless places most American schools are, how oppressive and petty are the rules by which they are governed, how intellectually sterile and esthetically barren the atmosphere, what an appalling lack of civility obtains on the part of teachers and principals, what contempt they unconsciously display for children as children (p. 10).

Six years later, in a recent issue of the *New York Times* (4/25/76), Zigler wrote:

> Some years after Silberman's *Crisis in the Classroom*, too many of America's schools remain joyless enclaves in which too many children experience little more than rebuff and failure.

SOME CRITICAL ISSUES IN PUBLIC SCHOOLS TODAY

It is impossible to discuss, or perhaps even to list, all the issues in public school life that need to be examined critically. Our decision to search for specific themes that permeate the atmospheres of public schools has been based on a number of factors: the idea (as Blatt stated earlier in this volume) that children cannot be understood apart from the institutions in which they live; the need to continue the process of understanding the natural culture of schools that Sarason has begun so well; and the notion that, despite the myriad of severe problems they encompass, the public schools remain the institution with the most significant potential for the lives of our children.

Aside from the obvious reason that there are unlimited issues but limited space, the reasons for our choices of specific themes are summarized below.

Children with Special Needs. While the issues that follow (indeed any issues we might choose) have obvious implications for all children, we confess that the specific application to children with special needs was an important element in the selection of each of the critical themes. We were concerned with the meaning of our issues in terms of the options they implied for responding to the range and depth of individual differences.

Emotional Lives of Children and Adults. A second prime consideration was the expected impact of particular issues on the emotional lives of the children and adults who spend their days in public school settings. Our bias undoubtedly shows here, as this reason reflects our belief that the inner lives of all of us are important not only in and of themselves, of course, but also to serve as the essential base upon which to build a lifetime of learning.

Re-Entry Problems. Elsewhere in this volume (Biklen and others) and in other places, the problems of exclusion have been discussed. Here we are more concerned with the process by which children can re-enter the public school system and, most importantly, the factors that determine the success or failure of that process. This is a particularly important area of concern now, in light of the legal advocacy that is enabling more children to remain in school and the mainstreaming movement that strives to have more children with special needs placed back into regular public school settings.

Adults in Schools. This is an area of concern that seems obviously crucial but all too often is ignored in much of the writing focused on public schools. In our choice of issues, however, we gave special consideration to the needs and problems of the millions of adults whose careers are embedded in the concept of public schools.

School/Community Life. What is the process by which schools and communities interact? Can they utilize each other's resources fully? Are they even aware of each other's strengths and weaknesses? We have been concerned about the "match" between school and community on a number of levels; the issues that follow clearly reflect these concerns.

The critical themes were chosen on the basis of the specific reasons listed above. Individually and collectively, they represent an attempt to examine and understand the public school experience, to analyze its functions and needs and resources, and to provide some general guidelines for continued scrutiny in the future.

Leadership

A variable that is critical to the life (or death) of any organization is the quality of its leadership. For a variety of reasons, strong positive leadership never has been one of the hallmarks of the public school system. Perhaps it's because of the organizational diffusion: The action is in your neighborhood school, all right, but the power and the resources and the "clout" are downtown somewhere, lost in the maze of school system bureaucracy. Then again, lately there has been more reason to believe that much of that "clout" isn't downtown at all anymore — it's tied up in the political machinations at your state capitol or hopelessly entangled in the web of the federal red-tapery in Washington.

There can't be much doubt that governmental officialism is a significant contributor to the crisis in school leadership. However, there are additional reasons — much closer to home — for the appalling lack of direction in so many of our schools. Unfortunately, many of those reasons are the principals of your local schools right now and, consequently, if we're going to discuss public school leadership, the principal's office is a good place to begin. The problem with principals is that they are often people in positions of potentially great influence and power who have neither the background and training nor the inclination to demonstrate the kinds of leadership their positions would allow. As Sarason (1971) says:

> The fact that a teacher has spent a number of years in a classroom *with children* is no compelling basis for assuming that it prepares one for a position in which one's major task is working *with adults*. Put in another way: being a "leader" of children, and exclusively of children, does not necessarily prepare one for being a leader of adults (p. 112).

Sarason cites additional factors (Teachers are "loners" who over time tend to accept schools the way they are. The motivation to become a principal often has little to do with the job itself but is tied more to the prestige and money and novelty of a new situation. Teachers' perceptions of the principal's role are often terribly incomplete.) that he feels combine to suggest that being a "good" teacher for a number of years may be *antithetical* to being an educational leader. And yet, as we know, this is the very process by which principals are chosen.

What are the implications of the lack of leadership in our public schools? First of all, schools without leadership all too often turn out to be settings devoid of purpose and of spirit as well. What kind of learning environment have we created when "the way it is" is always preferable to "the way it could be"? What kind of model for living are we presenting when children see adults who can only react but never act? And, of course, what kind of model are we presenting to teachers, some of whom may become principals themselves some day?

Secondly, leadership is a crucial element in the development of a school point-of-view or philosophy and, ultimately, an educational plan based on that viewpoint. One of the great tragedies in public school life is the failure of individual schools, for whatever reasons, to have a philosophy of education, to express it as clearly and completely as possible, and to develop and implement a process that maximizes the effectiveness of that particular viewpoint. This is not the task of the principal alone; all of the adults and, hopefully, the children

113

of each school should have the opportunity to participate in the goal-setting process. But there must be leadership to begin anything; there must be an active model for people to see, and a source of support for your efforts that people can feel.

What a difference there might be between a setting in which a principal serves as an administrator performing the typical housekeeping functions, carrying out the usual program, and another school in which a principal also takes on the leadership role we've been describing! The effects on both children and teachers could be striking, and persons in positions of potentially powerful leadership should be especially attentive to Silberman's (1970) words:

> What educators must realize, moreover, is that how they teach and how they act may be more important than what they teach. The way we do things, that is to say, shapes values more directly and more effectively than the way we talk about them (p. 9).

Decision-making

A second critical issue, closely related to Leadership, is focused on the area of decision-making in public schools. What kinds of decisions are made by school personnel? On what basis? At what point in time? More generally, this issue is concerned with the identification and resolution of problems in school life and the variety of decisions that should be made on a number of different levels.

One frequent kind of situation needing decision involves the determination of academic programs for students with special needs. Sometimes this occurs in a formalized committee process, but far too often decisions are made within the frighteningly narrow confines of one adult's mind.

You Don't Know Me

. . . You have me pegged before I walk in the door
You look at my grades
My aptitude tests
My IQ

You talk to other teachers about me and my sisters and brothers
And you have me pegged before I step in the door
How could I ever change your mind? . . . (Herbert, 1974)

We ought to know, by now, how devastating the effects of negative expectations can be on the lives of children. We ought to know how cautious we must be and how carefully we must consider each child as an individual when we're planning our educational programs. We ought to know a lot more about ourselves and the ways in which we think about others than we apparently do. Unfortunately, public schools are filled with the kinds of decisions Herbert phrased so well above and, as a result, great numbers of children are hurt every year.

But those informal assessments do not represent the only way decisions about individual children are made in public schools. There also is a much more formalized process for considering programs and placements for children who appear, at least to some adults, to be having difficulty functioning in their current school programs. Though the exact process varies, the usual sequence of events goes something like this: Adult (teacher, aide, etc.) notices some inappropriate behavior or academic inability of a child; referral is made to ancillary staff member (psychologist, social worker, resource teacher) who interviews or tests the child; a meeting is held by the standing committee that considers these "cases"; views are shared and a decision reached as to the most appropriate placement for the child being considered.

Although the manner in which all this happens and the roles of the people involved undoubtedly differ from school to school, it might be universally true that this formalized process may represent the most severe breakdown in decision-making in the public schools. So many potential problems are related to this process that we can only try to list some that are easy to recognize:

— The referral may be inappropriate. For whatever reasons — faulty observation, adult prejudices, a single "bad day" for the child, etc. — a child may be started on a totally inappropriate and potentially devastating process.

— The diagnostic work-up administered by the ancillary person may be inappropriate or inadequate. Appropriate psychological assessment, for example, requires much more than the speedy administration of an IQ test, but that is precisely what psychological assessment has come to be in many public schools.

— The information gathered and ultimately presented at the formal meeting may be incredibly incomplete. We have attended meetings in which teachers with differing viewpoints about the child being considered are not invited to participate. Meetings sometimes are scheduled on such short notice or at such inappropriate times that parents are unable to attend. Parents are sometimes not invited at all. In fact, often it is difficult for an "outsider" (someone who might be an advocate for the child) to be invited or even allowed to participate. Frequently, other school staff members who might have valuable inputs are not made aware of the meetings. Finally, though I have attended a great many of these meetings (usually through perseverance and insistence) I have never seen the subject child present nor have I ever heard a report of the child's input to this process.

— As a natural consequence of the problems pointed out above, the plan that is ultimately developed likely may be inappropriate. Aside from the incomplete or inaccurate information that goes into the plan, the major problem at this point may be the lack of alternatives available in so many public school systems. In many systems the choice is between regular classroom and special education classroom (for Emotionally Disturbed [ED] or Educable Mentally Retarded [EMR]). Sometimes the few choices that exist are already oversubscribed, with the result that, even if all earlier steps in this sequence have been performed appropriately, there may be no logical conclusion in the form of the right program for the child. Unfortunately, the "case" may be resolved by a statement like this: "Well, he can't stay here, and the EMR class has an opening — let's send him over there."

— Finally, and perhaps most critically, public schools demonstrate an astounding failure in following up on the decisions that do get made. In one instance of which we are aware, a decision was made on a Wednesday that a child would attend a special class in a different school beginning the following Monday. The mother was informed of the decision but given no assistance with the problem of transportation for her child to the new school. The child was told nothing except to clean out his desk and say goodbye. When the child arrived at the new school on Monday, it became apparent that no one had informed the school's administrative personnel, and the principal refused to accept him. The youngster went back to his original school for two weeks before the transfer finally was made.

It would be nice to think this example is a fluke, a process gone awry due to unusual circumstances, but Hobbs (1974) gives us evidence to the contrary. He discusses "turnstile children" — youngsters whose records are full of neglect, school problems, recommendations for special placement or care that never was provided. Hobbs found that children who were bounced back and forth between agencies showed a steady deterioration over time.

The failure of public schools to develop more effective and coordinated follow-up aspects of their decision-making process is a prime factor in the creation of "turnstile children." Decision-making without attention to implementation is worse than no decision at all. Decision-making without the understanding and assistance of all persons involved dooms the plan to failure and wastes the time and efforts of committee members. Decision-making of this type places all children in jeopardy.

Although many of the decisions made in schools focus on children, they almost always are made by adults. The kinds of decisions many adults, especially teachers, are allowed to or seem able to make are often restricted to their own specified working areas. Within the confines of general school district policy, teachers make decisions about their classrooms, janitors about when and how maintenance duties will be performed, social workers about which families to visit and when, etc. But so many of our public schools lack participation by staff members in the broader kinds of decisions, those affecting total school policy or programs.

This larger involvement may be missing for a variety of reasons: First, the big decisions might never be made at all, by anyone. Second, there may be no decisions to make — *all* policy may be set by the central administration. But the most critical reason, it seems to us, is the sort of "mindlessness" that Silberman (1970) refers to as the primary impediment to change in the public schools. In discussing major problems in education, and the inappropriate manner in which many educators perform their duties, Silberman says:

> If they make a botch of it, and an uncomfortably large number do, it is because it simply never occurs to more than a handful to ask *why* they are doing what they are doing — to think seriously or deeply about the purposes or consequences of education (p. 11).

How can we remedy this situation? How can we enable teachers and other staff members to see themselves as problem-solvers, as critical members of the school decision-making process, as developers of educational programs? We agree with Silberman that:

> We must find ways of stimulating educators . . . to think about what they are doing and why they are doing it. And we must persuade the general public to do the same (p. 11).

118

Support Systems

One way to encourage and stimulate teachers (or anyone else) is to provide a supportive atmosphere in which to work. Persons who feel the warmth and strength of psychological support from their co-workers are more likely to attempt new projects, more apt to persevere in the face of adversity, and more able to cope productively with the ever-present frustrations accompanying their jobs. Further, interpersonal support can add the energy and the spirit that enables a group of people to embark upon a creative, albeit risk-filled, venture that could result in major improvements to current conditions.

Generally, public school settings are nearly devoid of support for adults. The energy and creativity generated from supportive atmospheres are missing in schools. Instead, we are met by a sense of isolation and loneliness. The results often are tired old lessons instead of innovative, new projects; dull, listless, distant teachers rather than energized, active, spirited adults.

A number of reasons give rise to this unfortunate state of affairs; for example — the "closed door syndrome." In many schools one teacher and 25, 30 or 35 children live as a self-contained unit behind the closed door of their classroom all day. Among the important implications of this situation is that many teachers rarely see — let alone communicate with — another adult during their entire time at school. The communication that does exist often is quick and cursory, usually accompanying some other activity such as eating lunch. The effect continues to build over time, since for many teachers, the more time they spend in their rooms the harder it becomes to relate to adults. Adults who really want to be part of an interpersonal support system often are faced with a series of closed doors and, since there's no alternative, might well end up as additional isolated adults.

Another implication of the "closed door syndrome" is that the halls and alcoves of many public schools are usually empty and quiet. Consequently, it is difficult for "outside people" to feel comfortable in a school — a notion that may well acount for the difficulty encountered in trying to enlist "volunteer" assistance in many schools. Such assistance, if obtained, could be a significant source of support for teachers.

A second reason for the lack of support typically found in public schools can be traced to a particular organizational aspect of schools; there is simply no time set aside for adults to share perceptions, discuss important issues, listen to each other's problems. The infrequent breaks teachers may have are utilized for lesson planning, conferences with special teachers, correcting papers, etc. Faculty meetings, which could be a vehicle for this type of communication, are essentially administrative detail sessions. No one seems interested in meeting before or after school for *any* reason.

So the school day passes with no hint that adult-adult communication is important. Clearly, it's not a priority of the setting, and new teachers learn their lessons soon enough — make it on your own, without getting and without having to give the support all of us need. As a result, a lot of good people can't last long in public schools, and a lot of not-so-good teachers remain unseen and unreachable behind closed doors. Worst of all, the great majority of teachers who fall somewhere in between those two extremes are left to fend for themselves. Though some may in fact succeed and become "good teachers," we will never know how much better they might have been, or how many others would have joined the ranks as "good teachers," if their schools had offered them even a little of the support they'd been denied. Ultimately, of course, we must consider the effects of an army of unfulfilled, lonely, de-energized teachers who serve as major adult models for our children.

Community

Public schools are so big and omnipresent that, like most institutions, they have developed a life of their own. It's easy for lay people to forget, for instance, that school personnel work for the people of the community (who elect the board of education members who hire the superintendent who hires the administrators who hire the direct service personnel). Unfortunately, it has become increasingly clear that school personnel also forget about their relations with their own community and, as a result, those relationships sometimes cease to exist.

The impact of this failure to connect the school world and the real world can be severe and probably is most clearly expressed in terms of what does not occur now, but would more likely happen with the addition of "community focus" to the work of the public schools. Some examples:

— Adults don't spend enough time inside schools — as observers, as helpers, or as learners.
— Community resources remain unknown to children.
— Parents and siblings remain unknown to teachers.
— Some of the most relevant content is omitted from the curriculum.
— School and local social service agency personnel remain ignorant of each other's programs (although they're often involved with the same children).
— Communities remain disorganized, center-less.
— School buildings are not used efficiently, standing empty 16 hours a day while local groups are unable to find space for meetings, recreation, etc.
— Adults who would like to continue their education in some way have no place to turn.

The tragedy of this public school-community relationship gap is that it makes the work of the school so much more difficult and so much less meaningful. At any level of school endeavor, the narrow, totally independent style adopted by so many of our schools becomes an additional burden to children and adults. In regard to children with special needs, we know that focusing on a child for 5 or 6 hours during the school day is insufficient without additional focus on the family and

121

community in which that child lives the remainder of his day. Accurate and productive diagnosis and program planning are simply not possible without recognizing all areas of a child's life. When will we stop pretending that "school is school" — a self-sustaining entity?

The fallacy that serves as the basis for these problems with such powerful implications is widespread and firmly believed by far too many of us, including many public school administrators. The fundamental error is in thinking that public schools and education are synonymous. They are not. Education is a much bigger and broader concept than what the public schools have been doing all these years. "Education" is much too big to be owned by any one social agency or institution. It is especially important for school systems to recognize and accept the fact that a great amount of learning — perhaps the most significant learning — takes place outside of the public school building.

But schools must do more than accept the existence of outside-of-school learning. They, along with individual children and adults, and with informal neighborhood groups and official community organizations, must become active participants in a partnership dedicated to coordinating, and thus maximizing, the combined effects of all. More and more now, the conditions of our time mandate that schools embrace the notion of "Community Education" and become leaders in the effort to develop a "process that achieves a balance and use of all institutional forces in the education of the people — all of the people — of the community" (Seay, 1974, p. 11).

Vision

Finally (and obviously related to all that's been said), we reach perhaps the most critical issue in public schools: the *vision* of an organization, its plan for the future, its hope for realizing whatever potential it may have. Without long-range goals, without even a road-map to indicate the destination and route of the journey already begun, in the absence of the

122

vision of what could be, we also lose much of our ability to function effectively.

The vision of the public schools is narrow and constricted. The institution in our society that some hoped would become the "great equalizer" has accomplished that goal only by becoming a massive dehumanizer. Instead of adjusting to the variety of individual human differences, the public schools, as Silberman (1970) noted, ". . . have operated on the assumption that children should be cut or stretched or otherwise 'adjusted' to fit the schools . . ." (p. 81).

In fact, schools have become the greatest perpetrator of what might be called the "One Right Model" model. If it didn't originate in school, the idea that there is one "right" way for things to be done and, further, that all people must learn to do it that way, certainly has gained strength from public school programs over the years. The implications are severe and long-lasting, because this model leads to a rigidity of organizational structure and educational programming that can be nearly impossible to change. Further, the belief that children all can and must accommodate to the "one right way" implies that options do not need to be developed. As a result, alternative programs are perceived as frills and, if they're allowed to exist at all, they are frequently without sufficient financial and psychological support; their life-span often is short, understandably.

Perhaps the most serious implication of the "One Right Model" model is that it creates a situation in which it is absolutely certain some children will *not* fit. In this way, the public schools *create* children with special needs and then, incredibly but frequently, are unable to (even refuse to) respond to such children because of their perceived differences. Mercer (1974), on the basis of a long and comprehensive research program, has concluded that the public school is the "labeler" in the community. Even more stunning is her finding that great numbers of children whom the public schools labeled as retarded have *not* been identified as retarded in any other area of their lives. These persons hold jobs, have friends, join organizations and in general are typical, well-functioning citizens in their communities. The inescapable conclusion is that the public schools, through the "One Right Model" model, created and labeled a group of "school-retardates." The implications are ominous.

The narrowness of the public school vision is alarming not only because of the harm it has done, but also because of the great many potential benefits it prevents from occurring. The kind of community focus described above implies a variety of new and innovative kinds of educational programs that too many school systems are not willing to consider. The school is perhaps the institution with the greatest potential for preventing the severe emotional disturbances that represent such a mammoth problem in our society, but its efforts to date have barely scratched the surface of this crucial area. Finally, the restricted vision is a great contributor to the inability of public schools to create and implement comprehensive, functional educational programming today.

CONCLUSIONS

We have discussed five current issues that appear to have particularly critical importance to both the present and the future of public school life — leadership; decision-making; support systems, community, and vision. These issues point to the immutable conclusion that schools are filled with serious, longstanding problems, many of which seem strongly resistant to solution.

Without in any way diminishing the force behind those conclusions, we must also understand, in no uncertain terms, the overwhelming importance of the public school in our society. Smith (1974) tells us that for over 90 percent of our children, the public school is the *only* opportunity they will ever have for formal education. Our individual lives and our collective culture are inextricably linked with the public schools. A direct and powerful connection exists between the

HARRY JERSIG CENTER
OUR LADY OF THE LAKE UNIV.
411 S. W. 24TH ST.
SAN ANTONIO, TEXAS 78285

public school today and the kind of society we will have tomorrow. The combination of these two converging notions (that schools are both problem-filled and of primary importance to our lives) leads to the conclusion that if institutions are reformable, we surely must start with public schools; and if public schools are going to continue to exist and realize a significant proportion of their potential, they surely must reform. The needs are massive, the ideas are available, the strategies are being developed, and there are unlimited ways in which effective reform can occur.

We return to the issue of *vision* again, and the implications of a broader view of the educational environments that comprise the public school (Smith, 1974):

> The need for a plurality of modes of education to meet the needs of our diverse population has never been greater. The development of a diversity of optional public schools, each geared to be responsive to students with different learning needs and styles, provides one strategy for developing a new organizational structure for public education. The development of optional alternative public schools could provide choices for students, parents, and teachers in every community (p. 13).

REFERENCES

Children's Defense Fund. *Children out of school in America.* Cambridge, MA: Author, 1974.

Herbert, C. *I see a child.* New York: Anchor Doubleday, 1974.

Hobbs, N. *The futures of children.* San Francisco: Jossey-Bass, 1975.

Holt, J. *How children fail.* New York: Pitman Publishing, 1964.

Howsam, R. *Now you shall be real to everyone.* 17th annual Charles W. Hunt lecture, American Association of Classroom Teachers of Education, 1976.

Kohl, H. *36 children.* New York: Signet Books, 1968.

Kozol, J. *Death at an early age.* Boston: Houghton Mifflin, 1967.

Mercer, J. A policy statement on assessment procedures and the rights of children. *Harvard Educational Review,* 1974, *44,* 328-344.

Sarason, S. *The culture of school and the problem of change.* Boston: Allyn & Bacon, 1971.

Seay, M. *Community education: A developing concept.* Midland, MI: Pendell Publishing, 1974.

Silberman, C. *Crisis in the classroom: The remaking of American education.* New York: Vintage Books, 1970.

Smith, V. *Alternative schools, the development of options in public education.* Lincoln, NE: Professional Educators Publications, 1974.

Zigler, E. Children first or last. In *The 1976 New York Times Review of Education,* April 25, 1976, p. 20.

5

The Integration-Segregation Issue: Some Questions, Assumptions, and Facts

Burton Blatt

Question 1:
   What is the debate?

Assumptions:
   Many in the fields of special education and general education believe that children with special needs — all children — should live in ordinary communities and attend ordinary schools in ordinary classes. They may allow exceptions for that small number of children with extraordinary needs, agreeing that such youngsters may require specialized programs that could not be adequately provided in regular community settings. However, they would contend that, even for

---

This chapter originally was published in *Family Involvement,* October 1975, 8, 10-14. Reprinted by permission.

those children, every effort should be made to enhance their participation with typical children in regular school and other community programs.

Others (also in both fields) contend that children with special needs are best served in specialized programs, supervised by specially-trained teachers who employ special methods and use unique facilities and equipment. They believe it is the responsibility of both society, in general, and the schools to allocate the resources and support to permit special, oftentimes segregated educational opportunities for handicapped children. They believe that regular classes have many times been thoughtless places, dumping grounds for unwanted children who are forced to sit unattended, deprived of opportunities to learn. Some adherents of preserving specialized schools and programs are distressed by what appears to them to be an erosion of quality as the consequence of movements to decategorize, mainstream, integrate, and interrelate all children in heterogeneous settings. Their plea is to consider the handicapped child first and, secondarily, the philosophies of educational reformers with prejudices for integration.

They believe strongly that integration for many children with special needs is difficult to achieve and, for most of those children, unwarranted. They contend that the significant discrepancy in achievement level and rate of learning between handicapped children and typical children would cause unusual hardship and embarrassment for the handicapped, not to mention the severe pedagogical difficulties teachers would encounter in trying to provide for the individualized learning needs of widely heterogeneous pupils in integrated settings. They believe that many handicapped children have specific learning needs and disabilities requiring specialized pedagogical and curricula approaches. Consequently, they believe that teachers of handicapped children require unique pre-service training experiences which regular teacher education programs do not offer and, so they claim, neither do the newer noncategorical, interrelated special education programs.

128

In essence, critics of the integration movement in special education have concluded that such practices inevitably lead to general ignorance about individual differences, resulting in neglect of children who require individualized or unusual consideration. Capability for focusing on a child's deficits, dealing expertly with not only the deficits but his strengths in a clinical setting, accounting for disparities in his development as contrasted with typical development, attending to the special problems faced by families with such children, modifying classroom environments and procedures to promote successful experiences — these factors have been suggested as requiring specialized facilities, programs, and teachers. Consequently, many renowned special educators believe those are the elements which make special education special and, further, require much of special education to be separated from more conventional programs.

Facts:
Unfortunately, the one persistent fact in the integration-segregation issue is that no compelling research has been done in support of either approach. The best, the most, that can be claimed is that some children fare better in separate class programs and others do better in ordinary programs. This research, sometimes called "efficacy studies," leads to the general conclusion that special education programs — essentially special classes — as they are now constituted are no more beneficial for handicapped children than are ordinary classes. However, because of the equivocal data obtained from these studies, and serious defects with most of the research methodologies employed, the question remains essentially open and, possibly, unanswerable. And, for those who claim special education has not been given a proper chance to demonstrate its effectiveness, there are others who can equally claim, "neither have efforts to integrate children in regular programs."

The one situation in which I believe there is general agreement concerns segregated institutions. They are not good for people. To discuss this further in the context of "assumptions" and "facts" is to possibly create the illusion that there are compelling pros and cons to the question. There aren't — and I choose not to debate that assertion.

Question 2:
Then, what is the problem?

Assumptions:
There is no single problem or single debate surrounding the integration-segregation issue. There are problems; there are debates; there are assertions, facts, polemics, and solutions. With an issue grounded more in prejudices than in facts, more in values than data, more in fear (or love) than demographics, debate of the issue must deal with the many dimensions of human affairs: ideologies, missions, rights, development, resources, and politics. There is no central debate. There is no prepotent problem. And there is neither a single nor simple answer. There are problems and there are solutions. There are levels of integration that some would call segregation; there are levels of segregation that others would call integration. There is no black or white; there are no clearcut dichotomies or other subdivisions and boundaries to the issue. Consequently, assumptions and beliefs are important in understanding the issue, while "facts" are not always used on behalf of people.

Facts:
There are facts and there are facts. Although "some" facts and "some" knowledge can be dangerous, not to use the little we know may be even more dangerous, insofar as this issue is concerned. Also, I believe the truth lies not only in facts, or in accuracy, but in how the whole of a body of work permits one to see the truth. The words of a presentation, themselves, are almost nothing.

Question 3:
What are the competing values?

130

Assumptions:

Several levels of conflicting values are attendant to this issue. There are ideological differences between those who believe the state was created to serve human beings, to free them, and those who believe that, although we once created the state to serve us, we must not serve the state. Consequently, some claim the state must be responsible for, must control, social, intellectual and other kinds of deviance; others assert the right of any human being to do exactly as he pleases, to live exactly as he wishes, as long as he does not break the law. There are those who believe in total human freedom, who even appreciate the concept of anarchy; there are others who believe in human control, who even appreciate the concept of the totalitarian state. Most of the others — most of us — have values falling somewhere between those polarities.

Some people believe that folks are better off "with their own kind." Others believe the world becomes enriched as we engage in relationships with those who are different. These are the people who are disturbed because we have systematically excluded so many human beings from ordinary life. While there are some who decry our deliberate efforts to segregate and separate the deviant, or the merely different, from typical society, there are others who say we must exert greater efforts to separate out the deviant. They would claim that this is the only hope for the continuation of society as we know it. But their ideological opponents would ask why anyone wishes to continue society as it now exists.

We also have differences because of our selfish interests. Segregated schools and classes and, especially, segregated institutions require that architects design buildings and contractors build them and people administer them and teachers and social workers and psychologists work in them. Specialization incurs certain sacrifices that the specialist must make, but even they would not argue that there are not also benefits. There is, at least, a degree of self interest imposed into the substance of these debates.

131

Facts:

It is a fact that those closest to the issue — families who have children with special needs, teachers and administrators of special programs, and others who are intimately associated with programs for the handicapped — are most outspoken about their values relating to the issue. It isn't the general educator who is interfering with efforts to integrate disabled children in ordinary classes. Essentially, special educators — sometimes the parents — have been most responsible for the rather slow progress made in integrating children in the public schools. And who are the ones most loudly and eloquently defending the continuance of public institutions for the mentally retarded? The commissioners of mental health, superintendents of such institutions, and the directors, teachers, and matrons.

Persistently, we seem to blame Mr. Joe Citizen for all the abuse in our institutions, for our wastelands we call schools, for the so many abuses in our culture. Possibly Mr. Joe Citizen is too passive, too unconcerned, too busy to notice what is happening to abused children, and the neglected elderly and the suffering poor; but, also, he is untutored, possibly intimidated (by us), and much too trusting of his government, his experts, and his technicians. The professionals are much more responsible for the quality of our schools and the residences for the disabled. We have created them, and now we seek to preserve them. It isn't that professionals, parents, or other interested parties are dishonest, mendacious, or unfeeling. They are just as good as Mr. Joe Citizen — or just as bad. Further, they are not without self interest, and they each have their own perspectives and values. Let's not mistake those qualities for facts or morality.

What is the historic mission of people in the helping professions? It's so simple, yet so misunderstood or neglected: to help other people — not to judge whether they can or can't be helped but, explicitly, to believe they can be helped and to do everything in one's power to provide what they need. What is the historic belief concerning human educability? The evidence is so abundant, so clear: people can change, can learn; intelligence is educable, is a function of practice and experience and encouragement. Almost from the beginning, human beings noted that, with appropriate instruction and motivation, people can learn, can improve their performance. Yet, who will argue that, at least in our time, the most characteristic quality expressed by human beings is a pessimism — not only concerning others but, strangely, about ourselves, about our capabilities for changing.

The history is clear; the record is before us. Our mission as educators, psychologists, physicians, and others in helping fields is to help other human beings grow, learn, fulfill themselves. The goal is clear. Evidence aside, we must work as if people can change, as if our efforts will help them be better educated, healthier, better human beings. The need is clear: You have your values and I have mine; but the one point upon which rational people must agree is that it's better to be part of human society than be separated from it and, further, in the best of all worlds, variation adds color and zest to one's life, enhancing development.

If the mission we have, if not the facts, requires us to behave as if people can learn, and since there is little doubt among reasonable people that variance in life facilitates human development, doesn't logic — if not direct facts — make a compelling case for integration as the placement not only of choice but of necessity?

Question 4:
What are the practical concerns?

Assumptions:
The practical concerns arising from this issue are those embedded in all issues involving human affairs: money and politics. The two are inextricably related, bound to each other to solve problems as well as to create them. Some will claim that our institutional warehouses are the cheapest facilities society will tolerate. Some will claim that our segregated

133

special classes are the least expensive and most educationally enhancing facilities the public schools can provide. Some will claim we are today allocating greater and broader resources to community integrated programs. Some will claim that what we have now is what society wants.

Facts:

Segregation is *always* more expensive than integration, both in terms of real dollars and in terms of the preservation and enhancement of human resources. It is also a fact that most people want to live with their families and friends in ordinary communities. Simply, those are the facts about the dollars and the politics of people.

A good integrated special education program can be purchased for $2,000 a year per child. A poor segregated institution costs $8,000 to $12,000 a year, sometimes more. Is it for economy purposes that we continue to construct institutions at a cost of $30,000 to $60,000 a bed when, plainly, community residences can be less expensively purchased and remodeled to serve as group homes, halfway homes, and other living and developmental facilities? Is it for economy purposes that we continue to build segregated special schools for the trainable, the disturbed, and the deaf, while school enrollments are declining notoriously, resulting in unused classrooms and even empty schools? We have overbuilt; we have not considered the declining birthrates; and, yet, we continue to construct enormously expensive institutions and schools for which some of us are willing to pay a high price to separate one from another. How far will we permit those with vested interests, unreasonable interests, not only to rob our pockets but erode our values and convictions concerning human beings, their capabilities, and our interrelatedness?

And what of the politics? The politics are the people, and the will of the people should be felt, for then good may eventually obtain. The people know of what the world is made and what a human life needs.

6

Exclusion

Douglas Biklen

In many parts of the United States, people with special needs suffer and endure segregation and exclusion from community life and the dehumanization of inadequate or inappropriate services. To be sure, a few who have been labeled "retarded" or "disabled" secure adequate services and are able to maintain normal relationships with people in the mainstream of society, but the dominant pattern of treatment in this nation recalls the medieval practice of casting out the disabled into the woods. Though we speak of increasing professional and scientific competence, our society has effectively cast out those who are labeled as "special." And in isolated environments, far from the public eye, in state schools and state hospitals, these adults and children too often have been dehumanized. The responsibility for that dehumanization rests, in part, with the institutions and the professions, but primarily with a society that willingly segregates and excludes a significant number of its members.

Practices of excluding disabled persons pervade this society, from public schools and working places to closed institutions. Ironically, when special classes were first developed in schools, they were called "opportunity classes," on the assumption and hope they would provide disabled children with opportunities to develop their potential. They have, instead, become vehicles for schools to isolate disabled children from the mainstream. Similarly, in their early days, institutions were supposed to serve as training centers to prepare disabled persons for life in the community, but they quickly became custodial facilities. Today, as in past years, thousands of children receive no services because their parents justly refuse to institutionalize them and because schools exclude them.

Most recently, this legacy of exclusion and dehumanization has been dramatized, and hopefully mitigated, in several landmark court actions. In Pennsylvania, the Association for Retarded Children sued the State in federal court on behalf of all "retarded" children of Pennsylvania for the right to public education (*Pennsylvania Association for Retarded Children* v. *Commonwealth of Pennsylvania*, 1971). Plaintiffs in the Pennsylvania class action case were eleven "retarded" children who for years had been denied educational opportunities and who had been segregated from their peers. Not surprisingly, the case was based on the due process and equal protection guarantees of the Fourteenth Amendment to the U.S. Constitution, and *Brown* v. *Board of Education* was cited as a precedent for the right to equal education. A witness for the plaintiffs argued that all children, including the so-called "retarded," can benefit from education. The relevance of this case lies in the decision which mandated the right to education for retarded children and the right to due process during any hearings that might lead to a child's exclusion from public education.

Similarly, recent court action has brought to light again the shameful conditions within many state institutions, conditions which hundreds of thousands of people endure daily, sometimes for years on end. In Alabama, the guardians of a so-called "retarded" boy at the Partlow State School won a suit in federal court against the State for the right to adequate treatment *(Wyatt* v. *Stickney,* 1972). This case, argued by the National Legal Aid and Defender Association and supported by several professional organizations, including the American Association on Mental Deficiency, resulted in so many stringent stipulations between the State and the plaintiffs that henceforth it will be virtually impossible for the State of Alabama to incarcerate a "retarded" person without first showing that the person could not benefit from less-confined residential services.

Cases based on the right to treatment in institutions also have been filed against the Commonwealth of Massachusetts and the State of New York. In each case the plaintiffs have cited gross violations of human dignity and health within the institutions as bases for seeking legal remedies. In Massachusetts the court action *(Ricci* v. *Greenblatt,* 1972) was brought by parents of patients at the Belchertown State School, an institution that has been the subject of more than one newspaper expose and scathing state government reports. Two cases have been entered in federal court against the State of New York for conditions in its much publicized Willowbrook State School *(Parisi* v. *State of New York,* 1972; *New York State Association for Retarded Children* v. *State of New York,* 1972). In the *Parisi* brief, prepared by the Legal Aid Society of New York City on behalf of residents at the Willowbrook State School, the plaintiffs claimed breach of constitutional rights:

> By this proceeding plaintiffs and their class seek to vindicate their constitutionally-protected right to an equal opportunity to realize their developmental capacity including the right of each plaintiff and class member to receive appropriate developmental assistance adapted to his particular needs, their constitutionally-protected right to a formal determination with adequate procedural safeguards of the appropriate developmental program for each plaintiff and class member in light of his particular developmental capacity and needs, and their constitutionally-protected rights to be free from particular practices violative of the First, Fourth, Sixth, Eighth, and Thirteenth Amendments to the United States Constitution.

Plaintiffs and the class members arrive and remain at Willowbrook State School as a result of a realistically coercive pattern of forces and circumstances beyond their control and not of their own choosing, and because of the failure of the State to provide less drastic and restrictive alternatives. At Willowbrook the plaintiffs and the class members are denied appropriate developmental assistance, and many are, in fact, subjected to severely injurious and cruelly inhuman treatment. The net result is that plaintiffs and the class members are virtual prisoners in a human warehouse, condemned to incarceration for the rest of their lives without the prospect of ever attaining that measure of self-care and self-sufficiency of which they are capable.

Throughout the 55-page brief, attorneys of the plaintiffs cite inhumane practices of drugging and restraining patients, dehumanizing bathroom and dining facilities, the rampant spread of diseases such as hepatitis, totally inadequate medical and educational services, hindrances to parent visitation, institutional peonage, and so forth.

The Pennsylvania and Alabama (Partlow) decisions, have set precedents. Yet we know that nearly every other state has thousands of excluded school-age children. Moreover, in most states, Pennsylvania included, institutional life still resembles conditions described in Burton Blatt's pictorial essay *Christmas in Purgatory* (1974).

While working as a staff member at the Center on Human Policy of Syracuse University,[1] I have met many parents of disabled children. I have met parents who complain that their children have been denied adequate educational opportunities in public school classes, or who have been excluded altogether. Some parents say they have been encouraged or even coerced into incarcerating their children in state institutions.

Of all the parents and children with whom we have worked and who have suffered from these policies of exclusion and institutionalization, none is typical, none represents

---

[1]The Center is an advocacy organization dedicated to the promotion and study of open settings; it advocates the inclusion of children and adults into typical community settings such as schools, residences, and places of work.

all the others. In each case there are different disabilities, different individual needs of children, and different schools, communities and personalities involved. Yet, there is one common element in all of these cases: By categorizing and excluding many of those who have disabilities, schools, school boards, and school personnel have violated their charge to educate all children. Though each disabled child may have different needs, the pattern of treating these children is re-markably consistent. Thousands of children throughout the country have been denied services in public schools, and thousands of others have been segregated from their families and communities through a policy of institutionalization.

The following story about Mrs. Jackson and two of her children, Michael and Cindy, who are functionally deaf, por-trays clearly the almost overwhelming forces which often work against parents and children who want the public schools to provide education for the disabled.[2]

Mr. and Mrs. Jackson knew almost nothing about hearing problems when their son Michael, at the age of three, was diagnosed as profoundly hearing-impaired. They were even less aware of habilitative programs or the possible social implications of a disability to a young child. Their only advisor at this time was the diagnostician who recommended that they admit Michael to a residential school for the deaf in a city about 80 miles from where they lived. Though the Jacksons now view as a mistake that decision to institutionalize Michael, there were no alternatives at the time, no pre-school or nursery programs, and no possibility of private tutoring. Michael and his parents were caught in a bind of insufficient professional advice, lack of personal experience, and a choice between no community services and total institutionalization. Reluctantly, they chose institutionalization.

During Michael's first week in school, the parents became accustomed to the program and participated in seminars

---

[2]All names have been changed in order to protect the privacy of those involved.

where they were told that Michael would learn to talk and would be educated like other children. But Michael seemed unhappy. He had difficulty sleeping during that first week, perhaps from homesickness or fear of new surroundings, though in retrospect, Mrs. Jackson believes "he sensed something was wrong."

Michael's unhappiness turned out to be more than a modest case of homesickness, and the Jacksons' anxiety about his welfare continued. Whenever he came home on weekends, he never wanted to return to the institution. As Mrs. Jackson recalls, "He used to jump out of the car and run off in the fields. He didn't want to go back. He'd cling to us, and it was just heartbreaking."

As such incidents became commonplace, the Jacksons began to question institutional staff about Michael's progress. The institution "used to write us a note on Monday, and they'd say, 'Oh, he adjusted beautifully after you left.' Then you'd find out he was in the infirmary all week long. He'd be filthy dirty and have boils on the head, and we just couldn't clear them up." The staff at the institution told the Jacksons that Michael was simply run-down but that he would soon adjust to institutional life. Since the Jacksons saw no alternative to continued institutionalization, they left Michael at the school for two years, after which time his teacher wrote and said Michael was not learning, that he refused to participate in classroom activities. She suggested that the Jacksons take Michael to a doctor for further examination.

In the two years of institutionalization, Michael had learned to say only one word — "baby." The doctor who had originally diagnosed him and recommended institutionalization was amazed. He said, "If I had him, he'd be talking." Another doctor told them the decision to institutionalize Michael had been the worst thing they could have done to the child and suggested trying a public school special class. The Jacksons immediately observed several public school classes which they concluded were not adequate for Michael's specialized needs but which were at least more appropriate than the institution. Mrs. Jackson was somewhat disappointed to find that the "deaf" program was a melting pot for a variety of children who had different disabilities. The options still were limited to a single program (special class) or nothing; yet, the Jacksons considered their plight much improved from the time when Michael was institutionalized.

Before long, however, Michael began to resist attending this special class just as he had resisted placement in the institution. He refused to climb aboard the school bus and stayed home often, despite his parents' persistent encouragement. Since the Jacksons knew that Michael was bright (he had tested above average on IQ tests), they were at a loss to explain why he disliked school.

Late in the spring of his first year in this program, however, an incident occurred which threw light on his reluctance to join in classroom activities. He came home with a package of crayons belonging to another child in the classroom. Mrs. Jackson took the crayons back to the teacher of Michael's class and apologized for his having taken them. The teacher's response enabled Mrs. Jackson to understand Michael's reticence toward schooling. The teacher said, "That's typical of the deaf." This incident and Michael's resistance toward formal schooling might be regarded as isolated difficulties of a single child, little different from adjustment problems that many so-called typical children experience, except that this incident involved a teacher's prejudice against a disabled child. Michael's resistance seemed somehow reassuring.

During the next school year, another problem developed. The school board hired a new director of special class programs who encouraged institutionalization. He sent a letter to Mrs. Jackson stating, "It is my unpleasant duty to inform you that your son is being accepted into the hard-of-hearing class for this school year *only.*" The director further urged, "We hope that you have seriously reviewed our recommendation that Michael be enrolled in a school for the deaf." When Mrs. Jackson attended an open house at Michael's public school, the teacher told her, "I know you don't want to send him to an institution, but he's incapable of learning; he should be with other people like himself so he would have their companionship." Mrs. Jackson told me, "If I didn't have his IQ tests, I would have listened to this woman." The teacher claimed that Michael was not capable of learning, but when Mrs. Jackson noted that he had received 100% on all his spelling tests except one, the teacher's only reply was, "I think you're making a big mistake putting him into the public schools."

Pressure was mounting within the system to have the Jacksons place Michael in a state school for the deaf. Each month a rehabilitation counselor called Mrs. Jackson and urged her to submit an application to the institution. The counselor even threatened Mrs. Jackson and other parents of deaf children with court action to force them to institutionalize their children. The Director of Special Education warned that Michael would not be allowed in public school classrooms again unless the parents first attempted to institutionalize him. Only a formal written rejection of Michael by the institution would cause the Director of Special Education to reconsider. It appeared certain that Michael would be excluded from public school after the end of that school year.

By this time Mrs. Jackson had educated herself about the condition of hearing impairment and had read numerous reports about state institutions for the deaf. Her own experience with Michael as a three and four year old had served as an initiation to institutions. Moreover, she had read that "the American people have no reason to be proud of the education of deaf children. The most that they get is a third grade education." She knew that institutional conditions often were dehumanizing and frightening for children and that they learned little in such settings. She had seen such children labeled as retarded but knew they were not retarded; they simply had not been taught. In Mrs. Jackson's mind, such children were no more retarded than Helen Keller had been before a creative teacher discovered ways of teaching her to communicate.

This painfully derived understanding of deafness and its social implications led Mrs. Jackson to seek support among similarly situated families. She formed a group of parents to urge state and local education departments to supply educational opportunities for their children. The group submitted a grant proposal and received $20,000 to establish a pre-school program for hearing impaired children. But all of these activities were not solving the Jacksons' immediate problem — the school board's attempt to exclude Michael.

Their problem was exacerbated when they discovered that another of their children, Cindy, also was profoundly hearing-impaired. The examining doctor termed Cindy "very profoundly deaf" and suggested that she attend a weekly clinic at the hospital, at a cost of $30 per week. The Jacksons were unable to afford this.

Fortunately, changes in school district personnel provided Mrs. Jackson with another opportunity to enroll her children in public school classes. A new staff person at the board of education agreed to admit her children in a neighborhood school. The Jacksons realized that their present fortune was precarious and, even if the children were permitted in public schools, they might not receive adequate training. So Mrs. Jackson urged her parents group to extend its activities beyond the pre-school program to include child advocacy. The parents met resistance almost immediately, since they were entering a traditionally professional-controlled area. When they undertook a study of the need for deaf programs, all the school boards in the county reported insufficient need. According to the school boards, there were no more than seven to ten profoundly hearing-impaired children, and the majority of these already were institutionalized. The parents later learned that the number of hearing-impaired children far exceeded the seven to ten cited and that school officials had instructed school board employees to hide such figures from public disclosure. The parents group never was allowed access to information that would have enabled them to build a strong case for the need to establish special programs for the hearing-impaired. Further, officials at the local clinic that serves people with hearing impairments discouraged such programs, presumably out of fear that new programs in the schools would overshadow the clinic as a service center.

Although, according to Mrs. Jackson, "the parents groups never were able to accomplish a single thing," it is clear that they exerted extraordinary pressure on local education officials by seeking out information that usually is unavailable to consumers. Perhaps the greatest result of the organization was that parents informed themselves about alternative ways of providing educational services for deaf children. Mrs. Jackson's sister spent two weeks in California studying the programs for deaf children in 23 school districts. California was providing comprehensive services for deaf children in regular classes; it also had integrated hearing-impaired children into typical public school classrooms, providing them with supplementary services as well. For Mrs. Jackson's parents group, the California system became a model.

When Mrs. Jackson presented these findings to local educational and medical officials, she discovered that the California model and all the information about alternative services could not convince the professional educators. They stood adamant on the belief that a deaf child should be institutionalized. The educational and medical officials who wanted to segregate Michael and Cindy from community life were no different from the teacher who said Michael could not learn. The basis of professional insistence on institutionalization as the best answer to the needs of children with hearing impairments was not scientific, but cultural prejudices.

Michael and Cindy encountered more prejudice as they entered their new school. Without notifying the Jacksons, the principal placed Michael in a class for the "emotionally disturbed." The teacher of this class told Mrs. Jackson that Michael should be in a regular class, but the principal refused to change the placement. Michael was not even given textbooks, since there was a book shortage that year and the class for emotionally disturbed children was presumed to have less need for educational materials than other classes.

In the fall of the following school year, Mrs. Jackson again was instructed by the local communications disorder unit that her children should be sent to a state school for the deaf. A leading professional castigated the Jacksons during a public meeting "for denying the children education." He accused the parents of "doing a terrible thing, because the children will not be accepted in society." Much as blacks who challenge racist social policies were criticized during the civil rights movement of the 1960s for making life difficult for themselves, the Jacksons were blamed for the plight of their children, even though they sought tirelessly to secure adequate community services and community acceptance.

In August the school district's director of elementary education spoke to Mrs. Jackson. He said that her children did not belong in public school. Mrs. Jackson replied that she intended to keep her children in school, and that if the director ever decided to exclude them, she wanted the order in writing. In October the school principal called the Jackson home. "Didn't you get the school board's letter yesterday?" he asked. "Your children will not be admitted here any longer." Mrs. Jackson had not yet received such a letter, but soon it arrived, bearing a message, short and explicit:

> Enclosed are the completed Exemption Certificates for Cindy Jackson and Michael Jackson in accordance with Section 3208 of the Education Law and Article XXX, Sections 230-235, of the regulations of the Commissioner of Education.

While the school board had been preparing to exclude her children, Mrs. Jackson had been making appeals to the board of education for a special program for deaf children; she had been led to believe that the board was genuinely interested. Mrs. Jackson now believes that the school officials planned to neutralize her as a parent leader by forcing her children into

145

an institution, thus reducing the pressure from other parents. She responded to the exclusion order by appealing to a State Senator. The Senator suggested, "Put the kids on the bus in the morning. We'll work this out." That night Mrs. Jackson attended an open-house meeting at the school where the children were being excluded. "The principal beat a track to us right away . . . I told him, 'My children will be back here tomorrow.' He said, 'Oh no, you can't send them back here tomorrow.' So I said, 'Well, I'm going to.' Then the principal adopted another tack by arguing 'that they were removed because they're behavior problems.'" Mrs. Jackson was surprised, since she never had been informed that her children were disruptive in the classroom. She checked with the children's teachers that evening, and both teachers told her that Michael and Cindy were model students even though they were not receiving the special services that might benefit them. Then Mrs. Jackson accused the principal of arbitrarily excluding her children on false pretenses.

It would appear that the principal was willing to manipulate labels (i.e., from "deaf" to "behavior problem") in order to achieve an administrative end — namely, to strengthen or justify his actions. In the state where this story occurred, seemingly it is easier and more common for school officials to exclude children on the basis of bad behavior than because they have a disability. Most common of all is the exclusion of children who have been labeled with more than one disability (e.g., deaf and emotionally disturbed), simply because few specialized programs exist for multiply disabled children.

In the morning, when Cindy and Michael prepared to board the school bus, they were barred by the bus dispatcher. This dispatch supervisor later apologized to Mr. Jackson, explaining that the principal had called him the previous night with instructions to bar the children from entering. The children could not understand what was happening. The other Jackson children were equally upset when they saw their brother and sister denied entrance to the school bus. "I never really felt bad about the kids being handicapped because they had so much going for them," Mrs. Jackson said, "but that just did something to me. They couldn't control their tears. They had been denied their friends."

That morning, Mrs. Jackson called the superintendent of schools, who expressed his displeasure at being drawn into the case. But he became quite interested after Mrs. Jackson said, "It's pretty rotten when a principal will lie and say the children are misbehaving when the teachers say they are well behaved." The superintendent replied, "This I am interested in, and this I will look into." Ironically, his concern stemmed more from his interest in the principal's decorum than from his assessment of the children's needs.

Since Mrs. Jackson still was unsure what measures the superintendent might take, she again called the State Senator and complained that the State was pouring 12 million dollars into a state school for the deaf but that no money had been made available locally for public school programs. She also told the Senator that the exemption order for her children had been signed by a doctor who had never even met her two children. She was considering court action at this point, but the Senator convinced her that litigation would be a waste of time and money. He suggested they call for a hearing before the State Department of Education.

That hearing was attended by the local director of special education, the psychologist who had tested the children, the director of state educational programs for the disabled, and others. To Mrs. Jackson's surprise, the psychologist who had tested her two children suggested that they both be placed in a nearby state school for the retarded. Fortunately, this recommendation was not taken seriously by others present at the meeting, since tests indicated that the children exhibited "normal" intelligence. Others advocated placement in a state school for the deaf. Mrs. Jackson mentioned several recent reports in the field of hearing impairment which advocated integration of such children into normal classes, but the professionals attending the meeting told her simply that while it was difficult to part with one's children, it really would be

147

best for them to be institutionalized. In effect, Mr. and Mrs. Jackson were told they should be more accepting of their childrens' disability, and that they should show their acceptance by agreeing to segregate the children from their community.

Mr. Jackson responded to the professionals by saying, "One of the worst things you can do to these children is to deny them the companionship of other children." A neighbor of the Jacksons told the professional panel that after he had taught Michael how to play chess, he (the neighbor) had been unable to win another game against Michael. One of the doctors responded to this testimony by saying to the neighbor, "That's going to be a burden on you because these children are going to be retarded; they are not going to be educated, and it's going to be your fault because you're helping these parents to stand up for these children. They belong in an institution." Mrs. Jackson continued to plead that the State invest at least half the amount of money allocated for institutional education into public school education of children with hearing impairments. The local school superintendent agreed with Mrs. Jackson, but the state officials called such financing impossible and questionable. One official urged the Jacksons to move 50 miles so they could live near a state school for the deaf. The Jacksons refused, however, on the grounds that institutional life would be a detriment to the children, even if the children could live at home. They still wanted Michael and Cindy in public schools, believing that all children can best prepare for life in the community by learning to live with their peers.

Finally, at the end of this long hearing in the state capitol, the superintendent of schools offered a non-negotiable "deal": "You send these children to the state school for the deaf (50 miles from home) one day a week, and they can attend classes in the public school the other four days. Either you accept it or you get nothing." Mrs. Jackson was reluctant to accept. She did not want to send her children that far away, and she

feared the offer might be a ploy to have her children permanently institutionalized at a later date. The Jacksons then
consulted an audiologist, who said there could be no
therapeutic value in sending the children to an institution for
one day a week. Other families in the neighborhood promised
to raise money for a court case, if necessary, and prevailed on
the bus drivers to permit Cindy and Michael on the buses
regardless of the principal's present or future policies. Other
children in the school signed petitions to have Michael and
Cindy readmitted to classes.

During these tumultuous days, the other Jackson children
became upset; they threatened to confront the school officials
themselves, even though they were only of elementary school
age. Michael pleaded with his mother for an operation so he
could return to school. Knowing that an operation would not
improve his hearing, Mrs. Jackson grew more and more
frustrated.

As the Jacksons persisted, their neighbors told them to go
before the local board of education for a formal hearing on the
matter. The hearing was lively. The board president was
absent for the first part of the meeting but had instructed
another member to cut off debate early. The Jacksons'
neighbors had phoned this acting president beforehand, however, and she promised to allow free debate. Finally, the
superintendent of schools reversed the exemption order. He
said, "We will accept the children if you will agree to accept
the responsibility of educating them." Mr. and Mrs. Jackson
agreed to this proposal. It was a victory of sorts, a hollow one
at best.

When Mrs. Jackson went to the junior high school which
Michael was to attend, the principal asked her, "Mrs. Jackson,
what do you want us to do for your child?" This was one of
the rare occasions when a school official had conceded that
either Michael or Cindy would benefit from integration in a
regular school and in a regular class. Mrs. Jackson replied,
"Well, I just want you to treat him as a human being. He has
lived through many traumatic experiences, including being

149

institutionalized when he was young, and he just wants to be treated like other children."

Michael's recent school experience has been encouraging. His teachers apparently are pleased at his rapid progress in mathematics, English and art. One teacher said, "He overwhelms me — he's so eager to learn and he has such talent. And he's so persistent. I'm just amazed. I just wish I could do more for him." Both Cindy and Michael are now doing well in school. They receive only a fraction of the special therapy they need, but they are progressing nevertheless.

This case study provides the bare outline of how parents can hold local school districts accountable for the provision of adequate educational services to all children, regardless of their needs. Through the Jacksons' experiences, we can decipher a process for organizing around educational issues. The initial step in this process is to clearly identify the implications of various disability labels by observing the services available to specific groups of children. Most important, parents must not be deterred by existing policies and practices or professional advice, since professional practices often reflect administrative expediency rather than children's needs. To date, there is no scientific evidence that children benefit more from institutionalization than from community-based services. While certain current practices in special education may be scientifically based, more often than not we are prisoners of our past, locked into traditional policies of excluding children or seeking special placements, even institutionalization, when other alternatives might prove more satisfying in terms of preparing children for participation in the mainstream of society.

The Jacksons were willing to break away from this imprisonment. By forming a community of concerned parents, they sought to insure that children with disabilities not be shunned from society or lumped into classrooms for deviants.

At the time the Jacksons sought to find services in their own community, none of the now famous lawsuits on behalf of children with special needs had been conceptualized.

150

Perhaps today parents facing similar difficulties can carry the Jacksons' struggle a step farther by implementing a lawsuit to ensure that their children receive a local education. If, as has been suggested in this chapter, decisions about the placement of deaf children and others with special needs are largely based on administrative and political considerations, parents may want to avail themselves of political strategies.

If this case serves no other purpose, it should encourage us to question and, indeed, challenge special education services and medical policies which promote categorization, segregation and, ultimately, institutionalization.

REFERENCES

Blatt, B. *Christmas in purgatory*. Syracuse, NY: Human Policy Press, 1974.

Parisi, Patricia, et al. Plaintiffs brief, March 17, 1972, U.S. District Court, Eastern District of New York.

Pennsylvania Association for Retarded Children v. *Commonwealth of Pennsylvania, David H. Kurtzman, et al.* Civil Action No. 71-42, Order, Injunction, and Consent Agreement, October 7, 1971.

Ricci et al. v. *Greenblatt et al.* 1972 C.A. 469 F (M.D., Mass).

Ricky Wyatt v. *Stonewall B. Stickney, et al.* Plaintiffs brief, March 2, 1972, U.S. District Court, Middle District Alabama, Northern Division, Civil Action No. 3195-N.

7

Surplus Children

Douglas Biklen

Approximately a million children in the United States are excluded from formal schools for at least a portion of their school-age years. In Boston, for example, an estimated 10,000 children are excluded. What happens to these children? What problems do they face? Do they receive services elsewhere?

Some children who present management difficulties become potential surplus children, but these by no means account for all of the excluded group. Some never find acceptance in a public school or treatment program of any kind. Some must even wait to find admittance to an institution. Undoubtedly, the greatest difficulties in finding services are encountered by multiply handicapped children and their families.

Areas of special education and the administrative systems, of both schools and treatment agencies, that have developed in recent years tend to be differentiated by categories of disability (e.g., we have separate institutions for the retarded and deaf). Further, the institution for the retarded may exclude children who have been diagnosed as retarded and deaf; similarly, the school for the deaf may exclude the deaf and retarded child. In many states legislatures have passed funding laws which allocate state money to specific disability areas, thus intensifying the problems of a multiply handicapped child. Consequently, some children never find a place in the schools or in treatment programs.

The following interview with Mrs. Olson, mother of a handicapped child, Paul, speaks volumes about the difficult hurdles some parents must face if they want their child to receive even an hour a day of treatment/schooling. The author conducted this interview in 1971, as a prelude to establishing an advocacy service for such parents.

D.B.: Can you tell us whether or not, and in what way, it has been difficult for you to find services for your child? And how do you think your difficulties have differed from the problems other families experience with "normal" children?

Mrs. Olson: Yes, it's been very difficult to find services for Paul. First of all, it was difficult to get an accurate diagnosis, which I don't even think I have at this point (Paul was considered multiply handicapped). Services for Paul have been almost impossible to get, except for very strong personal pushing for everything. And as far as differing from the "normal" child, I really don't have to say much about that. When the child is "normal," he progresses through certain stages — at age five the bus comes and takes him to kindergarten, and the next year he goes to first grade, and then he goes to second. . . . Maybe he fails one — but it's an entirely different situation. There is just nothing available (for Paul) and what is available is often not the place where this child belongs. Sometimes you put him there because this is the only place there is; in the meantime, the child is getting older day by day.

D.B.:   What programs has your child been in to date?

Mrs. Olson: Paul is going to be nine on the 4th of July. He started school at three and one-half when I took him to the Association for Retarded Children — which was not really the place for him, but it was better than nothing at the time. Then he went into a Montessori program for almost two years. For a year we worked together with a patterning program. And then he was tutored for about half an hour a day with a teacher coming here. After the program was terminated completely, I used to drive him to a school in the suburbs for one hour's tutoring a day.

D.B.:   How old was he when he was getting one hour a day of schooling?

Mrs. Olson: He was seven. That was last winter. Just one hour a day of tutoring; just one to one.

D.B.:   Wasn't he eligible for public school?

Mrs. Olson: Yes, he was eligible, but there just wasn't a class for him. He was tested by a psychologist, and it was one of these disastrous things where Paul was unpredictable to begin with. This is one of the problems with the child. And there just wasn't a program for him. There are special classes, but he just didn't fit into any of the categories. So there was not a class.

155

D.B.: How about day care and recreational programs? Has it been difficult when you wanted to go out for the day to find some place where Paul could go and spend the day, or have you been able to get babysitters quite easily?

Mrs. Olson: I do not have a terrible problem with babysitters because of the physical setup here. I have a teenage daughter, and I have Paul's uncle who lives here, too. The problem is a bigger one — the day-to-day, month-to-month problem of a child who is growing up and who needs special training so he can develop his potential. I'm not worried about going out; I'm sure I could get someone to take care of him. As far as recreation is concerned, this is not that much of a problem either, because Paul is the kind of child who . . . I don't think that's the most important thing for him either. When he gets older, I'll probably run into that problem. I'm beginning to realize now that my problems are only beginning. I thought that when I got him in school, he would be going to school on the bus and coming home on the bus, and I could relax. I've had nothing but all kinds of problems. Like today, for instance, he isn't in school — not because he is sick, but because his teacher is sick. Now, if this were a "normal" child, there would be a substitute for his class. What if, in this entire school district, all the teachers out sick today had their classes cancelled? Somehow, I've gotten to believe that somebody, some mastermind, seems to think parents of children like this are superhuman. It's like they really believe this heaven-sent special child is sent to special people. I don't buy that. It's hard; it's tough. He goes to religious education on Sunday. I tried him in a swimming program, one to one with a boy. It didn't work out — the kid didn't have enough stamina to keep up with Paul. But, basically, I want to know right now if Paul will be going to school next year and the year after . . . I want to feel some security in the school situation.

D.B.: You're not certain of that?

Mrs. Olson: No, I'm not. Maybe it's just in my mind. I don't think so, because I know this is an unstable situation.

D.B.: Have you felt this problem before?

Mrs. Olson: Yes, I always felt that. Paul never went to school a full day until this year, and he is eight years old.

D.B.: You said he was in a number of programs?

Mrs. Olson: They were all half-day, two days a week — that's all. He never went to school a full day until this year, and I have a feeling this program is really an experimental thing.

D.B.: Which program?

Mrs. Olson: The class he is in now is a learning disabilities program. I know they're feeling it out, and they're feeling their way. I'm always holding my breath, thinking about what's going to happen next year. Suppose somebody on the school board decides this is too much money to spend for four or five kids. I've always got that hanging over me.

D.B.:

When you attempt to get services for Paul, what kind of reception do you get from the various service agencies? Do you find that they have programs ready for you?

Mrs. Olson:

Obviously, from what I told you previously, they don't. I think they do the best they can. In a sense, I will always be grateful to the Association for Retarded Children, because it was the only place I could turn when Paul was three and one-half — and they were marvelous, really. The program has expanded now, the building has changed, and things have changed. When I went there, they did the best they could with what they had. I have found afterward that everything is a struggle. You just don't go out and put the needs of this child in front of these people and expect them to take some wild interest in this child. You have to keep after it. You have to keep after the school system for bus service. If you want any kind of special funding for this child, you have to keep after the agency you're going through. Everything is a big struggle. I wonder, sometimes, how parents who don't have the stamina or the ability — what happens to them?

D.B.:

What would you do if you had it in your power to either resolve the kinds of problems you've had to date or help other families with similar problems?

Mrs. Olson:

First of all, I would like to see a lot of this lip service put into action. In other words, we read about these fantastic things that are being done, that are being plannned, but try to go find them! Try to take this child and

feel secure in a school situation! Earlier we
talked about day care — I know what you
mean about that. If you have a child like
this, it sometimes hampers the life of the
family in the sense that maybe they have to
get away for two weeks, and there is no
place where the child can go. I read, at one
point, about a state school that opens up its
doors to temporary stays. It's great, and this
shows more real sensitivity to the needs of
the child and the family. The child comes
first, of course. If the child can be established in a stable situation, that is primary.
But after that, the needs of the rest of the
people in the family are important, like the
effects upon the other children. I'm running
into that problem now. And it's hard, unless you know who to call — and even
when you call somebody, they just don't
have the answers at their fingertips.

As Mrs. Olson stated so well, even if you know the right
people, you may not find the right services or any services at
all. This example raises questions about the efficacy, comprehensiveness, and interrelationships (or lack of them) of
community agencies. The situation does not lend itself to
simple solutions; nor does the above interview reflect an
isolated situation. It is not a single incident experienced by
one child but, rather, the kind of situation facing thousands of
children in America.

A researcher (Sanzi, 1971) in Massachusetts examined this
problem in considerable depth as part of a statewide study on
the needs of "special" children. The following account, written by Sanzi,[1] of two families' struggles to find services

---

[1]Lauren Sanzi researched typical agency responses to "multi-sensory
disordered children." Her findings support the view that many children
simply cannot find adequate human services.

dramatizes the problems that emerged from the researcher's investigations (inquiries that went far beyond mere interviews with selected parents).

Family A's five-year-old son is the fifth of six children and is described as not responding to sound, legally blind, and brain-damaged. For two years and four months he has been placed in Crystal Springs Nursery. Prior to this placement, many contacts, described below (including parents' comments), were made.

1. St. Colleta Day School. Parents were told the child did not meet the criterion of a 70 + IQ.
2. Boston School for the Deaf. Parents were told the same thing.
3. Paul A. Dever State School. Might have accepted the child, but the family lived outside of their region.
4. Joseph P. Kennedy Memorial Hospital (inpatient). The family was told that there was no room in their program.
5. Wrentham State School. Family was told that there would be a seven-year waiting period. They visited the facility and their observations, plus the long waiting period, made them decide not to apply. They felt that it was depressing, plain, lacking in privacy and inadequately staffed. They were concerned their son would receive no attention or training.
6. Perkins School for the Blind. Following evaluation, the parents were told their son would not fit into the educational program, but were asked: "Do you mind bringing him back for further evaluations, because he is so interesting." They refused.
7. Institute for Human Potential (Pennsylvania). A year and a half before the boy was placed in Crystal Springs Nursery, he was evaluated at this institute. He was then "patterned" four times a day by four people for a year and a half. During this time, a full time nurse was employed by the family.
8. Other Treatment. For a period of six months the child was seen twice a month at the Hearing and Speech Clinic at Children's Hospital Medical Center. At age four months he had a cataract operation.

Two salient points are: (1) none of the above referred the family to another facility or agency and, (2) the family learned about each contact from other parents.

Family B has a five-year-old, non-ambulatory cerebral palsied son, the second of three children, who has been diagnosed as severely hard of hearing (wears a hearing aid), and has brain damage, an enlarged liver, and one "bad" lung. For the past ten months he has been placed in the Kansas Logopedic Institute, but may only be able to stay for another year. Family B's lengthy list of contacts follows:

1. Boston Children's Hospital Medical Center. At age 12 months he was seen for a neurological exam and some seizure activity was reported. There were no follow-up procedures or referrals at that time.
2. Joseph P. Kennedy Memorial Hospital. When the child was two, he was evaluated here and accepted into the day school program for one year.
3. Crystal Springs Nursery. Because of family problems, Family B applied for permanent placement at Crystal Springs for their son. He was accepted.
4. Joseph P. Kennedy Memorial Hospital. When hospital personnel learned of this possible placement (3, above) they accepted the child for a supposedly six-month inpatient pilot program for MSD (multi-sensory disorder) children. However, at the end of two and a half months, according to the parents, they "dumped him and left us out in the cold." The hospital made no referrals.
5. Walter E. Fernald State School. The family applied here because they had lost the placement at Crystal Springs and, still experiencing family difficulties, desired a permanent placement. Routinely, Fernald contacted Kennedy Hospital for records; "someone" at the hospital indicated that the child would not be a candidate for the Fernald program and he was not accepted.
6. Crotchet Mountain (New Hampshire). Kennedy Hospital then contacted Family B, referred them to this facility and made the initial appointment. Crotchet Mountain said they would accept him if he was toilet trained; he was not.
7. Pine Harbor School for the Deaf (Rhode Island). This facility considered taking the child after an initial parent interview. The parents felt that Kennedy personnel had indicated to Pine Harbor that their child should not be a candidate, and he was not accepted.
8. The family visited and contacted several more facilities both in and out of state, with no results.
9. Kansas Logopedic Institute (Kansas). When the family felt desperate, Kennedy Hospital suggested contacting this facility. The child was evaluated and accepted; he will be able to stay there as long as he is making progress.

Again, but with the exception of one facility, there was an obvious absence of follow-up and referrals. It must be re-emphasized that the preceding lists of contacts and circumstances are as the families have interpreted them. It is felt, however, that the experiences are real, and that similar situations are faced by many families of children with multi-sensory disorders.

Serious problems still face both families. In each, the sibling immediately older than the handicapped child suffers emotional problems which seemed to clear up when the MSD child was removed from the home. Because these parents have been advised by medical personnel not to bring the child back into the home, they feel they must seek long-term placement. When Family B faces the child's dismissal from Kansas Logopedic Institute, returning him to the family home or placing him in a short-term experimental program will be unacceptable. Ideally, both families seek long-term placement close to home with self-help training programs, where the children can develop to their fullest potential. Serious financial problems plague both families. Blue Cross-Blue Shield is currently covering two thirds of the $12.00 per day cost for Family A's son. Family B receives $7,000 per year from the Division of Special Education towards the $10,000 per year Kansas Logopedic Institute fee. The present problems will be intensified when Family A's Blue Cross-Blue Shield runs out, and when Family B's son is dismissed and the Division of Special Education will no longer be able to help maintain the child, who will then no longer be considered educable.

Both families have contacted the Division of Child Guardianship, but are not entitled to aid because of their income brackets. Neither family expects the State to assume full financial responsibility, but both believe they should continue to receive some support even when the child is no longer considered educable. Both families feel helpless and worry about the future and the possibility of being confronted with catastrophe. Family A suggested they might be exempted from that portion of their taxes which goes to help them support their child. The parents asked the investigator: "Does the State intend for an individual to provide totally for their multi-handicapped child indefinitely?"

To more fully understand the problems faced by these two families, the investigator placed a series of telephone calls to several facilities and agencies. Posing as a new state resident with a five-year-old deaf, partially sighted, non-toilet trained, ambulatory child, she called four state schools to gather information about waiting periods, cost, financial aid, and other possible placements.

I. Walter E. Fernald State School
    A. Waiting period — generally six months to a year. However, one child presently in treatment at Dixon State has been on the waiting list since 1965 (1965 to 1970). The social service office said this (the investigator's) case "has potential," though.
    B. Other referrals
       1. Crystal Springs Nursery
       2. Vesper Hills Nursery
       3. Te-lo-ca School (not recognized by the State)
    C. Training program — consists of little "apartments" each with six children (the investigator did not observe this)
    D. Cost — $12.00 per day
    E. Financial aid possibilities — Division of Settlement and Support, Massachusetts Department of Mental Health

F. Other comments — Stressed the necessity of a one year residency requirement

II. Wrentham State School
- A. Waiting period — about five years after evaluation of the child
- B. Other referrals
  1. Day care centers
  2. Nurseries
- C. Training program — none
- D. Cost — $12.50 per day
- E. Financial aid possibilities — Division of Settlement and Support

III. Belchertown State School
- A. Waiting period — extremely overcrowded, waiting list of years in some cases. Very doubtful that child would be admitted, especially if new in the state.
- B. Other referrals — Dr. R., West Springfield, for community placement (when contacted, he said he had no place to refer them either)
- C. Training program — none
- D. Cost — $10.50 per day
- E. Financial aid possibilities — Division of Settlement and Support

IV. Hathorne State School
- A. Waiting period — six months to a year
- B. Other referrals
  1. Avalon School
  2. Vesper Hills
  3. St. Coletta's day school
- C. Training program — none
- D. Cost — $15.00 per day, residential
        7.50 per day, day students
- E. Financial aid possibilities — Division of Settlement and Support

A second series of calls dealt with possibilities for financial assistance. The Division of Settlement and Support, Massachusetts Department of Mental Health, which had been recommended by the four state schools, was contacted first. The first person reached merely transferred the call to Miss K., who was supposed to furnish the necessary information. Miss K. explained that the investigator had contacted the wrong office, and should, instead, call the Department of Mental Health's Division of Mental Retardation because "they would know if there was any financial assistance available." This division, in turn, suggested a call to the Bureau of Retardation in the Governor's office. There, the secretary put the investigator's name on a mailing list for a brochure to explain funding to parents of a retarded child. She then connected the investigator with a man who suggested calling a Mrs. L. later in the day. Mrs. L. was unable to provide additional information and stated that the brochure would soon arrive. It arrived two weeks later.

A third series of calls, to inquire about financial assistance, began with a call to the Public Welfare Department Information Center. There, a woman suggested calling the Public Assistance Office, which, in turn, suggested calling the Division of Child Guardianship. A secretary in the DCG office immediately transferred the call to an unidentified man (called Mr. W. here), who said he was "not aware of all the criteria" concerning financial assistance, since he was in the "intake office" which gathers background information for the Special Services Department, in charge of placement. He evaded a question about where responsibility lies for decisions about financial aid. Mr. W. did describe a catalogue used by the Special Services Department in placing children, but when asked if the family could see it, he said they "absolutely could not see it because of the confidential nature," i.e., "description of the programs and a description of the types of children they accept." He stressed the focus on families with social crisis, but indicated that one worker, Mrs. P, deals with maintenance of mentally retarded children in the home. After trying several days, the investigator was unable to reach her and gave up.

When asked more about placement costs and individual costs such as operations, medication, etc. and whether DCG would cover them, Mr. W. said, "I shouldn't think so," but he would not elaborate. He did mention placement possibilities at Crystal Springs Nursery, Vesper Hills Nursery and some state schools. When inquiring into the possibility of calling the Special Services Department, he said that they would be able to supply no further information.

The Special Services Department was called anyway, but this time as a MACE representative. Mr. J. evaded all those questions about the determination and nature of criteria for financial assistance. He did offer the use of their placement lists but judged them to be inadequate. He named five state facilities for severely mentally retarded children, but, in contradiction to other information, told the investigator that his agency does not place children in state schools.

Two other agencies were contacted, Division of Preschool Hard of Hearing and Deaf Children and the Massachusetts Commission for the Blind. Because the first deals only with educable children, the call was transferred directly to the Division of Special Education. The investigator was told this division provides 100 percent funding for children in approved residential programs, both in and out of state, providing the child is educable or until he fails to progress. Children are then referred to the Department of Mental Health. The only exceptions are orthopedically handicapped and deaf children who are sent to Crotchet Mountain (New Hampshire) if they are toilet trained.

164

The person contacted at the Massachusetts Commission for the Blind was open and direct in providing needed information. She explained how to start financial eligibility proceedings in the case of a legally blind child. She also explained that financial assistance criteria are the same as for Public Welfare, and include the possibility of medical assistance for those under age 18 who need nursing home care.

Conclusions to be drawn from the last phase of this survey may be briefly stated. If one is to accept parents' statements about services and consultation offered regarding their multi-sensory disordered child, it must be concluded these are few in number and limited in scope. If the child has a specific label and is toilet trained, alternatives for services and funding are broadened. Regrettably, these conditions do not prevail for the group of children under consideration.

The typical situation involves lack of programs, long waiting lists and conflicting information dispensed by individuals who should be knowledgeable in the area. Frustrations are faced by all, with apparent gross discrepancies in treatment and consultation provided children with similar problems.

Those parents who have knowledge of the workings of bureaucracy or the fortitude to continue searching for help can usually find some solace. Frequently, though, the results of these efforts are minimal and there is always the fear of rejection, which means one must begin again.

Sanzi's research, including these vivid accounts of human endurance and determination and, occasionally, of defeat and rejection, suggests that there must be a better way for agencies to serve children. Indeed, many administrators and educators who read these pages may become more sensitized and therefore more responsive to parents and children who seek assistance. Yet, the most significant lesson in these portraits may not be for administrators of service agencies as much as for parents, consumers, and those who wish to become advocates. Mrs. Olson and parents A and B had little knowledge of their rights, of the legal responsibilities of the agencies they approached, or of the specific services their children needed. Further, while all of the parents felt strongly about their children and were persistent in their efforts, none had the availability of advocacy resources such as parent (consumer) action groups, legal aid, or training in social change.

This is not to suggest that confrontation and adversarial relationships between consumers and agencies should be developed *in lieu of* changing the service agencies from within but, simply, that the problems are of such magnitude and the agencies are so consistently unresponsive as to require a heightened accountability.

REFERENCE

Sanzi, Lauren. A survey of facilities and services for children with multiple sensory disorders in the Commonwealth of Massachusetts, *Massachusetts study of educational opportunities for handicapped and disadvantaged children.* (A study of the Massachusetts Advisory Council on Education; Burton Blatt, Director, Frank Garfunkel, Associate Director.) Boston, MA: 1971, pp. 200-210.

8

Missing Agendas in Social Policy : Head Start and the Handicapped

Robert Bogdan and Douglas Biklen

Policy mandates have become a frequently used tool of the social planning trade. Whether for equality in hiring of blacks and women or for antidiscrimination in schooling and health care, they have become an increasingly familiar element of federal programs.

One such mandate, the Economic Opportunity Act (Economic Opportunity Amendments of 1972), required that all Head Start programs engage in affirmative action to increase the enrollment of handicapped children to one of every 10 Head Start children. The Department of Health, Education and Welfare's Office of Child Development directed more than 3,000 local programs to comply by 1973. Handicapped children, as defined by legislation and guidelines, included "mentally retarded, hard of hearing, deaf, speech impaired, visually handicapped, seriously emotionally disturbed, crippled, or other health impaired children who by reason thereof require special education and related services" (Economic Opportunity Amendments of 1972 and Elementary and Secondary Education Act of 1965, p. 55). The legislation also required submission of yearly reports to Congress on the number and nature of the handicapped children enrolled. The intent of the mandate was to provide services to severely impaired youngsters in the regular Head Start setting. (For a history of legislation, see Lavor, 1972.)

The findings reported here are based on data collected during a year-long national study of the 10% mandate (Syracuse University, 1974). Sixteen site visitors who were trained in participant observation techniques (Becker, 1970; Bruyn, 1966; Bogdan, 1972; Bogdan & Taylor, 1975) and who went out as two-person teams to spend three days at each of 30 Head Start programs compiled extensive qualitative reports. The programs visited were located in various regions of the country and in both rural and urban areas. Programs varied in the number of children enrolled and the ethnic composition of the population served. A modified stratified random sample technique was used in choosing most, but not all, the programs. (For a complete discussion of sample selection, see Syracuse University, 1974, Appendix A.)

The mandate represented a major planning and policy thrust for the Office of Child Development. Its most important impact, however, may not have been to significantly change the lives of handicapped preschoolers, but to confirm the basically reformist nature of social planning in America. It was a planning and policy venture founded upon facts that were as much mythical as factual. Further, it was social planning that sought clinical solutions for a largely structural or political problem. In a number of ways, the 10% mandate exemplified typical flaws in human service planning and policy.

MYTHICAL FACTS

Immediately prior to our site visits, the Office of Child Development had mailed a questionnaire to all Head Start programs, requiring them to give the number of handicapped children enrolled, the handicapped conditions involved, and the services these children were receiving. On the basis of results of that survey, it was stated that: "Compared to last year, the number of handicapped children in Head Start approximately doubled" (Systems Research Incorporated, 1974). A report based on those findings which was submitted to Congress in April of 1974 stated:

> To date, children professionally diagnosed as handicapped account for at least 10.1 percent of the children enrolled in full year programs. In addition, 3.1 percent of children enrolled in full year programs are either partially diagnosed or reported as possibly handicapped. The distribution of handicapped children by category of handicap is as follows: 35 percent speech impaired, 20 percent health or developmentally impaired, 12 percent seriously emotionally disturbed, 9.5 percent physically handicapped, 7.9 percent hearing impaired, 7.4 percent mentally retarded, 6.6 percent visually impaired, 1 percent deaf, and 0.5 percent blind (U.S. Department of Health, Education and Welfare, 1974, p.iii).

The Office of Child Development declared it had surpassed its goal. For OCD the mandate was an unmitigated policy success. The impact of the mandate, however, cannot be understood by the figures in that report.

A basic, almost prejudicial, analysis with social planners is that they adopt at face value common definitions of "the facts" as if "the facts" were of natural origin and not social constructs which serve a specific interest group or class. Human resources specialists, for example, base elaborate training policies on the notion that America has a group of people which are "hardcore unemployed" — suggesting a problem in certain people that makes them hardcore unemployed; i.e., it is they who must change rather than the economy. This notion of the "unemployable type" emerges most often in times of high employment and low unemployment. The facts one chooses to consider (the number of "hardcore unemployed" rather than the number and quality of jobs available) reflect one's political ideology — not an objective condition. While one planner finds the cause of

169

unemployment in the worker (hardcore unemployed), another may explain unemployment as a product of a failing or oppressive economic system. As one changes the definitions of unemployment (Piven & Cloward, 1971), mental health or mental illness (Szasz, 1961; Scheff, 1966), juvenile delinquency (Platt, 1969) or women's roles (Millett, 1970; Friedan, 1963), one changes the policy and planning outcomes. Jessica Mitford (1974) provided a clear example of this phenomenon in discussing definitions of crime:

> When is conduct a crime, and when is a crime not a crime? When Somebody Up There — a monarch, a dictator, a pope, a legislature — so decrees. If one were to extend Ramsey Clark's imaginary map of high-crime areas into the adjacent suburbs, one might find manufacturers of unsafe cars which in the next year will have caused thousands to perish in flaming highway wrecks, absentee landlords who charge extortionist rents for rat-infested slum apartments, Madison Avenue copywriters whose job it is to manipulate the gullible into buying shoddy merchandise, doctors getting rich off Medicare who process their elderly patients like so many cattle being driven to the slaughterhouse, manufacturers of napalm and other genocidal weapons — all operating on the safe side of the law, since none of these activities is in violation of any criminal statute. Criminal law is essentially a reflection of the values, and a codification of the self-interest, and a method of control, of the dominant class in any given society. (One might suppose that some conduct, such as murder, is universally considered a horrendous crime and punished as such. Not so. Professor Laura Nader, an anthropologist, tells me that in some primitive communal societies murder is considered a relatively trivial matter, involving as it generally does merely a quarrel between two individuals; whereas polluting the river, which affects the whole community, is on the order of high treason.)

The same problem of definition plagues human service planners in the area of disabilities. Plans such as the 10% mandate assume agreement on what constitutes a disability. But an objective definition of disability is as illusive as the concept of crime.

Professionals dealing with the "handicapped" have had raging debates on the definitions of their diagnostic terms. While at any given time a definition may be said to be "official" (the one accepted by the most influential professional organization), there is never a clear consensus on the meaning of terms such as "handicapped" nor for the specific diagnostic categories falling under that heading. In addition, "official" definitions are changing constantly. Burton Blatt (1975) points to the conflict and change in the definition of the term "mental retardation," a sub-category of "handicapped." Reviewing the past 15 years of psychometric definitions, he states:

> Prior to 1959, there was more or less general agreement that the incidence of mental retardation is approximately 3%. That is, mental retardation was assumed to be normally distributed in the population and it was further agreed that the psychometric "cutoff" would be 75 IQ or 1½ standard deviations away from the mean. In 1959, the Association on Mental Retardation's Terminology and Classification Committee, chaired by Rick Heber, redefined mental retardation and, included in the revised definition, there was a statement that subaverage intellectual performance refers to a psychometric score which is greater than one standard deviation below the population mean on tests of general intelligence. . . .

> In 1973, a subsequent committee of the Association, now chaired by Herbert Grossman, again revised the definition to include as mentally retarded only those who are "significantly" subaverage in intellectual functioning with "significant" encompassing performance which is two or more standard deviations from the mean or average of the tests.

With a keen sense of irony, Blatt suggests that, with a stroke of a pen, Grossman (1973), enormously reduced the incidence of mental retardation (also see Heber, 1959). Further illuminating the problems of definition, he points to the fact that people who are legally mentally retarded in one state may step across the state line and no longer be "mentally retarded" and that children who may be in special classes for the mentally retarded in one country are not even considered retarded in others. Blatt (1975) gets to the heart of the problem of definitions for fields relating to the handicapped when he states:

> It's obvious; mental retardation and emotional disturbance, and even such seemingly objective conditions as blindness and deafness, are less objective disease entities than they are administrative terms; and, they are metaphors more than anything else.

Others have made similar observations. Jane Mercer (1973), Dorothea and Benjamin Braginsky (1971), Roger Hurley (1969), and Lewis Dexter (1964) have concurred in regard to the field of mental retardation. Richard Scott (1969) points to similar problems in the seemingly "objective" area of blindness. Szasz (1961, 1970), Bogdan (1974), and many others have pointed to the ambiguous and metaphorical terminology in the area of mental illness and emotional disturbance. (For studies of labeling of handicapped children, see Beeghley and Butler, 1974; Mercer, 1973; Edgerton and Edgerton, 1973; Richardson and Higgins, 1965; Scott, 1969.)

These definitional disagreements might seem insignificant were it not for the fact that they reflect obvious ideological interests. The number of persons labeled retarded, for example, increased by leaps and bounds during the period of social Darwinism, when testing came into vogue and when retardation was linked to moral degeneracy (Tredgold, 1908), ethnic background (Goddard, 1917; Gould, 1922; Brigham, 1923), and heredity (Galton, 1892; Goddard, 1912).

Today, identification of disabilities often becomes justification for segregating children with disabilities from their more typical peers (Blatt, 1973; Sarason & Doris, 1969), for tracking children into low-status life vocations, and for denying schooling altogether (Children's Defense Fund, 1974; Task Force on Children Out of School, 1970). In recent years, the increased interest in identifying individuals' handicaps has been accompanied by increased interest in the special education and related professions. In circular fashion, these professions expand the definitions of and thereby increase the number of people identified as "the hyperactive," the "emotionally disturbed," the "retarded," the "blind," and so on.

FINDING THE 10%

The confusion over how to define disabilities created considerable bewilderment for the Head Start agencies. The directives given to Head Start personnel in regard to the

172

mandate were not precise in defining "handicaps." Who were they supposed to label handicapped? Should a child with a "lazy eye," slow speech, or an umbilical hernia qualify as disabled? How about the extremely active child?

Prior to the mandate, some program staffs had used the term "handicapped" to refer to the majority of children enrolled in their programs. As one program director put it, "They tell us we have to serve 10 percent handicapped. Hell, we have 100 percent handicapped." In that sense of the word, he was referring to the fact that the program served children from a low socioeconomic background. But when the new mandate came, invariably the agency directors turned to professional diagnosticians for assistance. The identification of handicaps often reflected the diagnostic skills available to the identification process. If, for example, a community had a well developed speech and hearing clinic, more children would tend to be designated as having speech and hearing handicaps, since these well developed agencies were often called upon to give special assistance in assessment.

Head Start staffs in some programs, while comfortable in identifying and keeping records on children they defined as "really handicapped," were reluctant to label the more questionable cases as "handicapped." This was particularly true at the staff level which worked directly with the children. These staff members saw the diagnosis as having the same moral implications as name-calling but with longer lasting consequences. Some indicated they resisted labeling children as "handicapped" because they did not want the children to start their school careers with that stigma on their records. Labeling was seen as less problematic if children had demonstrable, major, physical defects; e.g., confined to a wheelchair, without sight, or with Downs' Syndrome (mongolism). But such children were few in number.

While there may have been confusion and anxiety over designating youngsters for the program, Head Start staffs, especially at supervisory levels (it was they who were required to fill out reports), felt they had to do so in order to meet

Washington's requirements. Some solved the dilemma (not wanting to stigmatize but needing to designate) by not telling parents, other staff and community agencies which children were on the "10% list" and by not referring to a child as "handicapped." In these cases, being handicapped was more an administrative matter than a programmatic concern or a stigmatizing label.

In other programs and for other children, this kind of resolution was not applied; thus, certain youngsters became known as "handicapped" who in the past would not have been so designated. Being listed as handicapped had a variety of effects. On visiting some centers, our observers were told by staffs that they were not sure whether a certain child was on the list or not. In others, being on the list made a child the object of special attention and made the staff more aware of special differences and needs the child might have. In some of those cases, it had the effect of bringing to the child services he or she would otherwise never have had. For others it meant being known as "handicapped" but not receiving any special services.

Our observations indicated that the majority of programs visited had made greater efforts to identify, recruit, and enroll children with special problems than they had in the past. Most made contacts with special disability agencies, notified medical and other clinical professionals, and sponsored advertisements. Yet, with the exception of the "really handicapped" children (who were in the great minority), identification of most children who became designated as "handicapped" took place after enrollment; i.e., children tended to be recruited with no known handicap. Typically, the condition of "handicapped" was conferred upon children after they entered the program, as the situationally derived criteria were applied. On a number of occasions, we heard staff members comment, for example, that "I didn't know we had so many (handicapped children) until we started counting."

All Head Start programs we visited reported that they had always included children now designated as handicapped. Children who, after the mandate, were seen as hearing impaired, emotionally disturbed, speech impaired and mentally retarded might have been recognized, prior to the mandate, through observation in the classroom and by professionals performing the regular and required initial medical examination, as having a problem, but the Head Start staffs had tended to see these children as having a specific difficulty rather than as being a "handicapped child." They had been casual about these specific problems and had not put children into specific categories. Prior to the mandate, Head Start kept no records on children's special problems. Since the word "handicapped" was not salient in pre-mandate years, few programs could give even an estimate of the number of children who could have been designated as handicapped.

Our primary conclusion of the mandate's impact was that the *overall nature of the population of children in Head Start changed only modestly, if at all, as a result of the mandate.* The major difference between pre- and post-mandate in regard to handicapped children was that more children were being either listed or labeled as handicapped than before. The mandate had precipitated head-hunting.

Our observers said that the great majority of children designated as handicapped might best be described as having "slight differences from typical children." Speech impairment was the largest handicapping category reported to our field workers.[1] Given the cultural diversity and differences among Head Start children and the possible effect of these differences on speech patterns, along with the factor of their being of pre-school age, our observers concluded that the speech impaired children they observed were far from being demonstrably different from the other children.

However, most programs defined themselves as having met the regulations of the mandate: They were serving and

---

[1]In the survey reported to Congress (U.S. Department of Health, Education and Welfare, 1974, p.5), 35 percent of the handicapping conditions were reported to be speech impairment.

175

had diagnosed over 10 percent of their population as handicapped.

Head Start directors understandably felt pressured to meet the congressional mandate. Less understandable and less excusable is the result — that the mandate led to labeling children, even when it is commonly accepted that labels have a decidedly pejorative impact. Was it necessary to label large numbers of children as handicapped in order to serve them in Head Start programs? Judging from our observations, there is no evidence that the labeling actually increased numbers of disabled children served, though there is considerable evidence that, through the 10% mandate, the process of identifying and labeling large numbers of children as handicapped became a customary practice. The point that severely disabled children did not profit significantly from the new mandate explodes the myth that labeling is a necessary evil in obtaining services for those who most need them.

One only can hypothesize about the long-range impact of this labeling process. The most obvious result is that the diagnostic categories have been reified and legitimized; e.g., children with the problem of over-activity become "emotionally disturbed" and children who are slow become "mentally retarded." The labeling process also may increase the influence of special educators and allied professions; it may result in further stigmatization of children as they enter public schools; it may cause certain diagnostic procedures (even psychological testing of this is of questionable validity) to become more commonplace in all pre-school programming; it may create self-fulfilling prophesies that spell failure for many children.

FROM CLINICAL TO POLITICAL PLANNING

Congress' 10% mandate resembles other social planning and policy efforts in that it falsely assumes basic agreement about the "facts" — in this case, the definition of "handicapped." And since various handicaps are defined as much by societal response to people's appearances and behaviors as by the appearances and behaviors themselves, the definition of handicaps must be a starting point for human service planning. It is just as crucial to understand how people interpret disability as to understand the social behaviors of crime, delinquency, mental illness, unemployment, achievement, and administrative excellence. But there was no agreement on the nature and implications of handicaps. And the Office of Child Development did not sufficiently explore that problem. Consequently, the Head Start mandate which began as an effort to mainstream handicapped children into typical settings never seriously challenged age-old beliefs about disabilities and traditional patterns of exclusion and segregation waged against disabled children.

Traditionally, American society has systematically structured the exclusion of handicapped children from the mainstream. Disability labels such as "educable," "trainable," "deaf," "blind" "emotionally disturbed," "autistic," "cerebral palsied," "multiply handicapped," and "learning disabled" have become cues to spawn special, often segregated educational and pre-school programming. The basic assumption has been that more severe handicaps require more segregated and more institution-like treatment settings. Severely disabled children have been channeled into institutional settings and private voluntary associations.[2] These are the children that Head Start was least able to find and attract.

Head Start's difficulty in drawing more severely disabled children reflects the intensity of segregation with regard to disability and the widespread development of ideologies that perpetuate segregation. Because, for example, voluntary associations have always experienced financial problems in meeting the needs of their clientele, they have had to rely on a

---

[2]That is not to say that all disabled children have been served. Literally several million children who have been excluded from public schools have not found any substitute, even in the private, segregated facilities.

combination of funding sources, including charity. Charity has come at a high price. As Pieper (1975) suggested, charity drives are too often characterized by pleas for pity toward the disabled and by overblown arguments that the disabled need highly specialized treatment. The "pity" image of charity has further dehumanized and ostracized the disabled. Just several decades earlier, the disabled had experienced more direct and brutal dehumanization at the hands of institution builders who viewed the retarded as wild, animal-like, potentially criminal, and morally depraved (Wolfensberger, 1975).

The claimed needs for extreme specialization gave rise to an argument that segregated settings could provide greater specialization at less cost in a single location. These assumptions never have been proven. Yet the same justifications of specialization and cost saving were being echoed by large institutions for the disabled. Here the argument fell down rather quickly, for institutions cost as much as $28,000,000 for a 750-resident facility. Today, while the voluntary associations still attract charity, the primary source of income for voluntaries and institutions (which have municipal bonds to pay off) come from State and Federal aid formulas, as well as from patients' Medicare payments. Not surprisingly, this fact, and the strong sentiments associated with the long history of building massive segregated service centers, have put present day institutions and voluntary associations in a protectionist positon where they must compete for children in order to survive. Head Start would need a powerful plan to reverse this tide of segregation.

The 10% mandate was more like a welcome sign on the Head Start door than a compelling social force to redefine present day conceptions of disability and treatment. Head Start lacked the mechanisms to reverse current segregationist patterns of service. First, the mandate came from above — from Washington rather than from the grass roots — and thus, local agencies rushed to comply with the directive but not to create social change in their communities. It was not their cause.

Second, the Head Start agencies did not mount a campaign to soften people's attitudes toward specialization, segregation, and disability. The voluntary associations viewed Head Start agencies as inadequately prepared to accept handicapped children who, it was argued, need trained experts for teachers. Head Start never confronted that challenge. Actually, most disabled children need only periodic special treatment such as speech therapy, physical therapy, sign language training and motor coordination experiences, and the remainder of a typical day can be spent profitably with typical children in typical program situations. But Washington had not prepared an education campaign to publicize this. Consequently, Head Start's open doors never were presented as an alternative to the segregated, pity-generating voluntary associations.

Third, even though public funds were their life blood, Washington never challenged segregated pre-school programs operated by voluntary associations, institutions, and even local public agencies. Admittedly, the Office of Child Development (as well as other elements of the Department of Health, Education and Welfare, including, most notably, the Bureau for Education of the Handicapped) publicly supported integrated programs for the disabled, but that support never took the form of sanctions against the segregated sector.

Fourth, the 10% mandate forced local Head Start programs to label children. In this sense, Head Start was not that different from typical disability agencies. The alternative would have been for Head Start agencies to provide all the necessary specialized programs (e.g., speech therapy and mobility training) without labeling the children. The concept of non-categorical programming could have been promoted as a radical departure from the segregated, stigmatizing programs currently available.

One can hardly be surprised that the 10% mandate developed by the Office of Child Development and Congress did not radically transform conceptions of disability and patterns of service. After all, as in most social planning, the real issue

179

at stake was one of power. Who has the power to control the lives of disabled persons? While the 10% mandate was one bid to create a new level of access to the mainstream, the power to define disabilities as pitiable, to characterize service as an undertaking for specialists only, to equate quality service with segregated service, and to reify and legitimize disability categories was left with practicing professionals, the disability institutions and bureaucracies, and voluntary associations. Power was the missing agenda.

REFERENCES

Becker, H.S. *Sociological work.* Chicago: Aldine Publishing, 1970.
Beeghley, L., & Butler, E. The consequences of intelligence testing in public schools before and after desegregation. *Social Problems,* June 1974, 21(5).
Blatt, B. *Souls in extremis.* Boston: Allyn & Bacon, 1973.
Blatt, B. This crazy business. In R. Kugel, *Changing patterns in residential services for the mentally retarded.* President's Committee on Mental Retardation, 1975.
Bogdan, R. *Participant observation in organizational settings.* Syracuse, NY: Syracuse University Press, 1972.
Bogdan, R. *Being different.* New York: John Wiley & Sons, 1974.
Bogdan, R., & Taylor, S. *Introduction to qualitative methodology.* New York: John Wiley & Sons, 1975.
Braginsky, D., & Braginsky, B. *Hansels and Gretels.* New York: Holt, Rinehart & Winston, 1971.
Brigham, C.C. *A study of American intelligence.* Princeton: Princeton University Press, 1923.
Bruyn, S.T. *The human perspective in sociology: The method of participant observation.* Englewood Cliffs, NJ: Prentice-Hall, 1966.
Children's Defense Fund. *Children out of school in America.* Cambridge, MA: Children's Defense Fund, 1974.
Dexter, L. *The tyranny of schooling.* New York: Basic Books, 1964.
Economic Opportunity Amendments. P.L. 94-424, 92nd Congress, H.R. 12350 (September 1972).
Edgerton, R., & Edgerton, C. Becoming mentally retarded in a Hawaiian school. In Eyman, R., Meyers, E., & Tarjan, G. (Eds.). *Sociobehavioral studies in mental retardation.* Los Angeles: American Association of Mental Deficiency, 1973.
Elementary and Secondary Education Act. P.L. 92-230, Title VI, 1965.
Friedan, B. *The feminine mystique.* New York: Dell, 1963.
Galton, F. *Hereditary genius* (2nd ed.). London: Macmillan, 1892.
Goddard, H. *The Kallikak family. A study in the heredity of feeblemindedness.* New York: Macmillan, 1912.

Goddard, H. Mental tests and the immigrant. *Journal of Delinquency,* 1917, 2, 243-277.

Gould, C.W. *America – A family matter.* New York: Scribner, 1922.

Grossman, H. (Ed.). *Manual on terminology and classification in mental retardation.* Washington, DC: American Association on Mental Deficiency, 1973.

Heber, R. (Ed.). Manual on terminology and classification in mental retardation. *American Journal of Mental Deficiency Monograph,* 1959.

Hurley, R. *Poverty and mental retardation.* New York: Vintage Books, 1969.

LaVor, M. Economic opportunity amendments of 1972, P.L. 92-424. *Exceptional Children,* November 1972.

Mercer, J. *Labeling the mentally retarded.* Berkeley: University of California Press, 1973.

Millett, K. *Sexual politics.* New York: Doubleday, 1970.

Mitford, J. *Kind and usual punishment.* New York: Vintage Books, 1974.

Pieper, B. What price charity. *The Exceptional Parent,* January/February, 1975.

Piven, F., & Cloward, R. Regulating the poor. New York: Vintage Books, 1971.

Platt, A. *The child savers.* Chicago: University of Chicago Press, 1969.

Richardson, W., & Higgins, A. *The handicapped children of Acamance County, North Carolina.* Wilmington, DE: Nemours Foundation, 1965.

Sarason, S., & Doris, J. *Psychological problems in mental deficiency.* New York: Harper & Row, 1969.

Scheff, T.J. *Being mentally ill.* Chicago: Aldine, 1966.

Scott, R. *The making of blind men.* New York: Russell Sage Foundation, 1969.

Syracuse University, Division of Special Education and Rehabilitation. Interim report on assessment of the handicapped effort in experimental and selected other Head Start programs serving the handicapped. Submitted to U.S. Department of HEW, OCD, by Policy Research, Inc., 1974.

Systems Research Inc. *The status of handicapped children in Head Start* (prepared for the Office of Child Development). Lansing, MI: Author, 1974.

Szasz, T.S. *The myth of mental illness.* New York: Hoeber-Harper, 1961.

Szasz, T.S. *Ideology and insanity.* Garden City, NY: Anchor Books, 1970.

Task Force on Children Out of School. *The way we go to school.* Boston: Beacon, 1970.

Tredgold, A.F. *Mental deficiency.* London: Bailliere, Tindall, & Cox, 1908.

U.S. Department of Health, Education and Welfare, Office of Child Development. *Head Start services to handicapped children* (2nd annual report to U.S. Congress, Washington, DC, 1974).

Wolfensberger, W. *The origin and nature of our institutional models.* Syracuse, NY: Human Policy Press, 1975.

PART TWO

ALTERNATIVE CONCEPTS AND SETTINGS:
the Promise

9

Research Orientations in Special Education

Burton Blatt

FOCUS

I will not forget a childhood experience, memorable because it was the first time I thought about language as being something other than words. I was made aware that human beings are circumscribed and bound, as well as freed, by their language — awesome stuff for a nine-year-old.

Someone visiting our home was telling my parents that he had decided to run for public office; in order to influence public opinion, he had bought a newspaper. Only days later did I understand the statement. Only days later did I comprehend how making a nickel purchase — something I had done many times — could in any way influence public opinion, much less help anyone to be elected to public office.

Not only children live in worlds circumscribed by their language, their understanding of the idioms of their culture, or what they think are the "rules of the game." Scientists, too, are culture-bound, as well as time-bound, grounded by their experiences and, undoubtedly, victimized as well as enriched by them.

Stated another way, all words, and the languages that words form, have antecedents. If there are no words to describe a thought, or a belief, or a wish, those ideas become unthinkable and impossible. Add to this limitation our human tendency to exhibit contempt or awe for what we do not understand and to wallow pridefully in our disdain or worship of the incomprehensible, rather than struggle to fathom it. Is it any wonder that we search for others' guidance, for any opportunity to avoid developing a unique solution? We prefer to implement the standard solution. Possibly the rarest gift of all is independence of mind.

For many years research of the issues contained in this book proceeded along experimental and other traditional lines. And, in spite of our inability to learn very much or help very much (not necessarily related matters), we continued to apply traditional approaches to the study of complex field problems — invariably with unsatisfactory results.

The problem of relevancy of research methodology has been particularly troublesome in the broad field of research on children with special needs.[1] With some rare exceptions, research on people with special needs has followed traditional lines of experimentation, survey analysis, and test construction and validation. Rarely have participant observation procedures, situation analyses, historical research, autobiographies, and process analyses been applied to these populations or problems associated with them. Traditional models have determined the type of research being conducted. I am concerned that the models are not determined by the nature of the problems studied. I also am concerned that traditional models determine the kinds of independent variables (i.e.,

---

[1]The remainder of this chapter is a brief summarization of the chapter (Blatt and Garfunkel) "Teaching the Mentally Retarded," published in the *Second Handbook for Research on Teaching*, edited by Robert Travers, Rand McNally, 1973.

sources of intervention and treatment) selected for study, and that they influence the scaling of independent variation.

In other words, researchers in the field of special education are confronted by problems connected with the assignment of children to treatments and of teachers to treatments. These problems become formidable when the researcher attempts to deal effectively with triads of teachers, children, and methods. Therefore, when one designs a classroom experiment that includes children (who vary), teachers and possibly some other adults (who vary), it is questionable whether there is a similarity in the way a treatment occurs in different classes with different teachers and different children. In traditional educational research strategy, the kinds of children and the personalities of the teachers are considered peripheral to the experimental comparison being made. The controls are employed to equalize the other potentially independent variables.

Here, however, I will discuss the assignment of major independent variables which relate directly to teachers and children, and intervening variables which relate to method and curriculum content.

For example, much attention has been given to the critical teacher-child relationship in the teaching process. An example of this phenomenon is the "Hawthorne effect" — the change which occurs in an experimental group as a consequence of the treatment itself. The Hawthorne effect seems to be more consistently related to improved performance than any particular method or curriculum. It is an experimental side effect that appears to have more research significance than so-called main effects. Consequently, one assumption the researcher should consider is that something like the Hawthorne effect is necessary to the development of a significant interaction. It can be specifically designed as an important component of educational research.

Although necessary, such an effect is not sufficient. Other questions must be answered: How do children spend their time in classrooms? How do they attend to what is going on?

187

How is their attention monitored? How are they dealt with when they succeed or fail? What kinds of questions do they ask and are asked? Rarely do we pose such problems.

The rationale for this chapter suggests development of research strategies that are in harmony with discovering and evaluating what actually occurs in natural settings, be they classrooms, clinics, institutions, homes, or neighborhoods. Possibly, this research orientation offers a solution to what Blackman (1969) described as the dichotomy between those who prefer experimentation as the method of proof and those who view education essentially as an art form which could lose its color and vitality if the movement to fractionate the teacher-pupil interaction achieves its apparent goal.

THE PROBLEM OF "FIT"

Individuals function differently in numerous ways. For some researchers, description is an end in itself. However, there is no unbiased description. For example, when several groups are given IQ tests, almost invariably they will have different averages. Are these objectively derived differences? We believe not! A good deal went into the development of the IQ test, selection of items, and procedures for administering the test. The testing format is, itself, a special structure for communication. Tests are validated in specific ways using specific criteria. They are developed to do *something*. The narrower that *something* is, the easier it is to validate the test; however, the test becomes more biased when used with different groups at different times.

We often talk about variability. What makes the greatest difference? Heredity or environment? School or home? Discipline or therapy? If a child has a problem, what (or who) had the most to do with it? What is the best way to undo the problem? Does what is wrong indicate what should be done? Reductions are not always useful, at least in the usual sense. Prescriptive education is a reduction. Therapeutic education is a reduction. Montessori, Frostig, Kephart, Cruickshank, Bereiter, A. S. Neill all offer reductions. Simply stated, reductionists say *this* is what to do with children who present in *this* manner. Whatever *this* is, the assumption is that *this* can be identified, described, and distinguished from something other than *this*.

Much confusion exists about what people should do, how they should do it, and when it should be done. Who is to judge? Are the judges' values my values? Or yours? How can it all be put together: poverty, delinquency, migration, retardation, language, values, disability, learning? Or can't it? Is it psychological, sociological, anthropological, epistemological? The first problem is to decide about fit — individuals who do not fit, groups that do not fit, individuals who do not fit groups that do not fit.

There are several differences between being an *individual* who does not fit, or match, and being in a *group* that does not fit. For example, the new field of learning disabilities has epitomized the Individual-no-match (Blatt, 1969): Find out what is wrong, then treat it; the patient subsequently will get better. Mental retardation always has been in the Individual-no-match category. Unfortunately, this was a strategic error and interferes with progress in our field. The black population of the United States illustrates an Individual-no-match category that did not begin to move out of a repressive society until it developed Black Power and pride — i.e., until it assumed a Group-no-fit strategy.

SUMMARY AND CONCLUSION

The literature in special education indicates that the preponderance of published research is experimental. Most studies of teaching have used traditional designs, whether efficacy studies, follow-up studies of children in special and regular classes, studies of different methodological approaches, or studies of different curriculum approaches.

We believe there are more appropriate ways to study teaching-learning in classroom or tutorial situations. However, it is well known that researchers engage not in what they want to do but in what they are able to do, what is possible, what is safe, and what gives assurance of completion.

We conclude that:

— There is nothing inherent in disability to produce handicap, i.e., a belief in one's incompetency. Further, it is not the primary responsibility of the behavioral sciences to determine the validity of the aforementioned statement, but to make it valid. We have supported far too many studies purporting to demonstrate differences between groups or the disorders of one child in contrast with another. All these years, we should have been promoting research that would seek to enable a child to learn after participation in a special program or curriculum.

— The study of particular methods for the purpose of demonstrating their efficiency is rather fruitless, and whatever is demonstrated eventually will be contradicted by subsequent research. Little is proven by such "all or nothing" studies of methodologies; i.e., studies which compare the efficacy of one method with that of another, or compare the superiority of one type of individual with that of another.[2] Only a naive researcher could conclude that the demonstrated superiority of his method had direct and specific transferability to other educational settings.

---

[2]Or, as Campbell and Stanley (1963) concluded, "We must increase our time perspective, and recognize that continuous, multiple experimentation is more typical of science than once-and-for-all definitive experiments . . . we should not expect that 'crucial experiments' which pit opposing theories will be likely to have clear-cut outcomes" (p. 3). On the other hand, we are not ready to suggest that there should be nothing but uniqueness in an educational setting. There must be the possibility for building generalizations because, if knowledge is an objective, we must be concerned with the degrees of non-uniqueness.

190

Our research preference is to study children and how they change in different educational environments. From evaluations of varieties of methods, with varieties of children in more or less formal and informal settings, utilizing teachers with heterogeneous backgrounds, hypotheses will be generated leading to viable theories concerning human development and learning. Through this kind of strategy, theory construction shifts from methodological to human interactive concerns.

We have attempted to discuss a relatively unpopular position among researchers, a position which assumes that human research should not be an activity separated from values and prejudices about people. Further, we believe it is impossible for the researcher to separate completely his beliefs from his research activities. Therefore, research with disabled persons should proceed, first, from a statement of values, then to an intervention and evaluation, with careful efforts to explicate the former, rather than to submerge it in contrived research designs.

What is our bias? That capacity is a function of practice and training. It is a task of researchers to validate this bias.

REFERENCES

Blackman, L.S. *A scientific orientation for special education.* New York: Teachers College, Columbia University, 1969.

Blatt, B., & Garfunkel, F. Teaching the mentally retarded. In R. Travers (Ed.), *Second handbook for research on teaching.* Chicago: Rand McNally, 1973.

Blatt, B. Learning disabilities. *Seminars in psychiatry,* 1969, *1,* 237-361.

Campbell, D.T., & Stanley, J.C. *Experimental and quasi-experimental designs for research.* Chicago: Rand McNally, 1963.

191

10

A Phenomenological Approach to "Mental Retardation"

Steven Taylor and Robert Bogdan

Recently, sociological perspectives have gained in importance in studying "mental retardation." Breaking from the tendency to concentrate on physiological and psychological dimensions of "the problem," social scientists such as Braginsky (1971), Edgerton (1967), Mercer (1973), and Goffman (1963) have studied and helped us understand "mental retardation" as a social phenomenon.

A particular sociological approach — phenomenological — represents a radically different way of approaching the subject matter, and has great potential for change in the field.

THE PHENOMENOLOGICAL PERSPECTIVE

Phenomenology is a perspective which attempts to view human behavior from the human actor's own frame of reference (Bruyn, 1966; Jacobs, 1972; Deutscher, 1973; Bogdan &

Taylor, 1975). The phenomenologist examines how people experience their world. For him or her, reality is what people imagine it to be. Perhaps the essence of this approach is best captured in the now trite phrase, "Beauty is in the eye of the beholder." If we are to understand beauty, we must study the beholder and not those who are considered beautiful.

From the phenomenological perspective, mental retardation, like beauty, is in the eye of the beholder. The phenomenologist distinguishes between intellectual or neurological conditions and societal definitions of mental retardation. As a concept, mental retardation exists in our own minds, rather than in the minds of those so labeled.

We have identified a group of people who, though different in many ways, may share some characteristics in common. We create a term, "mental retardation," to describe their condition. We begin to speak of "them" and "us," though we have no reason to assume that a person with an IQ of, say, 60 has any more in common with a person with an IQ of 20 than with a person with an IQ of 100. Nevertheless, we generalize about the "mentally retarded." Indeed, how many of us have heard the phrases, "The mentally retarded don't mind boring jobs," "Mongoloids are good-natured," or "The retarded like to be with their own kind"? We have even sub-divided the "retarded" into "educables" and "trainables," the "border-lines" and the "mildly, moderately, severely, and profoundly retarded."

The writers submit that the term "mental retardation" lends little insight into the nature of the people who have been categorized under that heading. To the contrary, it erects barriers to understanding the "mentally retarded" and perpetuates a mythology based on artificial distinctions. Our first involvement in this field began with observational studies of a state institution (Taylor, 1974; Bogdan et al., 1974). Staff members of the facility were eager to enlighten us, as naive newcomers. For example, they explained, "The retarded don't get hurt like you and me," "You can always tell when a full moon's coming 'cause they always act up," and "You can't talk nice to them 'cause they won't understand." To say the least, we learned little, if anything, about the "retarded" through such statements. However, we did learn a lot about the motives and assumptions of those who supposedly serve the "retarded."

The point is that we ourselves have created "mental retardation," a concept, a set of commonsense understandings held by members of our society. Since we have created it, we can "cure" it. As Burton Blatt has noted earlier in this book, one of the biggest breakthroughs in the treatment of mental retardation occurred several years ago when the American Association on Mental Deficiency redefined the concept and "cured" thousands of individuals overnight! Better than behavior modification, reality therapy, and thorazine combined!

To understand "mental retardation," one must view it as a social creation. In phenomenological terms, one must suspend, or "bracket," one's own assumptions and beliefs. Like the proverbial Martian visitor, one must experience everything as something new and strange (Bruyn, 1966). An excellent, but little known, article by Lewis Dexter (1964, pp. 37-49) illustrates this approach.

Dexter describes a mythical society in which a major target group of social discrimination is comprised of clumsy people, the so-called "gawkies." As we value intelligence, this society values grace. Dexter postulates that the technology of this society would be designed in such a way as to require grace for the successful performance of everyday tasks, simply because technologists would arrange to have things done that way. He speculates on what would happen to clumsy people in this society. School children would be ranked a grace quotient (GQ). Some would present an embarrassment to teachers and parents and be sent to special schools and institutions. Clumsy adults and children alike would be social rejects and ridiculed by pantomime jokes. Meanwhile, academicians would write scholarly papers on the "pseudo-clumsy" and form professional organizations such as the National Association on Clumsiness. Dexter even describes

195

the controversy that would surround researchers who conclude that people with subnormal GQs could live independently.

The lessons to be learned from Dexter's metaphor seem obvious, but often are ignored. As professionals, we have perpetuated the belief that there are two classes of people — "them" and "us," the "normal" and the "retarded." In short, a phenomenological perspective forces us to direct our attention to the social context and meanings of mental retardation.

METHODOLOGICAL IMPLICATIONS

A phenomenological perspective requires researchers to select methods which allow them to see things from other people's point of view. Although almost any research method could be used to accomplish this purpose, qualitative research methods are most compatible with the phenomenological perspective. By qualitative research methods, we mean procedures which produce descriptive data: people's own written or spoken words and observable behavior (see Bogdan and Taylor, 1975).

Qualitative researchers allow "subjects" to talk about what is on their own minds in their own words. Note how this differs from most other research methods. When we ask people to respond to formal questionnaires or inventories, we force them to respond to our questions and concerns. The qualitative methodologist first learns what is important to people themselves and only then begins to ask structured questions. Similarly, when we reduce people to statistical aggregates, we lose sight of their subjective feelings, perspectives, and experiences. Qualitative methods enable us to know people personally and to view them as they develop their own definitions of the world around them.

Participant observation and personal documents, especially unstructured interviewing, have served as the mainstays of qualitative research methods. Participant observation refers to research characterized by a period of intense social interaction between the researcher and subjects, in the milieu of the latter, during which time data are unobtrusively and systematically collected. Observers immerse themselves in the lives of the people they wish to understand. They engage them in casual conversations and encourage them to speak about what is on their minds. They allow data to emerge naturally, without forcing the subjects into the researchers' own preconceived notions and concepts.

Participant observation depends upon the recording of systematic, complete, accurate, and detailed field notes. The notes represent the researchers' attempts to record everything they can remember from the observation period. While observers are in the field, they force themselves to concentrate on what is going on around them, to record in their memories everything they hear, see, smell, feel, and think. After they have left the field, they record their observations on tapes which are later transcribed, or record them directly onto paper. Included in the notes are descriptions of people, conversations, and behavior, as well as the researchers' own feelings, preconceived notions, and working hypotheses.

While observers vary in the amount they can remember during an observation session, they are able to refine their observation and memory skills through training, concentration, and concerted effort. Some researchers use the analogy of a switch to describe the control they have developed to collect data in the field — they have learned to "turn on" the intensive concentration needed to conduct this kind of research. Finally, most observers, and especially novices, seldom spend more than an hour at a time in the field.

By personal documents, I mean those materials in which people reveal in their own words their view of their entire life, or a part of it, or some other aspect about themselves. Personal documents include such diverse materials as diaries, letters, autobiographies, and transcripts of long, unstructured interviews. In unstructured interviewing, as in participant observation, researchers allow subjects to give their own perspectives in their own words on a general topic or event.

The main difference is that interviewing is conducted in a quiet place apart from other activity.

Qualitative methods perhaps can best be explained by showing how this research differs from untrained observations of typical people during the course of their day. More specifically, how is the participant observation method different from what observant staff members do and what they notice in their work within an institution?

First, as noted above, the qualitative researcher attempts to systematically record everything that occurs in the field. Thus, a participant observation study is not an individual's off-the-cuff impression of a setting but, rather, a detailed analysis based on meticulously recorded field notes. Observers describe even the seemingly least significant aspects of the setting or subjects they wish to understand. In our own research, we have found that minor details can lend insight into the perspectives of staffs and administrators at state institutions: Furniture was constructed of metal, heavy wood, and hard plastic; television sets were mounted high on the wall; there were no curtains or decorations on the wards, with the exception of an occasional cartoon drawing; beds were pushed together, lacked pillows and, sometimes, sheets; residents and attendants used different water fountains; residents' bathrooms, in contrast to attendants' facilities, had no toilet stalls, seats on the toilets, toilet paper, mirrors, or soap. These and other features of that institution conveyed the notion that residents were child-like, destructive, and subhuman (see Wolfensberger, 1974).

Second, qualitative researchers study subjects in whom they have no direct personal or professional stake. The participant observer or interviewer conducts a study as a neutral figure, with no personal alliances or axes to grind. Regular participants of a setting carry personal biases and tend to see things from only certain people's points of view. One's formal role, such as a supervisor or counselor, also may preclude honest and open communication with people in other roles.

Qualitative methods are based on the assumption that researchers can establish with subjects a rapport characterized by trust, openness, and a free exchange of information. To accomplish this, qualitative researchers carry themselves in such a way that they eventually may become an unobtrusive part of the scene. They remain relatively passive throughout the course of their research, but especially during the initial stages. They ask non-threatening questions. They pay proper homage to the routines of their subjects. In short, researchers act as a mixture of an objective recording machine and an empathetic human being. Thus, attendants in our own studies have committed acts in our presence which they would hide from supervisors and even attendants on other wards and shifts. On numerous occasions they hit residents, drank beer, and pitched nickels, all in violation of institutional policies. Some attendants have expressed personal feelings and concerns to us which they wouldn't share with their fellow workers.

Third (and this directly relates to the phenomenological perspective), qualitative researchers question the concepts and assumptions which other people take for granted. For the phenomenologist and qualitative researcher alike, there is no truth or reality. "Reality" differs from person to person, from staff to resident, from administrator to ward attendant. In an institution behavior such as head-banging and rocking may be explained in markedly disparate fashion. One staff member may explain self-mutilation as a consequence of mental retardation. Another may point to boredom and lack of programming as the cause. Which is the "true" perspective? The researcher seeks to understand both of these perspectives, and accepts neither as true or false. On one ward where we studied, an attendant related an incident that supposedly had occurred prior to his employment at the institution:

Awhile ago one kid jumped off (a porch). He only broke his leg though. They don't get hurt like you and me.

199

Is it true that "they," the "retarded," don't get hurt like you and me? Irrelevant! The significance of this statement is that this attendant's belief had profound implications for his perspectives on and treatment of residents.

Professionals and paraprofessionals often operate under theoretical assumptions which color their observations. They may already "know" about "mental retardation." They may "know" that the "retarded" aren't like "us." They may "know" that "mental retardation" causes head-banging and rocking. This kind of "knowledge" obscures as much as it illuminates.

Finally, qualitative research requires more time, energy, and concentration than most people within settings have to offer. Most people must perform tasks with a certain degree of competence, which interferes with their ability to collect data. An occupational therapist must serve a number of clients; an educator must teach and confront problems that arise in the classroom; an administrator must direct and supervise. An observer often collects as many as 20 pages of field notes after a single hour of observation. At the conclusion of a study, a researcher may have collected over 1,000 pages of data.

This is not to say that participant observation and unstructured interviewing cannot be used to help people develop a clearer understanding of the settings in which they work and live. To the contrary, several successful studies, including Goffman's classic, *Asylums* (1961), have been based on research conducted by intimate participants of settings. However, we must point out that qualitative research demands a great deal of attention and a commitment to critical understanding.

THE PRACTICAL SIGNIFICANCE

According to phenomenologists, we view the world through rose-colored lenses. We see mental retardation because we believe in it, not vice versa. We must study mental retardation in ways that reflect this fact. One such approach is qualitative research.

Qualitative research represents less a set of techniques than a mode of relating to people and their experiences. On the one hand, it prescribes rules for inoffensive interaction between the researcher and subjects. Researchers must be sensitive to their effects on those they seek to study, and must employ strategies to gain the candor of subjects. As Robert Coles (1971) has remarked:

> Somehow we all must learn to know one another. . . . Certainly I ought to say that I myself have been gently and on occasion firmly or sternly reminded how absurd some of my questions have been, how misleading or smug were the assumptions they convey (p. 29).

On the other hand, qualitative research implies a certain empathy, a willingness to understand the world as it is experienced by others. In the field of mental retardation, this suggests several lines of inquiry.

As professionals, we must be aware that people's perspectives on mental retardation structure their action toward those so labeled. If one assumes that the "retarded" cannot learn, one will not teach them. If one regards the "retarded" as sub-human, one will ridicule them and, worse, congregate them in segregated facilities. If one assumes that the "retarded don't get hurt like you and me," one will mistreat them and ignore their suffering. Our perspectives act as a "self-fulfilling prophecy," thereby creating the conditions under which they will come true.

We also must learn to understand and value the point of view of those we have labeled "mentally retarded." As a society, we have been reluctant to listen to what the "retarded" have to say. We have been smug in our own perspectives. An incident related by Burton Blatt dramatizes this point. During the time he and Fred Kaplan were collecting material for their photographic essay, *Christmas in Purgatory* (1974), which depicts atrocious conditions at state institutions through pictures taken with a hidden camera, a resident discovered Kaplan's camera, which was secured to his belt and hidden by his sports jacket. The resident immediately reported the camera to an administrator whose attention Blatt had monopolized up to that time. The administrator laughed and dismissed the report with the remark, "Boy, these retardates can really have an imagination." The point is: To be labeled "retarded" is to be ignored.

More than this, we have been insensitive to the stigma imposed upon the retarded and their families (Goffman, 1963). In a society that values intelligence, "mental retardation" is a demeaning classification. As one former resident of a state institution said, "It never has been popular to be retarded" (see Bogdan and Taylor, 1976). Yet, professionals continue to label and diagnose, to degrade and demean. They criticize the community for intolerance, but perpetuate the myth of two types of people, "them" and "us." In our attempt to explain their "condition," we have added to the burden of those we label "mentally retarded." Can there be a "retarded" person who has not felt discrimination, rejection, and ridicule, due not to any individual characteristic, but merely because he happens to be one of "them"?

The authors have advocated a phenomenological approach to mental retardation, one that views people on their own terms, with a deep appreciation for their own perspectives and subjective experiences. In line with this, we have suggested adopting methods which allow us to talk with people and to hear what they have to say. To conclude, here is a statement (Bogdan & Taylor, 1976) from one who understands "mental retardation" better than we do — one who has experienced it:

> What is mental retardation? It's hard to say. I guess it's having problems thinking. Some people think that you can tell if a person is retarded by looking at them. If you think that way, you don't give people the benefit of the doubt. You judge a person by how they look or how they talk or what the tests show, but you can never really tell what is inside the person (p. 51).

REFERENCES

Blatt, B., & Kaplan, F. *Christmas in purgatory.* Syracuse, NY: Human Policy Press, 1974.

Bogdan, R., & Taylor, S. *Introduction to qualitative research methods: A phenomenological approach to the social sciences.* New York: Wiley, 1975.

Bogdan, R., & Taylor, S. The judged, not the judges: An insider's view of mental retardation. *American Psychologist,* January 1976, *31*(1), 47-52.

Bogdan, R., Taylor, S., de Grandpre, B., & Haynes, S. Let them eat programs: Attendants' perspectives and programming on wards in state schools. *Journal of Health & Social Behavior,* June 1974, *15*, 142-151.

Braginsky, D., & Braginsky, B. *Hansels and Gretels.* New York: Holt, Rinehart & Winston, 1971.

Bruyn, S.T. *The human perspective in sociology: The methodology of participant observation.* Englewood Cliffs, NJ: Prentice-Hall, 1966.

Coles, R. *Migrants, sharecroppers, mountaineers.* Boston: Little, Brown, 1971.

Deutscher, I. *What we say/What we do.* Glenview, IL: Scott, Foresman, 1973.

Dexter, L. On the politics and sociology of stupidity in our society. In H. S. Becker (Ed.), *The other side.* New York: Free Press, 1967, pp. 37-49.

Edgerton, R.B. *The cloak of competence.* Berkeley: University of California Press, 1967.

Goffman, E. *Stigma.* Englewood Cliffs, NJ: Prentice-Hall, 1963.

Goffman, E. *Asylums.* Garden City, NJ: Doubleday, 1961.

Jacobs, J. *Getting by: Illustrations of marginal living.* Boston: Little, Brown, 1972.

Mercer, J. *Labeling the mentally retarded.* Berkeley: University of California Press, 1973.

Taylor, S. *"Doin' a job": Attendants and their work at a state institution.* Paper presented at the annual meeting of the Eastern Sociological Society, Philadelphia, April 1974.

Wolfensberger, W. *The origin and nature of our institutional models.* Syracuse, NY: Human Policy Press, 1974.

11

Handicapism in America

Douglas Biklen and Robert Bogdan

In the past five years we have witnessed a revolution in public policy toward the education of children with disabilities (Abeson, 1974). Beginning with litigation (Gilhool, 1973), it was then forged through legislation. New federal laws ensure the right of every child to an education, the right of parental access to school records, due process rights for school and class placements, and the right of children to attend the most integrated (least restrictive) school program possible. But the battle to overcome years of blatant discrimination in the schools[1] must be viewed as part of a much larger struggle for equality. The roots of discrimination are founded in every area of our personal and social lives, not simply in the schools.

---

[1]Two million children, nearly half of them disabled, experience miseducation and exclusion daily (Children's Defense Fund, 1974).

For decades children with disabilities have been the focus of stereotyping, prejudice, and discrimination wherever they go. We have chosen to call these negative forces "handicapism." Handicapism can be defined as a theory and set of practices that promote unequal and unjust treatment of people because of apparent or assumed physical or mental disability. Handicapism manifests itself in relations between individuals, in social policy and cultural norms, and in the helping professions as well.

We do not presume to present, here, more than a scant sampling of "handicapist" policies, practices and behaviors. Nevertheless, we intend to present enough evidence to show that handicapism pervades our lives. We also will demonstrate that the concept of handicapism can serve as a vital tool by which anyone can scrupulously examine personal and societal behaviors toward disabilities. Further, the term "handicapism" offers leverage for changing the experience of people with disabilities. It provides the language to discuss an entire series of events and behaviors which previously might have aroused discomfort and frustration but which were not easily identified as part of a larger pattern of dehumanization.

HANDICAPISM IN OUR PERSONAL LIVES

We all have heard handicapist phrases throughout our lives, and — whether we like to admit it or not — most of us have contributed to them too. It often is said that the retarded are happier and better natured than the brighter child, a myth that also has been applied to other minorities, most notably blacks ("They are such happy-go-lucky people!"). Then there is the notion that disabled children will always remain childlike. The President's Committee on Mental Retardation issued a public service advertisement picturing a young person sitting in front of a birthday cake with eight candles. The caption read, "He'll be eight years old for the rest of his life." Similarly, disabled children are characterized as "God's special children." Wolfensberger (1975) calls these stereotyped

206

images of "the eternal child" and "holy innocent" myths. Ironically, if a person with a disability breaks out of the stereotypically dependent, incompetent, childlike role, he or she may be regarded as "extraordinary, amazing, unbelievable."

People often ask, "Well, how should I act toward a blind person or a mentally retarded person? I never know if I'm doing the right thing or not." A lot of the time, people without disabilities do the wrong thing.

First, there is a tendency to presume sadness on the part of the person with a disability. For example, one woman who has a physical disability and who, incidentally, smiles a lot told us of an encounter with a man who said, "It's so good that you can still smile. Lord knows, you don't have much to be happy for."

Second, there is the penchant to pity. You might have heard, "It is a tragedy that it had to happen to her; she had so much going for her." Or people sometimes tell us, "It is so good of you to give up your lives to help the poor souls." Or, "My, you must be so patient to work with them. I could never do it. They need so much." Each of these phrases reveals an underlying pity for people with disabilities.

Third, people without disabilities sometimes focus so intensely on the disability that it becomes impossible for them to recognize that the person with a disability is also simply another person with many of the same emotions, needs, and interests as other people. This attitude is reflected in the perennial questions, "What is it like to be deaf?" "It must be hard to get around in a wheel chair," and "You must really wish you could see sometimes."

Fourth, people with disabilities often are treated as children. Notice, for example, that feature films about people with mental retardation and physical handicaps are so frequently titled with first names: "Joey," "Charlie," "Larry," and "Walter." We communicate this same message by calling disabled adults by first names when full names and titles would be more appropriate, and by talking in a tone reserved for children.

Fifth is avoidance. Having a disability often means being avoided, given the cold shoulder, and stared at from a distance. The phrases, "Sorry, I have to go now," "Let's get together sometime" (but not now and not any specific time), and "I'd like to talk, but I have to run" are repeated too consistently for mere coincidence.

Sixth, we all grow up amidst a rampage of handicapist humor, which must take a psychological toll: "Did you hear the one about the moron who threw the clock out the window?" "There was a dwarf with a sawed-off cane . . .," "Two deaf brothers went into business with each other . . . a blind man entered their store. . . ."

Seventh, people with disabilities frequently find themselves spoken for, as if they were not present or were unable to speak for themselves. In a similar vein, people without disabilities sometimes speak about people with disabilities in front of them, again as if they were objects and not people.

In terms of personal relations, then, if you are labelled "handicapped," handicapism is your biggest burden. It is a no-win situation. If you fulfill the stereotype, you are pegged as a poor, pathetic, sad, forever childlike and dependent person, someone who should be spoken for rather than to, someone with an unending need for pity and charity. If you succeed in challenging, or even in escaping, the stereotype, you may be objectified in another way, as an unusual, rare case, amazing. You are not simply an ordinary person.

HANDICAPISM IN SOCIAL POLICY AND CULTURAL NORMS

Were handicapism a problem limited to personal interaction, its eradication might be accomplished by attitude change campaigns and a heavy dose of sensitivity training. But it is not so simple. Handicapism pervades our culture, public policy, and institutional practice.

In transportation, for example, despite the availability of technology to make mass transportation accessible to people in wheel chairs, neither the courts nor federal legislation has sided decisively with access. The federal law encourages "substantial" efforts to make transportation accessible (P.L. 88-365; P.L. 90-480). Currently, a legal rights group, the Public Interest Law Center of Philadelphia, is attempting to have the courts interpret federal statutes to require standards of accessibility.

Accessibility to phone booths, mail boxes, buildings (public and private), and bathrooms also has been impossible for many people with physical disabilities. Society has created handicaps even when the technology existed to wipe them out. This seems particularly curious in view of the fact that our country elected Franklin Roosevelt to the Presidency four times. Roosevelt was confined to a wheel chair.

For others, language, and especially the written word, has been a barrier. According to officials at the Laubach Literacy Center (1976), anywhere from 8 to 23 million Americans cannot read. They can't read street signs or other messages basic to daily life. Yet, our society seems to make a fetish of written signs. In many instances symbols would suffice. Americans who travel to Europe have for years been struck by that continent's preference for symbols in street signs. Then, too, we intensify visual disabilities by our unabashed use of small print. Phone books, insurance forms, even train, bus, and airline schedules promote this kind of handicapism.

More open discrimination occurs in the area of employment or, more accurately, unemployment. According to 1970 U.S. Census Bureau statistics quoted by Biklen and Bogdan (1976) — of people with disabilities, 85 percent have an income less than $7,000 per year and, of these, 52 percent make less than $2,000. Of people with disabilities, only 36 percent are employed. That leaves 64 percent jobless. For adults, the experience of being denied a job must be every bit as debilitating as school exclusion is for children. Whether in jobs, schooling, insurance, medical care, day care and preschool programming, and access to buildings and transportation, the message is too often "exclusion."

Naturally, we may ask where such societal indifference and discrimination originates. That is hard to say. But, whatever the source, we can at least identify how it is transmitted. The mass media contribute to handicapism.

News stories, for example, report the handicapist comments of public officials, often without criticism. When the U.S. Senate was examining Nelson Rockefeller for the Vice Presidential position, a senator asked the former New York governor if he could explain why New York mental hospitals and mental retardation institutions were so dismal. He responded, "It is very difficult to get people to devote their lives to take care of a human being while really in full fact it is no more than a vegetable and to do it 24 hours a day right around the clock" (quoted in the New York Times, October 10, 1974).

News reporting often links criminal behavior with mental retardation and emotional disturbance, so much so that many people now believe that a person's past history in special education classes can explain in part why the person committed a crime. One of the earliest proponents of this myth was Goddard (1915), who wrote a book entitled *The Criminal Imbecile: An Analysis of Three Remarkable Murder Cases*, in which he warned citizens to be on their careful guard for violent acts by people with mental disabilities. Schrag and Divoky (1975) have done research to show the continued popularity of this myth. Yet, there is no evidence that graduates of special education commit more crimes than graduates of regular classes.

Newspaper comic strips also promote handicapism, as do feature films. Comic characters yell out "stupid idiot" and "dummy" and make fun of people who have low IQs. Obviously, this kind of namecalling encourages children and adults to engage in similar behavior. The comic strips popularize prejudice. Films sell similar messages. Captain Hook and the patch-eyed pirates personify evil, as associated (presumably) with disability.

Another popular medium by which society communicates handicapism is the charity drive. Most of us have participated in charity campaigns either as organizers or donors. We have given to charity for several reasons — not simply out of pity or

210

guilt, but for compassion and social responsibility as well. But it is time for a change. Charity drives frequently highlight children with disabilities on telethons and national poster campaigns in order to evoke pity from potential givers. Children are paraded out to exhibition baseball games and photographed in promotional pictures with money trees, wishing wells, and related gimmicks. Services provided as a result of charity campaigns are viewed as privileges, not rights. Children remain indebted to the goodwill of their benefactors. So the price of charity runs high, in terms of human dignity lost and in human services afforded on a precarious funding base.

Handicapism, whether in the form of charitable contributions, uncharitable news stories, films, comic strips, or exclusionary social policies, has a unified impact. At the societal level, handicapism is discrimination.

HANDICAPISM IN THE HELPING PROFESSIONS

One would expect the helping professions to work toward abolition of handicapism. Instead, they frequently accomplish the opposite. The professions, like ordinary people and society at large, often intensify handicapism.

Educational professionals, for example, in their rush to meet specialized needs, have created separate classes and separate schools for disabled children. They have done this without any evidence that separation of disabled children will have any educational benefit (Bennett, 1932; Blatt, 1956; Cain & Levine, 1963; Cassidy & Stanton, 1959; Goldstein, Moss, & Jordan, 1965; Hottel, 1958; Pertsch, 1936; Wrightstone et al., 1959). In fact, the practice of segregating children with disabilities begins at the pre-school level in many communities. It then extends not only to school but to recreation programs and summer camps.

For teenagers and young adults, handicapism sometimes occurs in job training. Sheltered workshops, society's favorite placement for adults with disabilities, are segregated facilities "for handicapped only." Too often, the expectations for performance in those settings have a devaluing effect on the potential workers. We visited a sheltered workshop where people were assembling veterinary hypodermic needles. Upon talking to the trainees, we were told that the staff disassembles the needles each evening, and the trainees start their work anew the next morning. This "training" is really makework. It will not prepare the workshop client for industrial employment.

Perhaps the most extreme form of professional handicapism occurs in the form of institutionalization. Children and adults have been institutionalized in settings where mass treatment, lack of programming, unsanitary conditions, overcrowding, control by psychotropic medications, and boredom have become the order of the day (Blatt, 1973). Clearly, not all large institutions spawn dehumanization in such gross ways, but the overall pattern of institutionalization has been so miserable as to cause federal courts to rule, consistently, that children should not be institutionalized unless it can be shown that they are unable to benefit from less restrictive community programs and settings.

OVERCOMING HANDICAPISM

Handicapism, like other forms of prejudice, stereotyping, and discrimination, can be checked and eliminated. Many individuals already have become more aware of their own attitudes and are willing to correct handicapist statements of others.

Federal policies now mandate education for all. Courts have called for the integration of children with disabilities into regular schools as much as possible. The Department of Housing and Urban Development is preparing standards for accessibility in housing and other buildings. Federal agencies such as Closer Look have seen their role as one of spreading the word about children's rights. The National Association for

Retarded Citizens has discontinued its poster child campaigns.

Disability rights groups such as the Children's Defense Fund, Disabled in Action, the American Coalition of Citizens with Disabilities, the Center for Law and the Handicapped, the Center for Independent Living, and the Center on Human Policy have engaged in extensive organizing to overcome handicapist policies in the helping professions. Major professional organizations such as the Council for Exceptional Children, the American Association of Orthopsychiatry, and the American Association on Mental Deficiency have joined in fostering litigation to end discriminatory and dehumanizing practices.

The AFL-CIO International Union of Toy and Doll Makers has begun to organize workers in sheltered workshops to win basic rights such as health insurance, sick leave, paid holidays, improved wages, and more rapid placement of workers in industrial settings; the first workshop to be organized was the Skyline Center in Clinton, Iowa.

Sesame Street has included children with disabilities. Human Policy Press has issued several children's stories which portray children with disabilities in heroic roles. *The Exceptional Parent* and *Polling* magazines have published numerous articles by consumers of services. Individuals have begun to educate their local media about handicapist policies in the helping professions.

Obviously the list of advances against handicapism could go on and on. In almost every community, there are some signs that people are becoming more conscious of the moral imperative to end discrimination against people with disabilities. Certainly, there are enough signs of ferment in the air to warrant our optimism that social change will occur. We believe that by identifying the broad range of prejudice, stereotyping and discrimination waged against people with disabilities as handicapism, the goals of change will seem obvious. We present the following 10 points as a possible platform of action to abolish handicapism:

1. Learn to identify and correct handicapist statements in yourself and others.
2. Demand equal access to all services and facilities for all people, regardless of disability.
3. Support funding for only those agencies which operate non-handicapist programs.
4. Start a national publicity campaign to fight handicapism.
5. Support a moratorium on the construction and funding of segregating facilities and programs.
6. Identify handicapism in the media and mount boycott campaigns, if necessary, to eliminate it.
7. Hold professionals accountable for the elimination of handicapism in their own practices.
8. Demand that human services be considered a right, not a privilege.
9. Support and develop local, state, and national groups with enforcement power to monitor the abolition of handicapism in human services.
10. Organize an international committee to identify and eradicate handicapism.

REFERENCES

Abeson, A. Movement and momentum: Government and the education of handicapped children, II. *Exceptional Children*, 1974, *41*, 109-115.

Bennett, A. A comparative study of sub-normal children in the elementary grades. *Teachers College Contributions to Education*. New York: Columbia University, 1932.

Biklen, D., & Bogdan, R. *Handicapism: A slide presentation*. Syracuse, NY: Human Policy Press, 1976.

Blatt, B. *The physical, personality, and academic status of children who are mentally retarded attending special classes as compared with children who are mentally retarded attending regular classes*. Unpublished doctoral dissertation, Pennsylvania State University, 1956. (also University Microfilms)

Blatt, B. *Souls in extremis*. Boston: Allyn & Bacon, 1973.

Cain, L., & Levine, S. *Effects of community and institution programs on trainable mentally retarded children*. Washington, DC: Council for Exceptional Children, 1963.

Cassidy, V., & Stanton, J. *An investigation of factors involved in the education of mentally retarded children*. Columbus: Ohio University Press, 1959.

Children's Defense Fund. *Children out of school in America*. Cambridge, MA: Author, 1974.

Gilhool, T. Education: An inalienable right. *Exceptional Children*, 1973, *39*, 597-609.

Goddard, H. *The criminal imbecile: An analysis of three remarkable murder cases*. New York: Macmillan, 1915.

Goldstein, H., Moss, J., & Jordan, L. *The efficacy of special class training on the development of mentally retarded children* (Cooperative Research Project No. 169). New York: Yeshiva University, 1965.

Hottel, J. *An evaluation of Tennessee's day class program for severely mentally retarded children*. Nashville: George Peabody College for Teachers, 1958.

Laubach Literacy Center, Syracuse, NY. Oral communication, 1976.

Pertsch, C. A comparative study of the progress of subnormal pupils in the grades and in special classes. *Teachers College Contributions to Education*. New York: Columbia University, 1936.

Schrag, P., & Divoky, D. *The myth of the hyperactive child*. New York: Pantheon, 1975.

Wolfensberger, W. *The origin and nature of our institutional models*. Syracuse, NY: Human Policy Press, 1975.

Wrightstone, J., Forlano, G., Lepkowski, J., Santag, M., & Edelstein, J. *A comparison of educational outcomes under singles-track and two-track plans for educable mentally retarded children*. (Cooperative Research Project No. 144). Brooklyn, NY: Board of Education, 1959.

12

The Judged, Not the Judges
An Insider's View of Mental Retardation

Robert Bogdan and Steven Taylor

If one wishes to understand the term "holy water," one should not study the properties of the water, but rather the assumptions and beliefs of the people who use it. That is, holy water derives its meaning from those who attribute a special essence to it (Szasz, 1974).

Similarly, the meaning of the term "mental retardation" depends on those who use it to describe the cognitive states of other people. As some have argued, mental retardation is a social construction or a concept which exists in the minds of the "judges" rather than in the minds of the "judged" (Blatt, 1970; Braginsky & Braginsky, 1971; Dexter, 1964; Hurley, 1969; Mercer, 1973). A mentally retarded person is one who has

First appeared in *American Psychologist*, January 1976, *31*(1). Copyright 1976 by the American Psychological Association. Reprinted by permission.

been labeled as such according to rather arbitrarily created and applied criteria.

"Retardate," and other such clinical labels, suggests generalizations about the nature of men and women to whom that term has been applied (Goffman, 1963). We assume that the mentally retarded possess common characteristics which allow them to be unambiguously distinguished from all others. We explain their behavior by special theories. It is as though humanity can be divided into two groups, the "normal" and the "retarded."

To be labeled retarded is to have a wide range of imperfections imputed to you. One imperfection is the inability to analyze your life and your current situation. Another is the inability to express youself — to know and say who you are and what you wish to become.

Here, we present the edited transcriptions of some of the discussions we have had over the past year with a 26-year-old man whom we will call Ed Murphy. (For methodology, see Bogdan, 1974, and Bogdan & Taylor, 1975). Ed has been labeled mentally retarded by his family, school teachers, and others in his life. At the age of 15, he was placed in a state institution for the retarded. His institutional records, as do many professionals with whom he has come into contact, describe him as "a good boy, but easily confused; mental retardation — cultural-familial type." Ed now works as a janitor in a large urban nursing home and lives in a boarding house with four other men who, like himself, are former residents of state institutions.

AN INSIDER'S VIEW

When I was born, the doctors didn't give me six months to live. My mother told them she could keep me alive, but they didn't believe it. It took a hell of a lot of work, but she showed with love and determination that she could be the mother to a handicapped child. I don't know for a fact what I had, but they thought it was severe retardation and cerebral palsy. They thought I would never walk. I still have seizures. Maybe that has something to do with it too.

My first memory is about my grandmother. She was a fine lady. I went to visit her right before she died. I knew she was sick, but I didn't realize that I would never see her again. I was special in my grandmother's eyes. My mother told me that she (grandmother) had a wish — it was that I would walk. I did walk, but it wasn't until the age of 4. My grandmother prayed that she would see that day. My mother told me the story again and again of how, before my grandmother died, I was at her place. She was on the opposite side of the room and called, "Walk to grandma, walk to grandma," and I did. I don't know if I did as good as I could, but I did it. Looking back now, it makes me feel good. It was frustrating for my parents that I could not walk. It was a great day in everybody's life.

The doctors told my mother that I would be a burden to her. When I was growing up, she never let me out of her sight. She was always there with attention. If I yelled, she ran right to me. So many children who are handicapped must be in that position — they become so dependent on their mother. Looking back, I don't think she ever stopped protecting me even when I was capable of being self-sufficient. I remember how hard it was to break away from that. She never really believed that after I had lived the first six months that I could be like everybody else.

I remember elementary school; my mind used to drift a lot. When I was at school, concentrating was almost impossible. I was so much into my own thoughts — my daydreams — I wasn't really in class. I would think of the cowboy movies — the rest of the kids would be in class and I would be on the battlefield someplace. The nuns would yell at me to snap out of it, but they were nice. That was my major problem all through school — that I daydreamed. I think all people do that. It wasn't related to retardation. I think a lot of kids do that and are diagnosed as retarded, but it has nothing to do with retardation at all. It really has to do with how people deal

219

with the people around them and their situation. I don't think I was bored. I think all the kids were competing to be the honor students, but I was never interested in that. I was in my own world — I was happy. I wouldn't recommend it to someone, but daydreaming can be a good thing.

I kind of stood in the background — I kind of knew that I was different — I knew I had a problem, but when you're young, you don't think of it as a problem. A lot of people are like I was. The problem is getting labeled as being something. After that, you're not really as a person. It's like a sty in your eye — it's noticeable. Like that teacher and the way she looked at me. In the fifth grade — in the fifth grade my classmates thought I was different, and my teacher knew I was different. One day she looked at me and she was on the phone to the office. Her conversation was like this, "When are you going to transfer him?" This was the phone in the room. I was there. She looked at me and knew I was knowledgeable about what she was saying. Her negative picture of me stood out like a sore thumb.

My mother protected me. It wasn't wrong that she protected me, but there comes a time when someone has to come in and break them away. I can remember trying to be like the other kids and having my mother right there pulling me away. She was always worried about me. You can't force yourself to say to your mother: "Stop, I can do it myself." Sometimes I think the pain of being handicapped is that people give you so much love that it becomes a weight on you and a weight on them. There is no way you can break from it without hurting them — without bad feelings — guilt. It is like a trap because of the fact that you are restricted to your inner thoughts. After a while, you resign yourself to it. The trap is that you can't tell them, "Let me go." You have to live with it and suffer. It has to do with pity. Looking back on it, I can't say it was wrong. She loved me. You do need special attention, but the right amount.

One time, maybe when I was about 13, I was going to camp and had to go to the place where the buses left. My mother kept asking me if I had everything and telling me where my bags were and if I was all right. It is similar to the way other mothers act, but it sticks out in my mind. I was striving to be a normal boy, so it meant more to me. After my mother went back to the car, the others kids on the bus kidded me. They said things like, "Momma's boy." That's the one that sticks out in my memory.

I liked camp. The staff and counselors were good. I had this thing with my legs. They weren't very strong. When I fell back from the group on a hike, I was light enough so they could give me a ride on their backs. I had the best seat on the hike. Looking back on being carried, they would have lost me if they didn't. I was glad I was light because it was easier for them. I needed help and they helped. I went for many summers in a row, and they helped pay for the sessions when my parents were ill. I didn't mind being carried. The important thing was that I was there and I was taking part in the events like everybody else.

I remember the day the press came. It was an annual award day. They came to write up the story. The best camper got his picture in the paper. My name was in the paper. I got a patch for being a good camper. It was something that I had accomplished and felt pretty good about. My mother kept the article and the neighbors knew too.

In January of 1963, without any warning, my father died. A couple months later, Ma died too. It was hard on us — my sister and me. We stayed with friends of the family for a while, but then they moved. They told us we had to go. So they sent us to an orphanage for a few months, but eventually we wound up at the State School.

Right before they sent me and my sister to the State School, they had six psychologists examine us to determine how intelligent we were. I think that was a waste of time. They asked me things like, "What comes to mind when I say 'Dawn'?" — so you say, "Light." Things like that. What was tough was putting the puzzles together and the mechanical stuff. They start out very simple and then they build it up and it gets harder and harder.

If you're going to do something with a person's life, you don't have to pay all that money to be testing them. I had no place else to go. I mean, here I am pretty intelligent and here are six psychologists testing me and sending me to the State School. How would you feel if you were examined by all those people and then wound up where I did? A psychologist is supposed to help you. The way they talked to me they must have thought I was fairly intelligent. One of them said, "You look like a smart young man," and then I turned up here. I don't think the tests made any difference. They had their minds made up anyway.

Another guy I talked to was a psychiatrist. That was rough. For one thing, I was mentally off guard. You're not really prepared for any of it. You don't figure what they're saying and how you're answering it and what it all means — not until the end. When the end came, I was a ward of the State.

I remember the psychiatrist well. He was short and middle-aged and had a foreign accent. The first few minutes he asked me how I felt and I replied, "Pretty good." Then I fell right into his trap. He asked if I thought people hated me, and I said "yes." "Do you think people talk about you behind your back?" And I said "yes." I started getting hypernervous. By then he had the hook in the fish, and there was no two ways about it. He realized I was nervous and ended the interview. He was friendly and he fed me the bait. The thing was that it ended so fast. After I got out I realized that I had screwed up. I cried. I was upset. He came on like he wanted honest answers, but being honest in that situation doesn't get you any place but the State School.

When the psychiatrist interviewed me, he had my records in front of him — so he already knew I was mentally retarded. It's the same with everyone. If you are considered mentally retarded, there is no way you can win. There is no way they give you a favorable report. They put horses out of misery quicker than they do people. It's a real blow to you being sent to the State School.

I remember the day they took me and my sister. We knew where we were going, but we didn't know anything specific about it. It was scary.

To me there never was a State School. The words "State School" sound like a place with vocational training or you get some sort of education. That's just not the way Empire State School[1] is. They have taken millions of dollars and spent them and never rehabilitated who they were supposed to. If you looked at individuals and see what they said they were supposed to do for that person and then what they actually did, you would find that many of them were actually hurt — not helped. I don't like the word "vegetable," but in my own case I could see that if I had been placed on the low grade ward, I might have slipped to that. I began feeling myself slip. They could have made me a vegetable. If I would have let that place get to me and depress me, I would still have been there today.

Actually, it was one man that saved me. They had me scheduled to go to P-8 — a back ward — when just one man looked at me. I was a wreck. I had a beard and baggy State clothes on. I had just arrived at the place. I was trying to understand what was happening. I was confused. What I looked like was P-8 material. There was this supervisor, a woman. She came on to the ward and looked right at me and said: "I have him scheduled for P-8." An older attendant was there. He looked over at me and said, "He's too bright for that ward. I think we'll keep him." To look at me then, I didn't look good. She made a remark under her breath that I looked pretty retarded to her. She saw me looking at her — I looked her square in the eye. She had on a white dress and a cap with three stripes — I can still see them now. She saw me and said, "Just don't stand there, get to work."

Of course, I didn't know what P-8 was then, but I found out. I visited up there a few times on work detail. That man

---

[1]Fictitious name.

saved my life. Here was a woman that I had never known who they said was the building supervisor looking over me. At that point I'm pretty positive that if I went there, I would have fit in and I would still be there.

I remember the day that Bobby Kennedy came. That was something. All day long we knew he was coming, and he walked around. I got a look at him. He told everybody what a snake pit the place was, so it was better for a few days. At least he got some people interested for a while. I really admired that man. You take a lot of crusaders though, like local politicians, they go over to the State School and do a lot of yelling. They only do it when someone forces them to, like when someone gets something in the paper about someone being beaten or is overdosed bad. The newest thing at Empire was someone yelled sodomy. Some parent found out about it and called the legislator. Big deal. If they knew what was going on, it wouldn't be that big a deal — one incident of sodomy. Hell, for that matter they ought to look around them and see what the people on the outside are doing sexually.

It's funny. You hear so many people talking about IQ. The first time I ever heard the expression was when I was at Empire State School. I didn't know what it was or anything, but some people were talking and they brought the subject up. It was on the ward, and I went and asked one of the staff what mine was. They told me 49. Forty-nine isn't 50, but I was pretty happy about it. I mean I figured that I wasn't a low grade. I really didn't know what it meant, but it sounded pretty high. Hell, I was born in 1948 and 49 didn't seem too bad! Forty-nine didn't sound hopeless. I didn't know anything about the highs or the lows, but I knew I was better than most of them.

Last week was the first time I went into a state school since I was discharged as a ward of the State — which makes it about three years. I just went up to visit. I purposely avoided going there. I have been nervous about it. There are good memories and bad memories. The whole idea of having been in a state school makes you nervous about why you were ever put there in the first place. I'm out now, but I was on that side of the fence once. It has less to do with what I am doing than with how the game is played. Being in a state school or having been in a state school isn't fashionable and never will be. Deep down, you want to avoid the identification. If I could convince myself that in the end they are going to be cleaned up, I might feel better about it. You have got to face the enemy, and that's what it's like.

I have come from being a resident of a state school to being on the other side saying they're no good. It has been brought up to me — "Where the hell would you be if it wasn't for the State School." That holds water, but now the dam is drying up as I am on this side. Sure I had a need, but they kind of pitched you a low pitch. There wasn't anything better. I needed a place to go, but unfortunately there was no choice of where to go. When it's all said and done, there were those at the school that helped me, so I'm grateful, but still some other place would have been better.

I guess the State School wasn't all that bad. It was tough to leave though. You had all your needs taken care of there. You didn't have to worry about where your next meal was coming from or where you were going to sleep.

I don't have it that bad right now. I have my own room and I get my meals at the house. The landlord is going to up the rent though — $45 a week for room and board. I'll be able to pay it, but I don't know what Frank and Lou across the hall will do. They wash dishes at the steak house and don't take home that much.

It's really funny. Sunday I got up and went for a walk. All of a sudden Joan's name came in my mind. She's sort of my girlfriend. I don't know why, but I just thought of her moving in next door to the place where I live. That would be something.

Is there still any magnetism between that woman and me? I haven't seen her in three months, but there is still something, I can tell. We had a good thing going. I opened her up a lot mentally. I saw a very different person there than others see. I saw a woman that could do something with her life. If she could wake up one morning and say to herself, "I am going to do something with my life," she could. I don't think that retardation is holding her back so much as emotional problems. If she had confidence, that would make the difference. I know she could build herself up.

Her family had respect for me, at least to a point, but they don't think she should marry. We got pretty close psychologically and physically — not that I did anything. They don't have programs at the Association for Retarded Children that say to adults you are an adult and you can make it. She has been at the ARC for a long time now. She was a bus-aide, so in one way they showed her that she could work, but on the other hand they didn't build her confidence enough to feel that she could go out to work.

The last time I saw her, she didn't say a word. When she is pissed off at the world, she is pissed off. That's the Irish in her. In my opinion, she doesn't belong at the ARC. But one thing is her parents don't want to take chances. Like a lot of the parents, they send their 30-year-old kids with Snoopy lunch pails. They are afraid financially, and I can't blame them. If she went out on her own, they are afraid that her social security would stop, and then if she could continue, they wouldn't have anything. She could lose her benefits.

I first met Joan in 1970. It was when I started working at the ARC workshop. I sat there and maybe the second or third day I glanced over and saw her there. The first time I noticed her was in the eating area; I was having lunch. I looked around, and she was the only one there that attracted me. There was just something about her. At first she wasn't that easy to get along with. She put on the cold shoulder, and that made me think about her more.

One time I had a fight with one of the boys in the workshop. He was her old boyfriend. This day I was getting off the bus, and he said that I pushed him. He pushed me, and then when we went to the locker room, it got rougher. I yelled at him, "Get away from me." I started cursing and we started swinging. I guess he was jealous that Joan was spending so much time talking to me. He was a big guy, and he hit me in the mouth and cut it. The staff came and broke it up. They treated it like the whole thing was a joke. They thought it was cute, the two of us fighting over Joan. They ribbed us about it like they always rib about boyfriends and girlfriends.

It took awhile for her to understand how she felt. She didn't want to be too friendly. She didn't like me putting my arm around her. We went for walks during lunch, and she got pretty fond of me and I got pretty fond of her. One day I asked her, "Well, how about a movie?" She said, "All right," but she had to get her mother's permission. Then one day she said she could go. It was a Saturday matinee gangster movie. We arranged to meet at the bus stop downtown. I remember that I got down there early and bought the tickets before she came. I met her at the stop, and then I went up to the ticket office with the tickets in my hand. I was a little fuzzy, nervous, you might say. Of course, you were supposed to give the tickets to the man inside. The ticket woman looked at me — sort of stared and motioned with her finger. It was kind of funny, considering our ages. I was 22 and she was 28. It was like teenagers going on our first date.

Being at the State School and all, you never have the chances romantically like you might living on the outside. I guess I was always shy with the opposite sex, even at Empire. We did have dances and I felt that I was good looking, but I was bashful and mostly sat. I was bashful with Joan at the movie. In my mind I felt funny, awkward. I didn't know how to approach her. Should I hug her? You can't hug the hell out of her because you don't know how she would take it. You have all the feeling there, but you don't know what direction to go in. If you put your arm around her, she might scream, and you're finished. If she doesn't scream, you're still finished.

I never thought of myself as a retarded individual, but who would want to? You're not knowledgeable about what they are saying behind your back. You get a feeling from people around you; they try to hide it, but their intentions don't work. They say they will do this and that — like they will look out for you — they try to protect you, but you feel sort of guilty. You get the feeling that they love you but that they are looking down at you. You always have that sense of a barrier between you and the ones that love you. By their own admission of protecting you, you have an umbrella over you that tells you that you and they have an understanding that there is something wrong — that there is a barrier.

As I got older, I slowly began to find myself becoming mentally awake. I found myself concentrating. Like on the television. A lot of people wonder why I have good grammar. It was because of the television. I was like a tape recorder — what I heard, I memorized. Even when I was 10 or 12, I would listen to Huntley and Brinkley. They were my favorites.

As the years went by, I understood what they were talking about. People were amazed at what I knew. People would begin to ask me what I thought about this and that. Like my aunt would always ask me about the news — what my opinions were. I began to know that I was a little brighter than they thought I was. It became a hobby. I didn't know what it meant — that I had a grasp on a lot of important things — the race riots, Martin Luther King in jail. What was really happening was that I was beginning to find something else instead of just being bored. It was entertaining.

I didn't know that meant anything then. I mean, I didn't know that I would be sitting here telling you all this. When you're growing up, you don't think of yourself as a person, but as a boy. As you get older, it works itself out — who you are deep down — who you ought to be. You have an image of yourself deep down. You try to sort it all out. You know what you are deep inside, but those around you give you a negative picture of yourself. It's that umbrella over you.

What is retardation? It's hard to say. I guess it's having problems thinking. Some people think you can tell if a person is retarded by looking at them. If you think that way, you don't give people the benefit of the doubt. You judge a person by how they look or how they talk or what the tests show, but you can never really tell what is inside the person.

Take a couple of friends of mine, Tommy McCan and PJ. Tommy was a guy who was really nice to be with. You could sit down with him and have a nice conversation and enjoy yourself. He was a mongoloid. The trouble was, people couldn't see beyond that. If he didn't look that way, it would have been different, but there he was locked into what the other people thought he was. Now PJ was really something else. I've watched that guy, and I can see in his eyes that he is aware. He knows what's going on. He can only crawl and he doesn't talk, but you don't know what's inside. When I was with him and I touched him, I know that he knows.

I don't know. Maybe I used to be retarded. That's what they said anyway. I wish they could see me now. I wonder what they'd say if they could see me holding down a regular job and doing all kinds of things. I bet they wouldn't believe it.

———————————

Ed's story stands by itself as a rich source of understanding. We will resist the temptation to analyze it and reflect on what it tells us about Ed. Our position is that, at times and to a much greater extent than we do now, we must listen to people who have been labeled "retarded" with the idea of finding out about ourselves, our society, and the nature of the label (Becker, 1966).

Specifics that can be learned from stories such as Ed's are discussed by Allport (1942); Becker (1966); and Bogdan (1974). For example, his story clearly illustrates that mental retardation is a demeaning concept which leads to a number of penalties for those so labeled. These penalties include lowered self-image and limited social and economic opportunity. Also, his story shows the profound effect of early prognosis on how people are treated and on the way they think about themselves. It clearly demonstrates how segregated living environments and facilities such as state schools severely limit the basic socialization skills needed to participate in the larger society.

His story also illustrates how being institutionalized is a function of a variety of social and economic contingencies — family difficulties, lack of alternatives — more than the nature of the person's disability or treatment needs. It also touches on the difficulties faced by people who are "protected," and can more accurately assess the resentment and the restrictions this protection imposes. We also can see the profound effects of simple words of praise and rejection on the person's self-concept. Ed's story points to how some people who work "with" the so-called "retarded" develop joking styles that minimize the real and normal problems and conflicts with which the labeled person is attempting to deal, and how the object of these jokes feels about this. While his story mentions all of these specifics, two general points are noteworthy.

The first point is simple but seldom is taken into account in conducting research or planning programs: People who are labeled "retarded" have their own understandings about themselves, their situation, and their experiences. These understandings are often different from those of the professionals. For example, although cure and treatment might dominate the official views of state schools and rehabilitation centers and programs, boredom, manipulation, coercion, and embarrassment often constitute the client's view. In my own work in interviewing labeled people (Bogdan, 1974), and in Ed's story, the vocabulary of the therapist often contradicts that of the patient. The handicapped — the so-called "retarded" — respond to therapy and services according to how they perceive it, not according to how the staff sees it. Devaluing an individual's perspective by viewing it as naive, unsophisticated, immature, or a symptom of some underlying pathology can make research one-sided, and service organizations merely places where rituals are performed in the name of science.

The second point has to do with the lack of alternative ways in which those who are "different" can conceptualize their situation. The present condition of fields such as mental retardation is controlled by powerful ideological monopolies. As Ed's story suggests, there is a dearth of definitions in our society and few divergent agencies to provide individuals who are mentally and physically different and struggling and suffering, with ways of conceptualizing themselves other than the demeaning vocabulary of "sickness," "handicapped," and "deviant," of which "retardate" is a part.

The categories available to place individuals cannot help but affect how we feel about them and how they feel about themselves. When we present "subjects" or "clients" as numbers or as diagnostic categories, we do not engender in others a feeling of respect for, or closeness to, the people being discussed. Such views of human beings are not evil or unnecessary, but they comprise only a single view. Overemphasis on this view without presenting the subjective side distorts our knowledge in a dangerous way. (Social scientists presenting the alternative view include Coles, 1967a, 1967b, 1971; Cottle, 1971, 1972, 1973; Lewis, 1961, 1962; Shaw, 1930; Shaw & Moore, 1931; Sutherland, 1937; Thomas & Znaniecki, 1918-1920.)

Traditionally, social scientists have studied the retarded as a separate category of human beings and, by doing this, they have accepted commonsense definitions. It is assumed that the retardate is basically different from the rest of us and that he or she needs to be explained by special theories distinct from those used to explain the behavior of "regular" people. By taking this approach, social scientists have contributed to and have legitimized commonsense classifications of individuals as "normal" and "retardate." We have told the world that there are two kinds of human beings.

Ed's own words are a form of data and a source of understanding that permit us to know a person intimately. By sharing his life, we can approach the concept of intelligence in its more human dimensions. Through this intimacy we learn how the subject views himself or herself, and what he or she has in common with all of us becomes clear. Differences take on less importance. The person's own words force us to think of subjects as people, and categories of all kinds become less relevant.

REFERENCES

Allport, G. *The use of personal documents in psychological science.* New York: Social Science Research Council, 1942.

Becker, H. Introduction. In Clifford Shaw, *The jackroller.* Chicago: University of Chicago Press, 1966.

Blatt, B. *Exodus from pandemonium.* Boston: Allyn & Bacon, 1970.

Bogdan, R. *Being different.* New York: Wiley, 1974.

Bogdan, R., & Taylor, S. *Introduction to qualitative research methods.* New York: Wiley, 1975.

Braginsky, D., & Braginsky, B. *Hansels and Gretels.* New York: Holt, Rinehart & Winston, 1971.

Coles, R. *Children of crisis.* Boston: Little, Brown, 1967. (a)

Coles, R. Method. In *Migrants, sharecroppers, mountaineers.* Boston: Little, Brown, 1967. (b)

Coles, R. *The south goes north.* Boston: Little, Brown, 1971.

Cottle, T. *Time's children.* Boston: Little, Brown, 1971.

Cottle, T. *The abandoners.* Boston: Little, Brown, 1972.

Cottle, T. *The voices of school: Educational images through personal accounts.* Boston: Little, Brown, 1973.

Dexter, L. *The tyranny of schooling.* New York: Basic Books, 1964.

Goffman, I. *Stigma.* Englewood Cliffs, NJ: Prentice-Hall, 1963.

Hurley, R. *Poverty and mental retardation.* New York: Vintage Books, 1969.

Lewis, O. *The children of Sanchez.* New York: Vintage Books, 1961.

Lewis, O. *Five families.* New York: Wiley, Science Educations, 1962.

Mercer, J. *Labelling the mentally retarded.* Berkeley: University of California Press, 1973.

Shaw, C. *The jackroller.* Chicago: University of Chicago Press, 1930.

Shaw, C., & Moore, M. *The natural history of a delinquent career.* Chicago: University of Chicago Press, 1931.

Sutherland, E. *The professional thief.* Chicago: University of Chicago Press, 1937.

Szasz, T.S. *Ceremonial chemistry: The ritual persecution of drugs, addicts, and the pushers.* Garden City, NY: Doubleday, 1974.

Thomas, W., & Znaniecki, F. *The Polish peasant in Europe and America* (5 vols.). Chicago: University of Chicago Press, pp. 1918-1920.

13

Translating Psychological Concepts into Action

Seymour B. Sarason, Murray Levine, I. Ira Goldenberg,
Dennis T. Cherlin and Edward M. Bennett

There is an enormous difference between understanding on a theoretical level and in utilizing that understanding to make relevant interventions. In this chapter we try to indicate how psychological concepts can be translated into concrete actions in a classroom. More important than how that translation is handled is the significance of the classroom situation, which has enormous potential for bringing about change in children. The realization of this potential depends on intimate knowledge of a particular child in a particular peer group with a particular teacher in a particular classroom. When attempting to change or influence a certain situation, the psychological or mental health consultant must know that situation as intimately as possible.

Adapted from a chapter that originally appeared in *Psychology in Community Settings*, by Seymour B. Sarason, et al. New York: John Wiley, 1966. Reprinted by permission. ©Seymour B. Sarason.

Theories about a child and his behavior should be tested in a setting that constitutes a significant portion of the child's daily life. Psychodynamic concepts can be applied with a fair amount of control.

CONCEPTS → ACTION

The following examples indicate possibilities for translating psychodynamic concepts into action in the classroom to benefit the child:

SITUATION 1

Many books are available explaining the variables which affect learning to read. Seldom is any one variable the sole determinant; usually several variables interact to make reading a gratifying or upsetting experience. Once in awhile, however, it is possible to delineate specific conditions that have produced anxiety — generally a particular event in the child's young life of such magnitude as to influence significantly the future course of development. However, it is another matter to translate our understanding into appropriate remedial action. For this, we must have considerable control over the situation, which is more likely when teacher and psychologist work together in the classroom setting.

Johnny was a second grader whose teacher described him as "just about the nicest little boy you'd ever want to have in your class." He was bright and outgoing, immensely popular with his classmates and teacher, and had a warm, engaging smile. He often went out of his way to help another child in distress and seemed particularly sensitive to the needs of others. This sensitivity drew many of his classmates to him. Johnny was one of the recognized leaders of his class, a little boy with whom the other children wanted to be.

The only area in which Johnny appeared to experience any difficulty was reading. Johnny's inability to read, his unwillingness to learn, and his distress during reading lessons were a source of considerable puzzlement. Evaluated as superior in intelligence, he did well in every other area of work and was outstanding in arithmetic. Johnny had not been retained in first grade, with the hope that somehow his reading would catch up to his ability in other areas. However, as the semester wore on, it became evident that this hope would not be realized.

Each time the psychologist observed Johnny's classroom, he became more atuned to the impression that there appeared to be two distinctly different Johnnys. One Johnny loved school and everything in it, helped other children, reveled in doing his mathematics, looked forward to playing games, and enjoyed drawing. He appeared uniquely alive and exhilarated in the classroom, and learning seemed exciting and wonderful. The other Johnny seemed uneasy, restless, and anxious when reading occupied the class. Whenever the class went to the library, Johnny asked to be left in the room and became belligerent when his request was denied. When the children read silently at their seats, Johnny's eyes wandered about the room and he squirmed in his seat. Whenever his reading group met with the teacher, he suddenly developed a short attention span and became withdrawn.

The psychologist shared his observations with the teacher. Although originally she had believed that not paying attention was Johnny's problem, she soon became convinced that other variables were present. Although both teacher and consultant tried to talk with Johnny, neither could gain any helpful information. Johnny simply told them he did not like reading, that it was boring, and that he would rather do other things.

Because the situation was not improving, the teacher thought it might be helpful to meet with Johnny's mother. The teacher and the psychologist soon found themselves face to face with a woman who seemed frightened and anxious, fidgeting with her clothes and obviously ill at ease. Immediately she informed them that she knew the meeting had something to do with Johnny's inability to read and that there was no reason for her son's difficulty. She suggested that he might be "just lazy" and would do better if the school would put more pressure on him or would punish him more severely whenever he would not try to learn. The mother said she had become particularly close to the boy after the sudden death of her husband three years before. She also said that Johnny had an 18-year-old sister with whom he was close. The mother, on the verge of tears, wanted to get out of the situation as quickly as possible, and the meeting was terminated.

At the mother's suggestion, the teacher and the psychologist met Johnny's sister. Considerably less anxious, she immediately apologized for her mother, who she said had become extremely nervous after her husband's death. She then related the following story about the circumstances of her father's death:

On New Year's Eve, when Johnny was five and about to enter kindergarten, the mother was in the bedroom getting ready for a party. The father, already dressed, was sitting in the living room with Johnny. Suddenly he groaned and his head dropped to his chest. Johnny shook his father and then ran to the bedroom and said that "Daddy is acting funny." When the mother came out, the father already was dead. Johnny's mother was overcome by the tragedy. She became extremely depressed, rarely left the home, and frequently cried, wrung her hands, and stared into space. The mother did not want the children to forget their father. She often gave Johnny one of the family albums to go through and made him point out every picture in which his father appeared. The sister was asked what Johnny and his father were doing in the living room the night the father died. "Johnny was sitting on my father's lap," she said, "and Dad was reading him a story."

The psychologist discussed with the teacher the connection between the father's death and Johnny's inability to read. The teacher felt she could now begin to work with Johnny by helping him deal with his feelings of guilt and anxiety with respect to reading. However, this was not the kind of situation with which to confront the mother, who appeared too involved with her grief. The psychologist then turned his attention toward the older sister. She seemed to be the most appropriate person to help Johnny outside the classroom. The psychologist and the teacher discussed with Johnny's sister how Johnny's problem in reading might be related to memories of his father's death. They indicated how she could encourage Johnny to express to her his feelings about reading. The sister was extremely anxious to be helpful but somewhat hesitant about her ability to handle the situation. It was therefore decided that the three of them would meet regularly to compare notes.

SITUATION 2

When it is possible to observe a child over a long period of time, especially when he can be seen in a variety of different settings, it is easy to detect changes and inconsistencies in the child's moods. This is particularly true in the classroom, where if variations in behavior occur over a period of time, they signal a change in the child's characteristic way of relating to himself and/or to others. Teachers often can spot potential areas of difficulty in this manner. Psychologists have learned to use the danger signals as bases for preventive and remedial intervention.

Rhoda was a six-year-old who attended a kindergarten class the psychologist visited regularly. She was a small, plump, cherubic child who seemed to enjoy her days in school. Although she was somewhat mischievous at times, the psychologist always saw her as an extremely engaging and outgoing little girl. Over the course of time in which he visited her classroom, he had become accustomed to seeing her rushing around the room amiably poking her nose into everyone's business.

One day he was taken aback to find Rhoda not actively involved with any of the other children. She was seated quietly at her desk scribbling aimlessly on a piece of paper. She appeared sad, almost forlorn. He was struck by the vast difference in her behavior but decided to observe further to see whether this new attitude would persist. Throughout the morning there was no change. Regardless of the activity, Rhoda remained passive, withdrawn, and somber.

The teacher already had noticed the change in Rhoda's behavior and had investigated. She reported that Rhoda's best friend for the past two years had moved to Florida. Although the child was to return in six months, Rhoda was positive she would never see her friend again. Consequently, she went into "mourning."

The teacher was quite concerned with Rhoda's behavior, although she believed the child would get over it in a few days. The teacher related that she had tried talking to Rhoda, reassured her that her friend would return, and had made her the "assistant teacher," but Rhoda did not respond to the increased attention and the teacher's attempts to boost her ego.

In discussing the situation with the teacher, the psychologist used the term "separation depression." He spoke about Rhoda's loss of a love object and her subsequent depression and withdrawal. The teacher quickly thought of several other children who had formed close attachments to some of their classmates and, given today's rate of family mobility, she was sure these children already had experienced or would soon experience the loss of a love object. For Rhoda, we agreed that it was necessary to express her feelings of depression in a manner appropriate to her own needs and to the needs of the absent child so they could share each other's experiences. It seemed important that Rhoda get a chance to understand that her friend would be returning in six months, and to maintain whatever realistic relationship remained between herself and the other child.

After thinking about the situation, the teacher came up with an idea that seemed to meet all the requirements. She would organize a formal learning experience around the subject of communicating with friends or members of the family who recently had left the neighborhood. She would have each of the children write a letter to someone who had moved away and someone whom he would like to retain as a pen pal. Because none of the children could actually write such a letter, the teacher would have each of them paint a card and would go around to each desk and ask the child to tell her what to write. The children were to bring to class the address of a friend or relative, and the card would be sent away as soon as possible.

The teacher implemented her plan. Each child made a card. When the teacher came to Rhoda's desk, Rhoda was eager to dictate her letter. In a moving way she said how much she missed her friend, wished that she had never left, and wondered if she ever would "come back home again." The teacher faithfully wrote down everything. When the activity was over, the children sealed their letters, placed stamps on the envelopes, and sent them away.

Much to her surprise, Rhoda received a letter from Florida. The letter, written by her friend's mother, but in her friend's words, was similar to the one Rhoda had "written." Her friend really missed her and wished that Rhoda could have come to Florida with her. Florida was "very nice," but her friend was looking forward to their reunion when she returned to the neighborhood. Rhoda was overjoyed with her letter. She immediately went to the teacher and asked if she could "write another letter back." The teacher felt it would be a good idea for Rhoda and her friend to correspond while they were separated, and volunteered to be Rhoda's writer.

In a rather short time Rhoda came out of her depression and soon became her old self.

SITUATION 3

The subject of sibling rivalry serves as an introduction to our next example. Sibling rivalry is common among children in the same family, especially during the early years of development. The classroom is another setting in which a form of sibling rivalry can be detected as children fight for the teacher's attention. The teacher becomes the parent substitute, and the child's unresolved sibling conflicts often are worked through with this new substitute parent. Teachers become acutely aware of this type of conflict and often are able to utilize the classroom to deal with these problems.

One of the most common variations of sibling rivalry — we might call it "presibling rivalry" — occurs when an only child is informed that he will soon have a little brother or sister. If the child is unable to deal with the situation at home, he often will utilize the classroom as the arena in which to act out his feelings. He also may use the teacher to obtain information and reassurance. The teacher's ability to understand and deal with the situation becomes an important variable in determining the child's current and future adjustment.

Jody, a small, frail-looking, seven-year-old girl, was essentially uncommunicative in the classroom. She was repeating kindergarten because of the school's feeling that she was not ready for the first grade. The school hoped the additional year in kindergarten would allow Jody to develop those verbal and nonverbal skills which would enhance her prospects of succeeding in the first grade.

After an initial period of difficulty, Jody appeared to be making a rather good adjustment. She quickly developed a close relationship with her teacher, an extremely gentle woman who was experienced and competent. During her first two months Jody began to talk and was learning to interact with many of the other children. She no longer remained isolated for prolonged periods and had begun to develop some friendships. Although she was not able to do her formal kindergarten work as well as had been hoped, Jody was beginning to act in ways that were much more appropriate to her age and the classroom setting.

One day in the middle of November, things changed abruptly. Jody came into the class and immediately withdrew into her shell. She would have nothing to do with any of the other children and began behaving in a manner reminiscent of the previous year. She sat by herself and gazed out the window. The teacher tried talking with her on several occasions, but the child ignored her. A short time later Jody began to display a host of aggressive and assaultive behaviors. She approached other children very directly and, with little or no observable provocation, tried to hurt them. This behavior continued and, over a period of time, the other children in the class began avoiding her.

The teacher thought it would be a good idea to meet Jody's parents. The father could not take the time from his work to attend the meeting, so only Jody's mother was present.

Jody's mother told the teacher and the psychologist that she also had noticed a recent change. The mother was quite unhappy about this, for she had thought her daughter was "getting better." Further, the regressive behavior was occurring at a time when the parents were least prepared to deal with it. The mother said she was nervous and anxious herself, "what with being pregnant and all that." This was the first time the psychologist or the teacher had known that Jody's mother was expecting another child. The mother spoke of all the trouble she had experienced in carrying and delivering Jody. Because of their anxiety, the parents had done little more than tell Jody that she was going to have a little brother or sister. It was clear that they were too involved in their own conflicts to deal with their daughter's concerns about the situation, nor could they perceive the effects of their behavior on Jody.

The psychologist began to view Jody's classroom antics as an expression of the child's questions and feelings about her position with respect to other children, within a setting that might better tolerate this type of behavior. Jody was quite concerned about what would happen to her when her sibling arrived on the scene.

The teacher felt that, under the circumstances, it was imperative that she deal with Jody's questions in a way the parents could not. She initiated a "share and tell" activity in which each child discussed what he liked and disliked about his younger siblings, how it felt to be the older brother or sister, and the kinds of questions he had about them. The teacher also began to spend some time each day with Jody and confronted her with the problem. She shared with Jody some of her own past feelings upon learning she was going to have another brother, and told how she was able to help her mother care for the new child. Jody gradually began to respond. She began by sitting on the teacher's lap, patting the teacher's stomach, and asking if the teacher was going to have a baby. The teacher explained to Jody "how a baby lives inside Mommy," how it grows, and when it is born. Jody asked more and more direct questions and finally inquired if the teacher's Mommy still liked her after her brother was born.

Throughout this period, Jody's classroom behavior became less and less unpredictable. Although she did not renew her friendships with the other children, she stopped her assaultive behavior. She began drawing pictures of babies and immediately took them to the teacher, an act the teacher always responded to as an invitation to talk a bit more. The teacher told Jody's parents about Jody's concern and, without putting undue pressure on the parents, tried to make them aware of how they might be helpful. Throughout the remaining months of the mother's pregnancy, the teacher continued her involvement with Jody.

As it turned out, the delivery was not difficult and there were no complications. The child was a healthy little boy. After the birth, Jody's parents became markedly less anxious and fearful and even began thinking about having another child in the near future. The more relaxed the parents became, the more relaxed Jody became. Her regressive behavior vanished, and she was able to continue the progress that had characterized her earlier months in kindergarten.

SITUATION 4

More often than not, it is the "troublesome" rather than the "troubled" child who quickly comes to the teacher's attention. The troublesome child disrupts classes, frightens or annoys other children, and makes teaching difficult, if not impossible. Teachers, not surprisingly, most often ask assistance for the troublesome child.

The troubled child, on the other hand, is much less likely to be noticed immediately. Although he may have as disabling a problem as the troublesome child, his behavior is neither dramatic nor interfering. More often than not, his symptoms have a passive quality. He usually is withdrawn, unobtrusive, and silent. Both troublesome and troubled children, in their own ways, are dealing with problems which interfere with their abilities to learn in the classroom. Because of the nature of their symptoms, however, the troublesome child usually is the one whose cry for help is acknowledged.

It is a sensitive and perceptive teacher who can step back from the immediate needs of the teaching situation to take note of those unobtrusive but troubled children who need help. Even when this occurs, however, the problem is in translating psychodynamic understanding of the child's problems into a helpful and appropriate plan of action.

Michael was a nine-year-old third grader whose class the psychologist had been observing for a long time. During that time he had never focused much attention on the boy because he was more concerned with several of the other children. This was a problem class. Several of the difficult third graders had been funneled into it because the teacher was extremely capable, experienced, and willing to deal with children who were difficult for others to handle. She was in complete command of her class. She provided an atmosphere in which learning became an exciting and wonderful adventure to many children whose previous school experiences had been uniformly unsatisfying. Michael was one of the "good" children in the class. He did his work and never was involved in any of the periodic flare-ups characterizing the behavior of many of the other children.

During a coffee klatch, the teacher asked the psychologist if he had spent any time observing Michael. He told her that he had not and asked her why she had Michael in mind. She seemed a bit hesitant but said there was something about the boy that bothered her. He was not a behavior problem and was certainly no trouble in class, but he was just "too, too polite — not at all like a nine-year-old boy." His politeness and extreme deference made her a bit uneasy. She then displayed some of Michael's drawings. Each one, regardless of content, was replete with undercurrents of violence, blood, and murder. Many showed a striking preoccupation with mutilation and torture. The drawings looked like the creations of a violently angry, sadistic, and hostile little boy. The psychologist decided to spend more time observing Michael.

The psychologist's observations soon began to yield a different picture of the boy. Although never directly or openly aggressive, his behavior was covertly hostile, sadistic, and sneaky. When a little girl next to him dropped her pencil and bent to pick it up, Michael, ever so deftly and nonchalantly, moved his foot and kicked the pencil further from her grasp. When a boy was hurrying down the aisle to get to the front window, Michael looked the other way, "accidentally" stuck out his foot, and tripped the youngster. When the youngster fell, Michael smiled, apologized, and helped the boy get up from the floor. Again and again we saw Michael do or say something which invariably hurt another child. On each occasion his actions would be apparently accidental and without malice or forethought. It became clear, however, that his "accidents" were too numerous to be unmotivated.

Meanwhile, the teacher had met Michael's mother. Her primary impression was that the mother was an extremely rigid and proper person. The mother spent some time telling the teacher how important she thought appearances and manners were and how the modern generation was not being

244

brought up to show appropriate respect for its elders. She related how, in her household, Michael and his younger brothers understood the uselessness of temper tantrums and obstinacy. Outbursts of anger and aggression were not tolerated; unless the child could "quietly discuss his problems like a little adult," he was neither listened to nor recognized.

The psychologist came to feel that Michael was learning to deal with his feelings by masking them behind a fragile facade of civilized living. Anger and aggression clearly were unacceptable. He was made to feel that these expressions were neither healthy nor normal for a little boy. However, it seemed difficult for Michael to disown these feelings completely; they did not dissipate with time. They found expression in subtle, indirect, and frightening ways.

The psychologist then began to think of ways to use the classroom setting as a means of intervening in a process that was detrimental to Michael's development. He felt it was necessary for the boy to experience feelings of hostility as neither unhealthy nor unacceptable — feelings which need not always be hidden. He wanted Michael to be able to get angry, ask questions and express ideas about violence, and use the learning situation as a way of testing his fantasies.

The teacher began having the children talk about their dreams and fantasies in a series of "share and tell" sessions. Each child began by sharing information about what he liked and disliked, feared and hated, and wondered about. During this activity many of the children brought up themes of violence, murder, sadism, and anger. After each session the teacher summarized what the children had talked about and indicated how most of them had similar feelings and questions. They then discussed in very simple terms when each of these feelings was appropriate and the conditions under which they could be expressed.

Michael soon started talking about many of his own feelings and the things he would do secretly. He related some of his fantasies about killing and death and some of the things he did to small animals. The children were intrigued with his deeds but soon began discussing similar things they had done or contemplated. When Michael began talking about mutilating animals, the teacher artfully turned the discussion into a session on anatomy and other related subjects. The "share and tell" sessions continued. Michael looked forward to them and seemed anxious to be called upon. The more he talked about his experiences, the less sneaky his behavior became. He loosened up and dropped some of his excessively deferential and reserved behavior. He began laughing a little more spontaneously and became much more like a child than a "little adult."

With the passage of time, Michael became more popular with his schoolmates. He began joining them in their ball games and spent less time alone. His drawings were more benign in character. Although his overall behavior was more openly aggressive, it was less ominous in its implications. He became angry and sometimes fought, but he did not rely solely on indirect and potentially dangerous maneuvers. The teacher, although aware that she now might have to contend with Michael's newly exuberant and potentially disruptive behavior, was much happier in knowing that he was becoming more the healthy little pest and less the unhealthy little adult.

SITUATION 5

This example involves stealing — a common problem with children of all ages, particularly younger children. Usually the stealing is not serious and involves small objects such as a pencil, crayon, puzzle or, more rarely, money. Few teachers are inclined to punish a very young child for such an act, since he may not understand its moral implications. Any action that may be required is designed to show the child that stealing is wrong. Those oriented toward psychodynamic concepts tend to view stealing as symptomatic of some disturbance.

246

A first-grade teacher approached the consultant about a little girl who had been taking small things from the other children. On one occasion she had taken something from the teacher's desk drawer. The teacher did not know how to handle the problem. Brief investigation indicated that the child's parents had been divorced a year or so previously and that the mother was soon to remarry. This information supported the inference that the child was anxious about losing the affection of important people in her environment.

The consultant suggested that the teacher take the child aside and tell her that she was concerned about her taking things. The teacher was to show acceptance of the impulse to steal by saying she could understand that the child would like to have the things she had taken. However, she was to explain that it was not right to take anything without asking, and that if the child should want anything, she was to ask the teacher for it. The teacher might have to say "no" sometimes, but usually she would be able to give the little girl what she needed. The teacher followed through and reported that the child did not say much but looked very serious. On subsequent occasions, the teacher was to call the child over and ask if she wanted anything.

The teacher later related an incident in which the child was alone in the room with the teacher's purse, which was open. The girl went to get the teacher, in the next room, to tell her she had forgotten her purse. The teacher praised her effusively for her thoughtfulness and reinforced the idea that if the child wanted anything, she was to ask the teacher. The teacher reported that she followed through on the suggestions, with the result that the child's stealing stopped entirely.

SITUATION 6

In the following example a teacher dealt with a child's anxiety by teaching a lesson concerned with the problem with which the child was struggling. Open consideration of the problem in the classroom permitted the child to express and master his difficulty.

A first-grade child had for some weeks been moody and relatively ineffective in class. One morning he asked to go out to the bathroom but was asked to wait a short time because the bathroom was in use. When he asked again, he was permitted to go. After awhile, when the child did not return, the teacher became concerned. As she was considering sending someone to look for him, the principal received a call from the child's mother saying that he had come home. Then the teacher discovered a small puddle under the boy's seat, evidence that he had wet his pants. The child clearly was distressed, both by that specific situation and by other events, judging from the unusual behavior he was exhibiting.

The mother brought him back to school, and at that point revealed that she had recently returned from the hospital where she had undergone surgery. The child had stayed with a grandmother during that time. The mother indicated that she probably would have to return to the hospital for a few days for further medical procedures. She said the child had known about her impending hospital visit the first time, but that she hadn't told him exactly when she would go. She entered the hospital one day while he was in school, and he returned home to find her absent. According to the mother's report, the child cried when he learned she was in the hospital, but after that he was obedient and apparently happy. Upon her return he became whiny and clinged to her, asking many questions about whether she would go again and about how she was. The mother was wearing a surgical dressing on her neck and was unable to carry out her normal duties around the house. She usually drove the boy to school regularly, but now that she was not well, she was unable to do so. The child seemed to deeply resent that his mother was not doing some things for him that she did before, and there was some suggestion that he was worried about whether she would be at home when he got there.

On the basis of this information, the consultant advised the teacher to tell the child he was wrong in leaving the building without permission but she could understand that he was worried about his mother. The consultant and teacher then worked out a plan whereby the teacher would conduct a lesson on illness, surgery, and going to the hospital. Several children were able to contribute hospital experiences. The teacher also included some discussion about the process of recovery, indicating that sometimes it took a long time for people who came out of the hospital to be completely well. The child apparently contributed some of his own experience and asked a number of questions about how people recovered. According to the teacher, he seemed much involved in the discussion, and at the conclusion appeared calm and satisfied. From that time until the end of the term, the child's mood changed to one of normal exuberance, and his work improved steadily. He didn't wet his pants in class again and seemed totally at ease in school.

SITUATION 7

In the following example a hypothesis developed from projective tests was used as the basis for finding a satisfactory activity to help satisfy a psychological need in a constructive fashion.

A first-grade child's test protocol suggested that his aggressive behavior partly reflected his desire to identify with symbols of strength. He wanted to be able to ward off threats of aggression directed against himself. The child frequently attacked other children, often without obvious provocation. He was difficult to manage in class, and his mother implied that he could be controlled only when his father threatened to beat him for misbehavior. The parents had recently separated, and the father was not available. As part of a general effort to work with the child, the consultant and teacher discussed some of the test results. The consultant explained the child's fantasies relating to aggression and asked how the child could be instilled with a feeling of physical strength without fighting other children. The teacher suggested that she give him the task of moving chairs following the reading group. He was to be given the job because he was strong, and she was to emphasize her pleasure at seeing him exercise his strength in this fashion.

This child's problems were quite marked, and no single effort would in itself make a significant difference. However, a good part of the disruptive behavior disappeared, and he eventually began doing some schoolwork. A highly significant factor is his mother's statement that the child was talking favorably about his teacher and his school and was quite upset when the mother discussed moving away. Somehow, the child seemed to feel he had found something for himself in this school with this teacher.

SITUATION 8

Incomprehensible or "crazy" behavior is always distressing. It is difficult to appreciate that such behavior also can be a signal of some kind of situationally determined distress.

A kindergarten teacher was working effectively with a schizophrenic child. She was maintaining him in the classroom and found that he would follow along with the group for many activities. However, the child was unable to do any work if left alone. He would engage in various forms of self-stimulating behavior including biting his hand, rocking, and masturbating. The teacher was able to tolerate a good deal of this behavior. Whenever the class was assigned a project involving handwork, she would try to help him. However, when she was working with him, he would sometimes make unusual noises that became progressively louder.

Discussion led to an interpretation of the noises as a distress signal indicating the child's feeling of inability to handle the work. The consultant suggested that the teacher work with him until he began making the noises. She was then to tell him she understood that he felt he could not do

250

the work, and therefore they were stopping at that point. After trying this tactic, the teacher never again complained about the noises. She felt that she now was aware of a method of handling the problem and that it was comprehensible to her.

SITUATION 9

Sometimes teachers must handle difficult situations on the spot. In the following example the consultant happened to be available to help a teacher think his way through a difficult situation. The consultant had been working with the boy and his teacher for several weeks preceding the following incident.

A fourth-grade boy told his teacher that he had found a hunting knife in the street. He voluntarily gave it to the teacher to hold for him until after school, exacting a promise that he would get the knife back after school. Both consultant and teacher had considerable concern about the boy because he had been involved in a number of fights and once had been accused of chasing a girl into her house with what he claimed was a toy hatchet. The teacher felt he was beginning to develop a good relationship with the boy, and he was worried about damaging this relationship if he did not return the knife. The consultant suggested that the boy was in fact seeking protection against himself and that it would be serving the boy's interests to hold the knife. The teacher and consultant then worked out an approach in which the boy would be told that the teacher knew it was illegal to carry a weapon, and that the boy would be in great difficulty if the police found him with the knife. (Since the boy already had been picked up by juvenile authorities on several occasions, he could understand the reality of that statement.) Moreover, the teacher was to take the boy to the principal, who was to be given the knife to hold, and was to commend the boy for his good sense in giving the knife to the teacher.

The incident did not mark any particular turning point in the relationship between the boy and his teacher. The boy accepted the teacher's decision and seemed at least as friendly after the incident as before.

SITUATION 10

Sometimes academic and intellectual limitations are such that not much progress can be anticipated in a given situation. When the school has already provided a child with remedial help and he has received psychotherapy culminating with the recommendation that he be treated as nearly normally as possible, the school is left without recourse when he continues to have academic difficulties and/or get into trouble. In the following instance it seemed the boy's behavior in school was in clear response to his feeling of inadequacy in dealing with his school situation.

This fourth-grade boy presented a longstanding problem of underachievement. Also, he had been aggressive in the neighborhood, with many complaints coming into the school. His teachers reported that he had a short attention span and was hyperactive. He had been under psychiatric care, had been tutored during summers, and had received remedial reading — all to little avail. Observations in class showed that he participated eagerly in those few things he knew, but soon got lost in the material. He then would dawdle, daydream, or just sit over his work. Following a series of conferences with his parents, it was decided to remove the pressure from him by taking away all extra services. His teacher agreed to program for him at his level and to grade him much less strictly, to avoid feelings of failure. He already had been retained in the grade and did not show much progress as a result of the retention.

After the pressure was removed, he produced some modestly good papers, and as his work in school improved, his mother indicated that he was doing homework without argument. He seemed to feel more at ease in the classroom and mentioned that somehow he was catching onto the work more easily. Observation in class at the end of the year confirmed that he appeared happier, attentive for longer periods of time, and much more receptive to criticism. In terms of measured achievement, he did not improve that much, but his attitude and feeling about school certainly changed for the better.

SITUATION 11

Sometimes we not only translate the child's needs into some kind of program in the classroom but also help others to think about the dynamics of their interactions with the child. Sometimes the very act of considering what is going on makes the difference. In the following example the mother came to the school because she was having difficulties with the child, who complained that she did not like school, and who was beginning to feign illness.

A Jewish teacher began the conversation by saying, "She's my only Jewish child, and it's a shame the way she acts." The child was resistant, negativistic, somewhat disrespectful, and was turning in work the teacher felt was unworthy of her. The teacher initially was critical of the mother, whom she felt spoiled the child and, consequently, she found herself either pushing the child hard or ignoring her. The teacher indicated to the consultant that she was worried about several personal problems of her own, one of which was the failure in school of a nephew toward whom she felt very close. She had been trying to help her nephew continue his education, and he was not responding to her efforts. The consultant made no effort to interpret the teacher's possible transfer of emotional reactions from her family to her student but merely indicated that he felt certain the teacher would be able to cope with the child after her mind was settled about the other issues.

Following this discussion, the teacher began changing her tactics. She stopped pressing the child about her work, began giving her extra tasks around the school room, and praising her profusely. In about two weeks the teacher reported that the child had attained the highest score in her class on the annual academic achievement test. The teacher was pleased with this progress and made it a point to advertise the child's achievement widely in the building. The child's mother made it a point to tell the consultant about her daughter's accomplishment and then began to question whether she had been too hard on the girl herself. For the remainder of the school year and through the following year, the child's performance in school was excellent and attempts to feign illness ceased. The mother made no more complaints about behavior at home (although this was no certain indication that the home problems were settled).

The intervention in this case really was quite mild. The consultant had a conference with the child's mother and one with the teacher, calling the problem to the teacher's attention. The teacher brought sufficient evidence to support the hypothesis of a transference of her personal concerns to her perception of this child's difficulties. The opportunity to talk aloud helped the teacher reconsider her treatment of the child, and after she shifted her tactics, the child's response changed markedly. To attempt any kind of interpretation of the teacher's reaction can be treacherous. Often it is enough for the consultant to understand what is happening and for the teacher to receive support in what she is fully capable of doing.

SITUATION 12

A small but significant number of teacher requests for help from the consulting psychologist relate to character problems of their students which do *not* disrupt others in the classroom. A teacher may seek out the psychologist about a student's joyless perfectionism, friendlessness, or general nervousness. The psychologist may redefine the referral question. Thus, what the teacher perceives as nervousness or prattle may reflect the unexploited creative enthusiasm of a richly endowed child. The daydreaming and friendlessness of a youngster may be more potentially serious than the teacher realizes. After the teacher and psychologist have reached a working agreement about the possible meaning of a child's problems, the psychologist often plans a set of diagnostic interventions which the teacher can carry out to assess the child's self-understanding and his capacity to modify his behavior, without more direct involvement by the psychologist.

A well-developed first-grade black boy periodically became sullen and stubborn in school. Every two or three weeks his moody uncooperativeness manifested itself with no clear triggering incident. In the last quarter of the school year, when the usual pattern showed no signs of softening despite the good relationship between teacher and child, the teacher discussed Orio's periodic negativism with the psychologist. The teacher never had discussed the matter with the boy lest she uncover more than she could handle, but the psychologist, in his observations, was impressed with the accessibility of the child to discussion. The psychologist had theorized aloud with the teacher about the possibility that Orio was extremely angry during these periods and did not know how to think about or use his angry feelings at such times. By backing off from the boy's difficulties, the teacher was in effect reinforcing Orio's own neglect of his inner life at such times.

Taking reassurance in the psychologist's assessment and his availability if any deep-seated conflicts should arise, the teacher waited for the next bout of moodiness. Later, with great excitement, she reported to the psychologist that she had followed the plan. Orio had talked about his parents' periodic quarrels which came to blows regularly. He was able to tell the teacher that he didn't know how to tell his parents how angry he was with them and, instead, took it out on others in school when he felt that way. The teacher told the boy that he also took out his anger on himself by becoming sullen. After several such talks Orio could speak about his anger instead of smothering himself in it, and his uncooperativeness diminished considerably during such periods. The teacher's intervention may not have resolved the boy's home difficulties, but it did strengthen his forebearance at considerably less cost to himself.

Several features of the teacher's approach should be stressed. She had not relied on a single contact with the child but had followed through on subsequent occasions. Teachers, as well as psychologists, sometimes make the mistake of assuming instant learning with a child and regard a discussion as fruitless unless it has an immediate payoff. This teacher, moreover, had not simply labeled the undesirable behavior and persuaded the child to alter it. She had instead explored its significance, building on the child's understanding and vocabulary for the problem. Finally, by permitting the child to talk out his angry feelings, the teacher was encouraging a model of emotional functioning for the boy that stressed insight and sharing instead of festering feeling, self-punishingly expressed. The child's grasp on such learning can be strengthened, while his shame is diminished, by participating in a lesson or group discussion on problems common to the daily life of the children. Thus, teachers have been able to deal with the problem of absent or drinking fathers, parental discipline, and questions of ethnic affiliation and skin color.

Before the psychologist recommends teacher intervention in exploring a child's emotional reactions, teacher and child must have a reasonably sound relationship which in itself has not contributed to nor altered the child's undesirable behavior. Second, the preoccupations that have been interfering with the child's work and happiness are explored to permit him to ventilate his concerns. The teacher is not encouraged to probe for unconscious meanings. In short, the psychologist keeps track of the teacher's interventions to ensure that she is not taking a psychotherapeutic role for which she is not trained, a role that could easily produce more distress than it eliminates in the child and teacher.

THE TEST REPORT

Very few recommendations contained in psychological test reports and psychiatric evaluations are specific and suitable to the classroom. Recommendations for treatment at a child-guidance clinic with a year's waiting list are of little direct help to the classroom teacher. Recommendations for "individual attention" say nothing and appear to the teacher as impractical burdens. Mental-health professionals are singularly ignorant about the school situation and do not recognize its potential for constructive change.

To the teacher, and probably to others, the sight of a psychologist without his test kit is sufficiently strange to cause confusion about who he is and what he does! A teacher generally sees the school psychologist only long enough to point out the child to be tested. Frequently, a school psychologist will ask to see a child, after no social contact with the teacher other than a perfunctory greeting. Periods ranging from weeks to years may go by before a referral is answered, depending on the school system, the pressure of referrals, available personnel, attitudes of the principal toward testing, and the personal relationship between the principal and the school psychologist.

The typical product of a psychological examination in the schools is a written psychological report. If a child in fact has a low IQ, the teacher is reassured that his difficulty in learning is not her fault. If his IQ falls in the normal range, the test report sometimes will allude to the child's anxiety, his dependency, or some other emotional problem, in a fashion that may place the blame for the problem within the child. The concrete fact that the child has been tested is sufficient for some school personnel to categorize the child as either disturbed or dull. In either case the teacher's responsibility for doing something is minimized. Clearly, if he is dull, he cannot be expected to learn. If he is emotionally disturbed, he does not fall within the teacher's jurisdiction and she need feel no guilt about this lack of progress. It seems that tests are not valued so much for suggestions in classroom management as they are for the emotional support which the test procedure provides the teacher.

Only when the consultant appreciates the degree to which a teacher is left alone with a problem can he understand that she is not necessarily cruel or unconcerned. It is difficult to see how a teacher can adopt other than a defensive posture, in the absence of concrete help and someone with whom to share a problem, and in the tradition that teaching consists primarily of the preparation and presentation of material for normal children. The occasions in which a teacher works with great dedication to help a difficult and troubled child are tributes to the capacity of the human spirit to transcend adverse circumstances.

In contrast to the typical situation in the schools, the consultant who was the subject for examples in this chapter never accepted a referral for testing until he had first discussed the child with the teacher and observed the child in the classroom. This particular attempt to break through the loneliness of the situation was not immediately successful. Although some teachers welcomed the opportunity to try something new with a child, others did not initially receive this variation in procedure with great enthusiasm. In instances in which the teacher desired testing to determine whether a child should be placed in a special class, the consultant's refusal to test at once was seen as an unnecessary obfuscation or as questioning the teacher's judgment that the child needed help. Only close and continued contact with the teacher permitted corrective discussion when misunderstandings arose.

Even though a teacher requests help, and even though help in the form of testing is given, it is all too easy to underestimate the degree to which a teacher may misunderstand the nature of psychological tests. Most teachers have only a superficial familiarity with intelligence tests and no knowledge at all about projective tests. At times a teacher may even be threatened by the contents of a test report, although the issues are couched in the most careful language. The teacher may read criticism into a report where none is in-

tended. At times the consultant may need to provide a cap-
sule course in psychological testing to explain his meaning.

At its best, the testing process brings together the teacher,
child, parent, and consultant as partners in an enterprise in
which all have a mutual interest. After the consultant has
discussed the referral with the teacher, observed the child in
the classroom, and the child seems particularly suitable as a
candidate, the teacher and consultant interview the parent.
The interview is presented as a mutual problem-solving situation. The teacher briefly describes the child's problem in
school, and the parent is asked to contribute whatever information he (she) can to help the teacher understand the child's
behavior in school. The interview frequently brings out relevant information. At the conclusion of the first interview, the
parent is requested to give permission for a psychological
examination, with the understanding that no specific action
will be taken until the results of testing are discussed with the
parent and teacher.

The child is then assigned to an examiner who is instructed to tell the child explicitly that his teacher is concerned
about his performance in school and wants him to do the best
he can, and that the examiner wants to understand how he
thinks and works so he can help the teacher. After a few
months the consultant becomes a familiar person in the school
building, and the children know him. Most go with him for
testing quite readily. If someone other than the consultant has
to conduct the testing (as is sometimes the case), the consultant makes it a point to introduce the examiner to the child in
the presence of his teacher. Every effort is made to minimize
the unfamiliarity of the situation for the child. In almost all
instances the children thoroughly enjoy the testing experience
and look forward to spending further time with the examiner.
The teacher experiences the repeated examinations as a form
of working with the child, especially since the consultant
makes it a point to make some comment about each session
and inquires about the child each time he sees the teacher.

When testing is completed, the consultant and the teacher (and the graduate student, if one has been involved) arrange for a conference. The conference is structured as a sharing of ideas, and the teacher is encouraged to contribute his observations and comments as the test findings are reported. It is stressed that the teacher is not to let the consultant slide by with generalities of jargon which are not understandable. The teacher is encouraged to ask questions and require that the consultant be specific, concrete, and understandable. As the findings are discussed, the consultant makes it a point to ask the teacher about how particular ideas may be translated into action feasible in the classroom. In many instances the specific form of the recommendation for action comes from the teacher.

During the conference, the consultant and teacher also discuss what the child may be told about the test findings, and schedule a conference to interpret them. Such conferences are carried out with children as young as first graders. The child usually is told by the consultant that he did very well and that the examiner and teacher were pleased with his cooperation. No matter what his IQ, a child always is told that the tests showed he is not dumb, that he can learn, but that sometimes it may be difficult for him to understand the work. When a child is intellectually more capable, he is informed of that, but again he is cautioned to expect that he may have difficulty in learning some things. In other instances some of a child's behavioral characteristics are interpreted, with suggestions on how he may handle himself differently in a particular situation.

The child also is told that his mother (or father) will be asked to return for a conference and that, in essence, she will be told the same thing the consultant has told him. In most instances the child is eager for his parent to have the conference, because the report always is couched in as favorable terms as possible without actually denying clinical realities. Both teacher and consultant meet with the parent for the post-testing conference, and discuss various recommendations. By this time (sometimes three or four months after the referral), parent, teacher, and consultant are familiar with each other, and the conference is an expected climax to a series of activities rather than being a shock to the parent.

It is important to note that the teacher is brought in as the consultant's colleague and partner at every step in the process. The consultant attempts to remain in touch with both teacher and child in the implementation of recommendations.

Typically, in the way schools operate, a child who is to be placed in a special class is tested, and if he qualifies by having a sufficiently low IQ, his parents are called in and informed of the decision by the principal. The usual expectation is that the parent will protest the placement and the principal then will have to "sell" the idea to the parent. After the parent agrees to the placement, the child is sent to the special class without any preparation. His previous teacher's experience with him is in no way utilized, and the special-class teacher is given a child with no information other than that he has been failing and has an IQ low enough to qualify him for the special class. Rarely are the two teachers involved in any joint effort to work together in expediting the child's placement. Wherever possible, the consultant should break into this situation by including the special-class and the regular classroom teacher in conference together to plan the child's transfer.

14

What Teachers Need to Know

Frank Garfunkel and Burton Blatt

We can be surer that children learn than that teachers teach. Individual learning differences can be meaningfully demonstrated, although their significance in planning educational programs is not clear. Despite the discrepancies between measurable behaviors and educational goals, there is enough concordance between the processes and results of learning to indicate that somehow the system works.

This is not at all the case with regard to teaching. Attempts to relate teachers, teaching, and learning have been largely unsuccessful. A great deal of energy has been expended to describe teacher-pupil interactions and to compare classroom protocols with theoretically derived constructs. But such descriptive work is a prelude for evaluating effectiveness, unless teaching concerns only what takes place overtly rather than what happens to students covertly.

In short, the system for obtaining *useful* knowledge about teaching (not teachers) does not work. The concept of teacher competence is unverifiable. Although one would assume there are professionals who can clinically judge competence, there is no reliable way to judge the judges. For the teacher this may mean that, if others cannot judge him, he cannot be confident of his own insights into what he is doing. Consequently, teaching becomes a question of faith.

THEORY OF CURRICULUM DEVELOPMENT

The determinants of cognitive learning may well be extraneous to teaching; and the reason why teaching competence cannot be identified may be that it has no direct effect on cognitive learning. Teaching involves continuing relationships between children and adults, so the dimensions of competence will have to be explored within these relationships. However, learning depends on past learning, motivation, and values, all of which are affected by home lives, peer relationships, and personality development. The teaching of a particular person is a miniscule part of a complex system.

The principal contributors to *learning* variance operate independently of *teacher* variables. Several implicit assumptions are present here. For example, a given teacher (1) presents students with appropriate materials, (2) can, and (3) does communicate with children. The orderly presentation of materials is sufficient, given any particular group of students, to outweigh teacher variation if the criterion is related to the materials being taught.

The often demonstrated "Hawthorne effect" is an example of situational variance dominating the effects of individual teachers. Studies of teaching methodology also have failed to show recognizable teacher effects. Studies of interventions into the lives of children of different ages and social conditions have shown minimal effects. Large classes are the equal of small classes and various studies of grouping have never arrived at the "one-tail-test" stage. We are still trying to ascertain direction.

The hypothesis that the teacher's competence has no direct effect on the amount of student learning is disturbing. But how does one study this hypothesis? We would suspect that research findings gathered from the study of teacher and method effects are more a result of prejudice about the teacher ethos than they are the outcome of either empiricism or theory.

VARIATIONS IN COGNITIVE BEHAVIOR

Clinically, we see differences between teachers. We intuit that some teachers have radically different effects on students than do others. However, research on teaching has not systematically described this variation or its relation to pupil functioning. This means that the training and selection of teachers is chiefly the result of prejudice. For the teacher, it suggests an interface of "competence" separating his knowledge from its usefulness for teaching. For the researcher, it means that the wrong questions are being asked.

It is noteworthy that, in the teaching profession, rewards are based on criteria not directly relevant to teaching competence. In public schools rewards usually are based on straight seniority; in universities, on publishing. *The equation of good teaching with learning, when the former is not determinable and the latter is, provides a foundation for incompetence.*

The variables of social class, family adequacy, sex and age (developmental) account for considerable differences in school achievement. Previous achievement obviously is an important source of present achievement. There are also variables relating to the operation of schools which, at their extremes, show correlation with achievement. However, these, again, are not teacher variables.

Evaluations of teachers are characterized by unsupported reliance on the criteria of cognitive changes in children. It has been argued that such changes are correlated with several variables, but not with differences in teaching. Although the literature gives many explanations, the most obvious is that cognitive learning is independent of teaching competence. Nonetheless, it has been argued that it is desirable to measure competence so as to inhibit incompetence, even though it probably has minimal effects on achievement. We must then ask new questions and find new criteria for *competence.*

Let us think of competence as the teacher's effect on the learning climate. The object is to focus on the kind of climate that unfolds under a teacher's influence. We assume that the development of superior climates is directly connected with learning in non-cognitive areas, since desirable non-cognitive abilities are part of a successful climate. Climates can be thought of as evolving naturally or the result of manipulations. If we are to get beyond the myth of the "born teacher," we will have to institute experimentation with climate control in training programs.

FOCUS ON THE EDUCATIONAL SETTING

Through the years, we continually have been confronted by discrepancies between what teachers get in their training programs, what they want, and what they need. It is not unusual to hear graduating students remark that their only valuable training experience was their student teaching. This is a direct appeal for a one-to-one relationship between what goes on at the university and what will go on in their future teaching positions. Students rarely complained (until recently) of the relevance of their liberal arts courses. They seem to have assumed that university students should receive a broad liberal education in addition to any specific professional preparation.

The gap between college course work and vocational experience in education is no different than in other areas of endeavor. However, education students expect help of a relatively specific nature; they tend to ask for more useful methods courses than those which are currently offered. Few education students and teachers have strong backgrounds in developmental psychology, learning theory, personality, group interaction, perception and motivation. Yet, these areas represent the various fields in psychology that have addressed themselves specifically to the problems of learning in group situations — problems which would appear to be most relevant for classroom teachers.

In trying to make sense out of how teachers are trained and what they seem to want in their training, many underlying issues interfere with direct inspection. The problems of teacher training institutions are intimately connected with the theme of this chapter and, consequently, cannot be avoided completely. These problems are so closely related to our educational establishment that we cannot understand one unless we understand the other. Much could be learned by comparing the professional training of teachers to the training of other professional workers. Professional schools are necessarily traditionally oriented, because of their struggle to gain recognition for distinct professional fields with university status. This traditionalism is reinforced by complicated certification procedures which sharply curtail innovation in the schools, as well as in the professions themselves.

Our purpose in reviewing some of the more general ideas about professional training is to free us from the restrictions that inhibit innovations in that training. Freedom is facilitated only when the participants become aware of the kinds of restrictions under which they are working. As a matter of fact, most of us in teacher preparation are more interested in what *we* think teachers need than in what *they* think they need, or what they get. We must convince teachers of the possibility of new ways to view their needs, ways which are different from present formal teacher training or a liberal arts curriculum that excludes formal teacher training.

It is not surprising that studies of teacher effectiveness have failed, in light of the highly diffuse nature of teaching. Many different areas of activity comprise what is loosely referred to as "teaching": leading discussions, lecturing, presenting materials, counseling, being an adult model, controlling behavior. There is little indication of a general factor cutting across these various areas. The global assessment of teaching can be valid only if salient characteristics are correlated to each other and to some meaningful measure of competence. However, viewing teaching as a collection of independent behaviors and attributes does some violence to the phenomenon we are trying to understand.

The researcher's dilemma of trying to decide what should be studied, and how, is intimately connected with the teacher's decision to choose materials and present them in diverse ways. Because of this presumed connection, the present chapter continually swings back and forth between research and teaching. Too often, a clinical approach is unaffected by empirical findings. Extensive literature on studies of teaching (Gage, 1963) shows that diverse aspects of educational methodology are insignificant determinants of academic success, when compared with developmental or social-cultural factors. This is not reflected in the curricula of teacher training institutions. Even more striking, it is not reflected by current educational practices.

We are not suggesting that particular findings must lead to recommendations as to how teachers should be trained, how children should be taught, or how teaching should be studied. Quite the opposite — for the above-mentioned literature suggests that repeated differentiation is desirable. The uniformity pervading teachers' colleges implies some substantively empirical support for common practices; there is none. Current practices should reflect the equivocal nature of past findings with a labyrinth-like assortment of programs. Many alternate strategies are possible for training teachers and for studying teaching (and children), but one cannot be employed without the other.

Notwithstanding the essential integrity of the teaching process, we must operationally distinguish between cognitive and non-cognitive areas, study them separately, and train teachers to excel in one or the other. Teachers have been expected to fulfill both of these functions without being trained for either. The teacher generalist has enough developmental psychology, learning theory, social psychology, and methodology to be mediocre in everything. Teachers are as good or as bad as they were when they started training, with little possibility that they will achieve anything resembling professional excellence. Whether one views teachers as artists or as applied psychologists, there must be a study discipline that becomes the foundation for what will follow.

We propose the development of specialists who are distinguished both by their pedagogical style and by the children being taught. The more specialized the training, the more exclusive will be the selection of children. Unfortunately, the converse of this is often true: As a technique becomes more specialized and as it becomes more explicitly articulated, it develops an aura of universality, a growing belief that the technique can be helpful for all children who have any kind of disability. This distortion is enhanced by the religious fervor often accompanying the process of educational specialization. Great teachers and innovators have a charismatic effect not only on children, but also on their disciples. The right combination of teacher and method with a child can be startlingly effective, but how "universal" is either the teacher or the method? For children without disabilities, one can almost assume that specialization is not needed unless extraordinary learning is the goal.

WHAT DO TEACHERS WANT TO KNOW?

At every level of teacher education and inservice training, we are confronted with individuals who want to know what is best to do in specific situations. Many education students feel their training is seriously lacking because it does not dwell enough on the realities of the situations into which they will be going. The continuing call for specificity seems to rest upon the assumption that most teachers and students believe there are answers to their specific questions, but that instructors and supervisors are unwilling to share this information with them because of ignorance or reticence. Criticism is leveled at teacher educators that they are too distant from the classroom and that, even if they once taught, they now are ill prepared to serve the needs of prospective teachers.

The common judgment of teachers that student teaching was the most important single aspect of their training raises serious questions about the ability of teachers to come to grips with the problems of their own training. In the first place, they are looking for a kind of teaching at the college or inservice level which they would probably find inadequate even at the elementary or secondary level.

Most teachers would agree that the most important thing they can teach students is how to learn. No student will learn everything about geography or arithmetic. However, children might learn enough skills and technical language to pursue areas of inquiry as they arise later, even if they have not been specific subjects for school study. The only way to develop this kind of transfer of learning is to teach at an abstract enough level so that what is learned can apply to a great variety of situations. The generalized intelligence score obtained from aptitude tests is a better predictor of future achievement in a specific area than specific aptitude tests in that area. The children who will learn more and better in any specific area are those who have acquired general abilities to learn, rather than specific subject matter. Learning to read, for example, will enable the pupil to study subjects with which he has had no contact in his formal schooling. Similarly, arithmetic enables him to deal with quantitative concepts in many ways.

In view of the universality of reading and quantitative concepts, we are asking whether the best way to teach reading is through a specific approach to words and sounds; or, on the other hand, whether reading should be taught more globally so it is learned as a general ability which can apply to other languages as well. In such a system, children receive language training rather than reading, writing or any other specific

270

components of the process. We need not uniformly agree that all children should be taught general bodies of knowledge in general ways. It is enough to agree upon the principle that children should be taught in maximally theoretical *ways* and that they should be taught maximally theoretical *things*.

How does one stimulate maximal transference in a particular situation? Most teachers do not seem to recognize the importance of avoiding concrete situations while they are learning, if their training is to be maximally effective. On the contrary, most teachers pursue specific courses which would make them "specialists" for dealing with particular kinds of children in specific situations, rather than teachers who are trained to deal with many different kinds of children.

Perhaps the crux of this matter is the failure of university education to be sufficiently general. In very specific ways throughout the liberal arts and professional education of university students, great demands are placed upon students for what can be called "controlled learning." The assignments are neatly spelled out on an assignment sheet passed out during the first week of classes. The readings often are specified, page by page, in the textbook and in a variety of library books. Examinations often are rigidly laid out to conform to specifications. In light of this, it is easy to understand that students do not make an about-face when it comes to learning how to teach. In their professional education courses and practicuums, they seek the same kind of specificity they have received elsewhere.

On the other hand, most course work involves extremely theoretical subject matter which has no specific application. This suggests a discontinuity between the general subject matter of liberal arts courses and the mode of presentation. This and other discontinuities are not inherently bad, but they are destructive when they lead to critical impotency.

WHAT DO WE TELL TEACHERS?

In the face of the demand of teachers and students to be taught things of relevance to the classroom, and in consideration of the fact that most teacher trainers were at one time teachers, it is not surprising that most professional education is fairly concrete. The very titles of methods courses imply that this is a substantive area and that methods can be communicated to students in a university-level classroom situation. Teaching methods courses are viewed as a transmission process. At the same time, the professional education community pays lip service to the idea that all individuals are different and teaching must be tailored to their personal needs. Great stress is given to textbook and workbook teaching, which necessarily assumes homogeneity of students, teachers, and situations. If the homogeneity does not already exist, it certainly will be enhanced by the process of inculcating into future teachers the idea that a subject such as methods of teaching social studies is, in fact, a legitimate substantive area of university education.

Assuming that student teaching experiences are considerably more valuable to students than any of their other training experiences, we conjecture that this is because either the student teaching experiences are of high quality or the professional education courses are of low quality. Since student teaching usually is handled in a massive way, with relatively indiscriminate placements and, generally speaking, is fairly mediocre, then course work relating to methods of teaching and to educational psychology must be quite inferior.

At any rate, it is much simpler to give students the things they want than to use other approaches which may be resisted because they are gross departures from other experiences which students have had in schools and universities. Students, as well as other people, have great anxiety about getting into situations of which they are unsure. Going into a classroom without knowing what to do is extremely threatening. The usual argument for specific approaches is that they give the teacher something to do until he becomes familiar enough with the milieu and the children to "take off" on his own. However, the orientation of telling teachers what to do, of giving them textbooks and workbooks which they can then automatically follow, is in direct contradiction to teaching them to view the teaching situation itself as a problem-solving situation.

The textbook and the workbook offer initial security which is increasingly difficult from which to retreat. This false security is insidious because it is subverting the learning process. The workbook is just as harmful to the child as it is to the teacher in that the child, too, gains a false sense of security defined by clearly foreseeable steps to learning and a finite goal — the last page of the workbook. In this way, the process of learning how to learn is systematically inhibited by the garments of security and presumption without ever really being born.

However, maybe we are stuck with a model for training teachers which is an outgrowth of a huge "numbers game" which completely distorts the interpersonal characteristic of the teaching-learning situation. A teacher has to be extremely gifted and dedicated to develop his own materials throughout the year for 30 to 40 children, no matter what the rewards may be. Similarly, the teacher educator is continually faced with huge numbers of students, and the procedure used in teaching these students is much more a result of the numbers than of any explicit philosophy of teaching.

Thus, what we teach certainly is a function partly of our experiences and the realities of situations, but it also is an indication of stagnancy which tends to insist upon uniform teacher training for all students who go through a particular school of education. To the extent that a program commitment does not permit some groups of students to receive special kinds of training, even the best aspects of a training program will become so diluted by numbers as to end up being another kind of mediocre expression.

WHAT DO TEACHERS NEED TO KNOW?

We cannot argue with the idea that every well-thought-out methodology will be effective in the hands of some teachers with particular children. In some cases, results will be obtained from teachers who are pleasant or unpleasant, warm or cold toward children, highly directive or permissive, well organized or relatively disorganized in their approach, or any one of a variety of other ways. We do not dismiss the idea of a "programmed" teacher or an orthodox Montessori teacher or any other kind of teacher with a prescribed methodology. However, we do see inherent limitations in any prescription, because — either directly or by suggestion — it can be convincing evidence to the teacher to view the teaching process as the teacher fulfilling prescriptions which have been laid down for him by other people or agencies.

Our choice of strategy in this matter is partly aesthetic in that we get little satisfaction from working with and studying teachers who are not operating as free agents. We view the teacher training situation in the same way we view the child learning situation— namely, as a problem-solving opportunity where the most important resources available are those within the teacher and the child. These resources have to be drawn out as dictated by requirements of the interactions and the milieu.

We are not addressing ourselves to a situation in which a teacher with certain given abilities to deal with a certain number of children, and certain possibilities for obtaining materials, has to do everything in his power to stay in the same place. We do not desire to isolate ourselves in an ivory tower but only to admit and recognize situations (perhaps most of them) where the notion of creative teaching in consideration of interactions and individual differences is a total myth. But we also *are* assuming the existence of situations in which the realities are not so oppressive as to inhibit creative and developmental activity on the part of the teacher.

One way of exploring the possibilities for teacher training and for what teachers need to know is to utilize the analogy of mapping, which bears a certain literal resemblance to the processes of cartography. The teaching-learning process, whether the teacher's or the child's, can be viewed as a series of constructions, readings, and use of different kinds of maps. In every case, the student — whether a child or an adult — needs, as an end product, to become thoroughly familiar with various kinds of maps which will aid him in a variety of different kinds of trips. If he understands the general principles of mapping, it won't be necessary to teach him the characteristics of each map he encounters. He will be able to apply the generalities to strange maps because of a universal system which connects all maps. If the *general* principles are taught, any *specific* map used as a teaching aid is, in itself, trivial.

We can break down the process into several components which, again, are directly analogous to the teaching situation. A person who views a segment of reality — whether geographical, verbal, quantitative or historical — then can abstract from some wide area of knowledge to gain some reasonable and germane continuity. A "map" is then presented to the student, who can use it either as a general model enabling him to read other kinds of maps, or as a specific instrument enabling him to deal with the problems presented in that particular map without generalization to any other map.

This suggests only one of the problems in generalization — namely, the use of a variety of maps because of the knowledge of the principles upon which they are commonly based. The other problem pertains to a more crucial dimension of the mapping process — the construction of maps in the first place. If students are made aware of not only the principles of given maps but also the principles of map construction itself, they will be in a position to generalize within the language matrix of a given series of maps and across different kinds of languages represented by different kinds of maps.

To be more explicit, it is one thing for a student to learn the principles of road maps and therefore to be able to use many different road maps without having previously studied them. It is another matter for him to be so familiar with the total mapping process that he can proceed to understand topographical maps or other kinds of geographic maps or, to extend it much further, to be able to understand totally different kinds of maps and be able to construct them for his own uses. The last extension of knowledge, for us, is the ultimate in problem solving. The concept applies as readily to methods as it does to maps, and to teachers as it does to children. Furthermore, it suggests the intimate connection between the way teachers learn and the way children learn.

The newly trained teacher who goes into the classroom and asks what he should do may be saying that he does not know how to begin to solve the problem with which he is confronted, or that he has not been provided with the specific map upon which he can draw to find direction. It is our contention that when a teacher does not know what to do when confronted by a new situation, he is failing because he asks the question in the first place.

What do teachers need to know? As a limited goal, they need to know how to read maps and to use them. They have to be taught, or have to discover, how maps are created for any medium and for any subject matter. This analogy is a generality, but it gives direction to teacher training programs and should help students find what they need to know. Unless we aim in that direction with some intensity, we always will be aiming far below the potential of teachers and the needs of teaching situations.

Perhaps an abstract theoretical orientation for the training of teachers will fail for many students because they cannot let themselves be that free and because they are really aiming at becoming technicians rather than scientists or artists. But we suspect that we will necessarily fail with these people no matter what approach we use. So, perhaps it's better to fail with a glorious ideal than with a useless, overspecified, sterile one. We always shall be haunted by the prescribers and the programmers who want to develop a prescribed, programmed society. Maybe the chief ingredient of their inevitable failure is to be found in the minds of young children who resist us in every way they can. When we have observed the programmed lesson, we have seen children resisting such teaching. The beauty of this resistance is that it's a logical reaction to the requirements of uniformity.

REFERENCE

Gage, N.L. (Ed.). *Handbook of research on teaching* (a project of the American Educational Research Association). Chicago: Rand McNally, 1963.

276

15

Psycho-Educational Assessment, Curriculum Development, and Clinical Research with the "Different" Child

Burton Blatt and Frank Garfunkel

Development of superior procedures to assess children and to design curricula for them depends upon the quality of collaboration fostered in these endeavors — collaboration of teachers with supervisors; and both teachers and supervisors with psychologists, language specialists, social workers, and other professionals. Such collaboration, however, does not guarantee either effective or meaningful results. The existence of classes of children, teachers, psychologists, and other specialists in an open, cooperative system provides the raw materials. Effective collaboration ensures that the potentials will not be dealt with haphazardly.

An important way in which classrooms differ from each other is the extent to which daily activities are a result of materials which have been supplied because of certain *normative assumptions* about the children, rather than *specific evaluations* of the children. The fifth-grade class that receives fifth-grade readers and fifth-grade workbooks clearly is using materials which have been developed with an "average" fifth grade in mind. At times, it appears proper for the teacher to ignore the variability of a particular group or an individual in that group. However, to the extent to which assumptions are made about groups of children — and the resulting curricular procedures — important dimensions of variability obtain between different kinds of classes and different teachers.

At one extreme is a group of students, possibly a college class, which does not vary much in age, abilities, or motivations. Lectures are delivered to the entire class; there is a standard textbook; and the final examination is objective. The teacher has made certain assumptions about each student's life, family, perspectives, intelligence and, possibly, even his religious convictions. Obviously, problems as well as virtues accompany this kind of "normative teaching."

At the other extreme is a class of children varying greatly in age and ability. The teacher clearly sees that each child must be treated quite separately. However, if the members of this group are taught individually by the teacher, and in each case different standardized reading books and workbooks are used, normative assumptions still are being made. The assumptions do not apply to the group as a whole but to the individuals in the group. Use of normative materials means only that lessons have been more or less predetermined for a particular child rather than especially developed for him. Even individual tutoring can be an example of normative teaching.

However, in some cases, specially developed lessons for particular groups or children might very well be ineffective, while the teaching of packaged materials might be extremely effective. The question of how materials are developed and where they come from is not necessarily crucial to the question of quality. Further, some teachers likely perform more competently when using normative materials than when using a diagnostic approach to teaching. Regardless of what approach the teacher finds most comfortable and successful, his insight into the possible risks involved in choosing particular strategies is a much more important consideration. He must recognize and be sensitive to continuous "educational feedback."

We will admit our bias in this matter, if it is not already apparent. We believe it is desirable for the teacher to become involved in developing, *to some extent,* materials for the children in his class. He will not necessarily develop "better" materials than those commercially available, but he will have to study children more carefully and learn a great deal about them — how and what they learn. Active participation in gaining this knowledge will make the teacher better able to improvise if and when the teaching-learning process is unsuccessful. Standardized materials provide fewer ways to deal with failure. Failure, unlike success, may occur for various reasons and in a variety of ways.

DESIGN OF A THEORY FOR ACTION

Teachers need a theory of action which is general enough to apply to children characterized by extreme variation in performance, such as are found in special classes. Similarly, the well-ordered, relatively small, suburban elementary school class would become a special case of the more general theory which applies to the demands of any educational situation. If processes can be developed whereby teachers can design curricula for extraordinary situations and extraordinary children, it should follow that they will be able to deal effectively with more typical situations. However, one obvious point is that a generalized approach to teaching and learning cannot support itself with *a priori* prescriptive methods (i.e., methods prescribed irrespective of the particular child and his condition). If it did support itself, this approach would become another in a long list of normative ones. Therefore, the teacher must have the background and experience to make decisions

279

about what, when, where, and how children can best learn what he is trying to teach them. Closely related to how children learn is how *teachers* learn and how interactions take place in and outside their classrooms.

Although teachers have the responsibility for making decisions, they are restricted by their own logic in reaching a decision and in originating or planning activities. After they have made a decision, they need continuous feedback and evaluation regarding its effectiveness. Too often, the general pattern of teaching is opposite from the model suggested here. Teachers and allied educational specialists tend to be overly dependent on the selection of materials because school systems and clinics often designate certain specific texts and curricula for particular classes or groups, without consulting the teacher or considering the children. At the same time, teachers are visited on rare occasions, generally, with little concerted effort to provide them with regular feedback about what they are doing with children and its effectiveness. No matter how the teaching-learning process is conceived, it is difficult to see how it can become increasingly effective unless certain built-in features necessarily involve teachers and other appropriate professional persons for the purpose of changing the teachers and, consequently, for changing teaching and children.

CURRICULUM DEVELOPMENT

The concept of readiness is central to that of curriculum development. Learning cannot take place without readiness. But a child can be ready to learn — physiologically, experientially, conceptually, emotionally — yet fail to learn because of unfavorable external conditions. However, the distinction between internal and external factors is arbitrary, as is the entire concept of readiness and, consequently, the construct "curriculum." The question of teaching and learning (what, when, how, and the inevitable why) cannot be dealt with by appealing directly to any psychological laws of learning or teaching. Although a considerable amount of normative data have been compiled to relate when children tend to gain specific abilities, there are extraordinary variations of timing, sequence, and intra-child consistency. The mass-production nature of public schools, with their texts and workbooks and standardized examinations, is an inevitable by-product of a mass-education system.

Insofar as it is mandatory to educate all children to the age of 16, 17, or 18, it is necessary to staff schools with teachers having greatly varying backgrounds and competencies. The result is what we refer to as the "slot machine" approach to education. The system is like a machine which works when certain generalized stimulations are given to it. As long as the goals are fairly limited, the machine works both consistently and well. An individual goes through a four-year college program to prepare himself as a teacher. Upon graduation, he fits into one of thousands of classrooms and proceeds to distribute to students materials that are more or less similar to those used in all the other schools, without regard to such factors as where the students live, their social and cultural backgrounds, and their special strengths and liabilities.

There is no question that the "slot machine" approach is a great equalizer. There *is* a question as to whether this approach has anything to do with pedagogical excellence, and whether it is the method to be chosen for groups of children which show great evidence of failure. However, many of the "slot machines" work quite well, and teachers are capable of developing superior educational milieus which provide a setting for warm interpersonal relationships between children and their teachers. There also is little question that, in some of these situations, the children achieve what might be termed an ultimate goal of education: Children learn to teach themselves. However, the contention of this discussion is that the conditions of the mass-education system are quite different from the conditions that can be reasonably set up for a superior teaching situation — which is a necessity for the child with special needs.

Teachers may insist that they can use normative materials, and at the same time provide for other kinds of classroom experiences and needs. Many teachers and children have functioned effectively in this way. However, we see a contradiction between the goal of generalized learning experiences, where children learn in order to learn, and specific *a priori* prescriptive methods with specific textual materials and specific lessons assigned to all children. The contradiction is most obvious in classrooms for the disabled or disadvantaged, in which numerous children have problems which affect either their ability to attend to what is going on in the classroom or their motivation to accumulate academic skills.

To the extent that an educational environment presents a relatively heterogeneous situation with respect to pupil ability and behavior, we can loosely refer to that environment as a special educational setting. The problem facing the teachers, however, is in developing a construct which would provide guidelines for dealing with the most general type of teaching-learning situation — one which includes children who are relatively heterogeneous and who show a considerable variety of behavior over time and in different situations. In this kind of setting, the use of either age-wise normative materials or group-wise normative materials appears to be futile.

PSYCHO-EDUCATIONAL ASSESSMENT

The processes of *psycho-educational assessment* and *curriculum development* must coalesce. Whatever is involved in the assessment of a child is involved in curriculum development, and vice versa.

An adequate school program for disabled or "different" children must have both internal and external resources. Internal resources include the coordination and utilization of personnel and facilities existing *within the school system*. These resources should provide for careful, extensive, interdisciplinary diagnoses of children who have been referred for admission or who have been screened by some system-wide testing or recruitment procedures. After a child is placed in a special class or group, these resources should guarantee continuing supervision of program development and for curricular innovations especially appropriate for that child.

The diagnostic process which leads to placement and subsequent programming for an individual, or for groups, should lead to further diagnoses — both for purposes of re-evaluating *children* throughout the school program and for evaluating *programs* for children in different educational settings. Frequently, there is little connection between the diagnostic process and the curricular process. The diagnostic process leads to a child being placed in a special situation and usually stops there. Then the curricular process takes over, unfortunately with the assumption that the placement of the child was a correct decision at the time and will continue to be correct in the future. As a result, re-evaluation often is neglected.

There will always be a point at which internal resources become inappropriate or insufficient and the school or special unit personnel must obtain assistance from external resources, to best serve children with special problems. Certainly, most school programs would not be expected to develop their own mental health clinics, speech and hearing clinics, or pediatric-neurological clinics. However, the school staff should establish working affiliations with such service agencies. Proper utilization of external resources and relationships does take the energy and time of school personnel, both individually and in concert. Referrals all too often consist of a telephone call and a superficial follow-up. Unfortunately, this does more to remove the burden of the child from the school than it does to service the child's special needs.

Depending upon the size and budget of the school program and the school's accessibility to clinical facilities, its internal resources include supervisors, administrators, teachers, diagnosticians, therapists, and consultants (psychologists, social workers, speech and hearing therapists, art and music consultants, and sometimes research specialists). The staff should work closely with program supervisors and teachers to develop a fluid educational setting in which children with special needs can be attended to in an optimal manner. The system should include provisions for moving children from one situation to another when clinical considerations show this to be advisable. Adhering to the same principle, teachers or specialists should be ready to accept reassignments when warranted.

An effective school program obviously entails continual surveillance by qualified supervisory personnel. And, for a program to succeed, the competence and the dedication of individual professional workers must be supported by an active integrated program, with sufficient time and personnel to perform basic functions of diagnosis and educational treatment.

A MODEL

The following model deals directly with development of a multi-dimensional framework which could be the basis for assessment, curriculum development, and clinical research. The first two needs — assessment and curriculum development — have been shown; clinical research will become an increasingly important element of programming for the "different" child, in light of the ever-increasing public funds being appropriated for support of these programs and the subsequent reporting responsibilities which must be assumed by those who administer them.

This model considers both the molar aspects (overall performance and adjustment of the child in the school setting and at home) and molecular aspects (processes of learning, socialization, conceptualization, and language development) of different children. The model provides for analysis of both school and home behavior, in terms of a theoretical framework which would allow for the intentional manipulation of the behavior of children and teachers, and for the evaluation of their behavior.

With reference to the observed behavior of children and teachers and to theories of child development, a framework is constructed in order to provide a basis for action and evaluation. This tentative framework is used by teams of professional workers to evaluate children, teachers, and the curriculum. Finally, provisions for theoretical and curricular revisions are built into this framework. A description of the objectives, rationale, and design of this model follows.

Objectives

Objectives of the model are to stimulate development of curricula to offer maximum opportunities for the assessment of children, and to guide clinical research studies in program evaluation and child behavior. We assume that none of these objectives can be accomplished effectively and with validity without accomplishing each of the others.

In the past, some behavioral scientists have studied children under experimental conditions by which they attempted to control environmental factors. For example, an educator might study differences among several independent methods of teaching reading. He would design his study so that, through randomization procedures, a group of children learning to read by one method probably would be like another group learning to read by another method. He also would assign teachers to each group randomly so that one teacher would be more or less as well adjusted to his group and method as any other teacher would be to any other group and method. Consequently, the researcher would be able to claim that these two variables were held constant for all of the groups studied.

Research strategies similar to the one described are based on the assumption that the method of teaching is the most significant independent variable. Controls are set up to equalize the other variables. In such studies, the kinds of children and the personalities of the teachers are considered to be intervening variables with some importance, but are peripheral to the experimental comparison being made.

Our model presents a reversal of the above example; the basic design considers the independent variables to be the teachers and the children and the intervening variables to be the method and content of the curriculum. Although this approach would be suitable for studying any kind of classroom situation, it is especially suitable for disabled or disadvantaged children. In special classes, the usual curricular goals generally are subordinate to those pertaining to adult-child and peer relationships. Achievement is not the primary emphasis, and methods of teaching generally are not considered to be of greatest importance. The independent variables which should be given most attention in such settings — teachers and children and their interactions — are not readily subjected to careful measurement and control.

There are many good reasons for experimenting with only one or two fairly discrete variables at a time; but there are just as many good reasons for analyzing the complex interactions of children in realistic behavioral situations, as is our approach. Classroom situations will be intentionally manipulated in this model in order to answer questions raised by the theoretical orientations of a particular clinical research study and by the interactions between observers and teachers. The information obtained then will be used to vary programs and curricula for children in order to maximize the possibility of favorable behavioral changes in children. A careful study of the behavioral deficits and strengths of both the children and the program is an explicit part of the design. Through such study, the following questions are confronted: What anomalous behaviors are displayed by the children? How does the school program deal with these undesirable behaviors? What are the specific effects of various procedures upon individual and group behavior?

In essence, the total process of curriculum construction and evaluation for disabled and disadvantaged children should be continually re-examined for the purpose of setting a self-generating working model. It should include fragmental studies of all elements of the classroom "field" as well as an intensive study of the total "field." The problems of what and how to teach should be explored intensively.

A good deal of evidence leads to the proposition that the teacher-child relationship is critical to the teaching process. This evidence suggests that not only the "how" of teaching, but the relationships that develop between the teacher and both individual children and the total group are important. An example of this phenomenon is the "halo effect" which persistently appears in psychological and educational experiments. This effect seems to be more consistently related to improved performance than any particular method. An assumption of our model is that something like the "halo effect" is necessary to the development of a superior curriculum; one of our major objectives, therefore, is to build a "halo effect" into a curriculum.

But such an effect is not sufficient. Other questions must be answered. How do children spend their time in the class? Do they attend to what is going on? How is their attention monitored? How are they dealt with when they succeed and when they fail?

Rationale

Variables in the usual educational situation are such as to discourage the rigorous experimentalist from dealing with them. The classroom situation is antithetical to a controlled experiment that demands the rigid application of certain *a priori* conditions. Personalities of teachers and children, social interactions, and creative processes are examples of difficult-to-measure factors with which we have to deal if we are ever to be able to produce other than sterile descriptions of curricula. Since these factors cannot be measured easily, they usually are not included in the design of an experimental study.

The procedures of this model deal directly with both the process and the substance of interpersonal reactions as they take place in the classroom.[1] In studies of children, substance has received considerably more attention than has process. Thus, in terms of what is here called "substance," the literature is extensive in providing constructs which hypothetically and empirically describe how children differ from one another and how individual children change over a period of time.

However, the literature is not at all clear on how to produce changes most efficiently, especially when the children under consideration have cognitive or other disorders. Process has received less attention because it is less amenable to study. The measurement of the abilities of children (substance) is less difficult than the measurement of their social interactions or their motivations. Thus, psychologists and educators understandably have concentrated on variables that are relatively easy to measure, even though such variables may be of trivial importance to learning.

For example, an Intelligence Quotient is a good predictor of academic success, and generally is used as such. However, academic success is a function of both the substance and process variables. The latter, being difficult to measure, is more or less ignored. Why then is IQ such a good predictor of academic success if it measures essentially the substance and not the process? Obviously, process variables affect IQ in the same way they affect academic success, and the predictive efficiency of the IQ is due to indirect measurement of the process.

Clearly, it behooves clinicians to explore thoroughly not only the components of the IQ but also the components of academic success. This exploration calls for intensive investigation of the total field of behavior of children with, perhaps,

---

[1]For purposes of this model, *process* has to do with the ways in which relationships are initiated and proceed between individuals and the extent to which relationships exist; *substance* is concerned with the content of these relationships.

minimal attention to conventional aptitudinal criteria and maximum attention to processes. Such a focus is a reversal of what generally takes place in school evaluation programs. For most typical children the consequences of failure in academic and social activities are not catastrophic in that these pupils eventually will find jobs and will have friends, in spite of many failures. However, the educator is somewhat more anxious when confronted with children who will grow up to be intellectually and socially dependent — unless he can do something about the situation. Most teachers of typical children see no compelling reason to discover why some children do better than others. Instead, they "explain" the phenomenon by saying it is in the nature of things; they may point out that there are individual differences in aptitudes, value systems, and performance. There is no reason to discuss how we might change the status quo, and yet the status quo clearly is unacceptable for the disabled child.

This model focuses its attention on processes while it utilizes substantive constructs. Both serve as a basis for *what* is taught *when* it is taught. The model does not merely rely on a descriptive study of what is happening. Evaluation becomes a part of the program. A feedback system serves to involve teachers in every part of the evaluation so they cause changes and become changed. Parents are exposed to a program of group counseling which is designed to support the school program and is considered to be a part of the curriculum. The psychologist and social workers collaborate with teachers to interpret process and substantive constructs and to point out how they operate in classroom situations. The vehicle for changing the behavior of children is the teacher's increased understanding of the process and substance of the desired change rather than particular teaching methodologies or curriculum content. However, special percepts and concepts should be tested, and innovations should be made in the curriculum in order to treat deficits of particular children. The treatment should always be dependent upon the situation in which the behavior takes place.

Consequently, a design of teaching methodology or curriculum content should not be imposed on the classroom situation. Instead, the substantive data should be the tools that serve as sources for generating hypotheses and as bases for evaluating protocols. Different teachers would use the tools in different ways depending upon their perception of their roles as teachers. Some teachers might take an experimental approach, carefully evaluating specific deficits of particular children and treating them directly. Others might take a more clinical approach, concentrating upon their relationship with children and upon interactions within the group of children. Each class in the program should be autonomous, to the extent that the teacher and children of the class present a unique cluster of individuals and situations. Similarities in approach should exist to the extent that the cluster of individuals and situations overlap. The procedural core of this model should be a network of seminars and conferences in which substance and process would be studied, and uniqueness and overlap determined.

The rationale of this model, in summary, calls for development of assessment, curriculum, and evaluative procedures in harmony with what actually takes place in the classroom. Teachers should not be expected to fit into a predetermined mold. This recognition of individual differences in classroom situations is analogous to the recognition of individual differences in children. For research purposes, bases for comparison would be the variability existing among and between interactions rather than among and between either teachers or children.

Design

The design of a model based on the dichotomy of *substance* and *process* is somewhat artificial since neither can exist independently. However, this theoretical division does offer a workable way of discussing the design; therefore, we will take advantage of it.

290

Included under the category of *substance* are the abilities of children. Meyers and Dingman (1960) reviewed the literature in this field and hypothesized seven domains of expressive and receptive abilities of young children: psychomotor/whole-body; psychomotor/hand-eye; visual perception; auditory perception; receptive psycholinguistics; expressive psycholinguistics; and mental, including memory and thinking.

Pedagogical and diagnostic methods for dealing with these domains are not, by any means, pure, but numerous studies have focused on one or more of them. The result is a growing body of data on typical and atypical development and on the dimensions and structures of abilities of children. Although these studies have been encouraging in that they tend to offer support for agreement between the aforementioned hypothesized domains and empirical ones, the question still remains of how to apply the knowledge gained from the studies. Does the existence of more or less independent domains of abilities in children mean anything to the educator?

A good deal of research suggests there is no simple and direct application of these discoveries about abilities. The knowledge of a normative sequence of steps in which children tend to develop a particular ability domain does not have general application for individual children, for at least three important reasons: great individual differences in acquisition; motivational variabilities of greater importance than specific learning sequences; no guarantee that any transfer of learning will occur from teaching specific tasks. Further, the studies of ability domains give descriptive information about what children learn and when they learn, but they do not tell how learning takes place; nor do they indicate what is necessary for its transference. These ability studies are useful in providing educators with a necessary array of insights, but it is important not to ignore other operations that have to take place if learning is to be socially meaningful.

For the reasons given above, particular batteries of tests cannot be stipulated for utilization in an assessment program.

In general, the *a priori* listing of specific procedures in either the evaluation or teaching situation would be extremely unrealistic. Standardized instruments have not been developed for the complex problems which disabled children present to the evaluation team and, as mentioned previously, results of evaluations are not usually directly applicable to the classroom setting. Therefore, we need to modify existing procedures and attitudes if evaluation protocols are to be useful for teaching these children. Perhaps the greatest value in evaluative studies of ability domains of children is in their entre toward detailed study of children by members of the school staff. These studies should lead to development of a psychologically oriented curriculum based on the described variations that exist among children. The study of the *substance* of learning, in summary, is dictated by the type of children in the program, the kinds of behavior to be modified, and the extent of the behavioral modification. Selection and development of testing and teaching techniques should stem from studies of the ability domains of children. However, specific applications should depend on both psychometric protocols in each of the ability domains and clinical assessments of behavior of children in the program.

In terms of the *process* of learning, we include reactions between children and reactions between children and teachers, observers, and other individuals involved in working with the children. The interactions among children must not be isolated from contingent interactions of adults who are teaching and studying the children. The following diagram indicates the existence and direction of interactions.

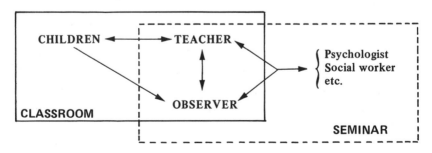

For each group of children in a class, there would be a teacher and at least one observer (who could be assigned to several classes). For each class, there would be a seminar which would meet regularly to discuss the behavior of the teacher and the children. Members of the seminar should be the teacher, the observer, a psychologist, a social worker, and other professional workers who are intimately involved with other children. They would deal with speech, medical, and other problems as they arise. The seminar would follow from the general description of Sarason, Davidson, and Blatt (1962, pp. 75-96), with modifications made necessary by the obvious differences in situations.

Essentially, our design for *process* provides systematically for communication between two group entities, the teacher and the observer. We find this to be a much more elaborate procedure than the usual educational model which consists of a teacher and the class of children and, at times, observers with whom the teacher may interact. The usual model lacks a system for facilitating communication and makes the process of teaching and learning completely dependent upon the personalities of the individuals involved.

Perhaps children with no unusual problems can afford the relative wastefulness resulting from an educational setting that leaves learning largely to chance. However, disabled children clearly cannot afford anything other than the most effective kind of learning situation. The first requirement for such a situation is that all the professionals know what is going on and when it is going on. Furthermore, there must be a strong beneficial and defined relationship between the teacher, who is continuously involved in a two-way relationship with the children, and an observer, who is involved in a one-way relationship with the children. In general, this supplies the model with an internal evaluative device which is the interaction of two elements in the system with significant variation in function but with a basic similarity in design.

REFERENCES

Meyers, E.C., & Dingman, H.F. The structure of abilities at the preschool ages: Hypothesized domains. *Psychological Bulletin,* 1960, *57,* 514-532.

Sarason, S. B., Davidson, R. S., & Blatt, B. *The preparation of teachers: An unstudied problem in education.* New York: Wiley, 1962.

16

Resistance to Change

Douglas Biklen

The newly emerging disability rights movement is achieving some breakthroughs, evidenced by major social policy changes in Washington and a proliferation of local, state, and national advocacy centers. The Education Amendments (PL 93-380) gave us due process rights for every handicapped child in the public schools; in other words, parents now have a vehicle — fair hearings — by which to demand dialogue with school administrators on crucial issues of testing, placement, and exclusion. More recently, the right-to-education legislation (PL 94-142) speaks of rights to "least restrictive" services, which means we now possess a clear mandate for normalization and integration. Where in past years controversy has ensued over the pros and cons of segregating or integrating children in schools and classrooms, we now have a moral imperative for integration. In 1973 the Vocational Rehabilitation Act included affirmative action and non-discrimination clauses, and what amounts to a federal order for state vocational rehabilitation agencies to stop "creaming" (serving the least handicapped clients first as a matter of convenience) and, instead, to serve the most disabled first. And the Privacy Act establishes strict standards pertaining to release of students' records, mandates the right of parents and children too, if they are over 18 years old, to complete access to their school folders and (importantly) opportunities to challenge specific entries in the school records.

In many ways, the new legislation and a congruent rise of advocacy organization at the grassroots reflects the past behavior of professionals in the human services. Obviously, not every education district or system has responded callously and monolithically to children with disabilities — we often have observed the opposite, that is, exemplary treatment — but the tendency has been for bureaucratic behavior to prevail. The consequence of bureaucratic intransigence has been a process of rendering consumers (in this case, parents and children) more and more powerless. Hence the need for protective legislation and a vital advocacy movement.

Clearly, it is time for reconciliation between parents and schools. That is essential if we are to move toward implementation of due process rights, least restrictive education, mainstreaming, right-to-education for all, productive uses of school records, and, finally, quality education. But reconciliation must evolve from equity. The time is past when parents will, in the words of one, "walk on eggs for fear of losing what we've gained." The powerless must become powerful and stand up for their rights; as Saul Alinsky (1967) said, "Reconciliation is when you get enough power so that the other side is reconciled to it." The true relevance of the disability rights legislation and the accompanying advocacy movement is that they suggest the possibility that parents can overcome traditional bureaucratic roadblocks to accountability and can change.

Following is a typology of "resistance to change," along with brief discussions of how such typically bureaucratic behavior contradicts the thrust of both national social policy and

296

grassroots advocacy and, therefore, how the arguments for resisting change can be refuted.

Type 1: *It costs too much and, besides, it isn't our responsibility.*

A parent recently sent me a newspaper clipping in which a special education director responded to parent demands for a program to serve children with severe disabilities by saying: "I don't believe in paying for a babysitting service just to relieve the parents' burden." On the same issue, an intermediate (regional) level school official complained that "we can't serve all handicapped kids at this point — not until all the districts are willing to pay." Of course, such excuses ignore the federal court principle established by Judge Waddy in the *Mills* v. *Board of Education* case in Washington, D.C.:

> If sufficient funds are not available to finance all services and programs that are needed in the system, then the available funds must be expended equitably in such a manner that no child is entirely excluded from a publicly supported education consistent with his needs and ability to benefit therefrom (quoted in Mental Health Law Project, 1973).

Moreover, the claim of insufficient funds directly contradicts the notion of equal access to education for all children. If you seek to deny one child an education on the grounds of inadequate financial resources, you must deny them all.

Type 2: *If we help your child, we have to help them all.*

In a memorandum from a State Department of Education official to a local school official, the reason for exempting one severely disabled child was the following: "The retention of Jane in the TMR class last year led to misinterpretation of the program within several communities, thus creating a difficult situation, as parents of other severely handicapped children began to demand admission to the TMR program likewise." Under the right-to-education legislation, these children must be served. New programs must be created or located. And if any disagreement arises between parents and schools over the issue of placement, parents can rely on due process hearings to challenge the schools.

Type 3: *Blaming the child.*

The following remark appeared in a State Department of Education memorandum: "Jane's deviant behavior within the classroom ('crying and screaming' upon occasion) was distracting to the children within the group." In another instance, a school district's record also locates blame in the youth: "This child is deeply troubled, but I doubt that there's anything we can do for her." Through due process procedures, parents may ask specifically, in descriptive terms, what is meant by "deeply troubled." And what programs would the school propose for remediation of this problem? And what part might the school environment have had in creating the problem?

Type 4: *The youth is not appropriate for our program.*

The most common excuse for denying children access to school and other human services programs is that the youth does not fit the school. One parent wrote to me about her daughter: "We are writing to inquire about the legal rights of our retarded daughter, Mary, particularly in regard to her right to training or an education with public funds. Mary was born November 6, 1960, in Metrocity and since that time has not received a single minute of training or education. She was diagnosed as severely retarded due to brain damage before or during birth. . . . As the time approached, we contacted the elementary school she would have attended and asked if they had special classes for retarded children, and the answer was no. This has been the only answer we have received for 13-½ years."

Another parent recently showed me an official form which excluded her son from public school. The child was excluded because the school did not develop an appropriate program: "This is to certify that I have made a careful examination of the above-identified child and find that unless recommended services are immediately provided, this child should be exempted from instruction for the period indicated, because of mental and emotional disorder." The form was signed by the Superintendent of Schools.

Under the education amendments and the right-to-education legislation, school districts may no longer act arbitrarily in these ways. They must provide due process hearings where parents may question their decisions, and they must either create new, appropriate programs or locate alternative ones.

Type 5: *Namecalling.*

The following are paragraphs taken verbatim from a child's psychological report in school:

> Alfred has been referred by all the Jackson J. H. Special Education teachers for evaluation and management and/or placement recommendations. . . . All three teachers see Alfred as a severe organizational distraction and question his adaptability to a public school program. Possibilities for achievement in a group setting seem to be poor.

What is a severe organizational distraction if it is not simply namecalling?

> Alfred requires constant attention and direction to maintain attention to a given task. Without this constant recall to focus upon a given task, he loses both the method and the content of the task.

Are there any specific examples of this?

> Alfred is a very pleasant, tall, red-headed boy who seems to crave attention and affection, however inappropriate the means of the response may be.

What does his red hair have to do with success or failure in school?

> His primary handicap . . . appears to be his anxious state which prevents consistent development of his mental and educational capacities, particularly in a group setting. Alfred is a severely emotionally disturbed boy whose function in the public school setting is dubious.

Still, the report offers no specific evidence of the boy's behavior.

Such arbitrary and subjective records may now be seen and challenged by parents. Further, parents can demand specific evidence. It seems in the spirit of the Privacy Act that the parents in this case could request that the school include data on Alfred's strengths as part of his record.

Type 6: *Fault finding: A study in bias.*

School records often seek to find fault in the youth rather than to formulate teaching and learning strategies. A major city school district utilizes the following rate scale. All of the categories are negative. Due process hearings and, indeed, school board meetings provide appropriate forums in which to demand a moratorium on the use of such biased forms.

Our experience has been that when parents ask to see children's school records, the bulk of the records seems to decrease, and comments that remain in the folders seem more descriptive than previously was the case. In other words, schools districts will become more judicious in their record keeping as parents use "the right to know" for purposes of accountability.

Type 7: *Blaming the parent.*

Have you heard the phrases, "You're too involved" or "Don't be so emotional; we must be objective about this"? Parents are all too familiar with such "put-downs." One parent who was exceedingly active in writing letters and demanding adequate personal services for her blind son thought it somewhat humorous when a school official submitted an editorial to the parent-teacher newsletter entitled "Parent Expectations":

> Almost every child is a genius in the eyes of his parents, and failure to achieve at a high level often is believed to be the fault of the school, since few parents will admit that heredity could be at fault. Far too many parents like to gain recognition through their children's achievements and use their child to this end.

LEARNING DISORDER EVALUATION AND RECOMMENDATION TEAM
TEACHER'S REPORT

ADDRESS _____ BIRTHDATE _____ INSTRUCTIONAL UNIT _____

PARENTS NAME _____ PHONE # _____ UNIT REPRESENTATIVE FOR _____ THIS CASE

NAME _____ GRADE _____

The following are some behavioral and physical signs which may indicate serious personal problems, learning problems, or emotional problems. Check only those which are appropriate. This single sheet is to be completed after all staff on unit responsible for student have consulted. This is a team referral!

Tardiness and absences
Failure to do homework repeatedly
Chronic scowl, frown, or grimace
Chronic "sad sack" expression
Bullying or threatening gestures to others
Persistent arguing with others and
  talking back to adults
Persistent refusal to obey
Temper tantrums
Inability to keep quiet
Inability to finish class assignments
Request or demands to leave the room
  for personal reasons
Being alone, avoiding others, and
  being avoided by others
Refusal to work with another because of
  race, religion, ethnic, or social class
Blank facial expression--seems out of it
Silence--often spoken to or questioned
Repeatedly being assaulted, victimized,
  or butt of jokes
Crying
Destruction of property
Physical assault on others
Physical assault on self
Stealing
Lying, exaggerating
Sudden, noticeable worsening of personal
  appearance
Clinging to parent, siblings, or other adults
Dressing like the opposite sex
Enuresis
Minor accidents causing oneself pain

Cheating
Fire setting
Nail biting
Nervous tics
Stuttering
Inability to enunciate properly
Thumb sucking, rocking
Physical complaints
Sexual play with others
Expressions of violence
Repeated verbal or physical contact with teacher or
  other adults
Drowsiness, falling asleep
Repeated claims of hunger in the morning
Repeated talking or humming to self
Repeated difficulty hearing
Chronic squinting
Inability to use school material or equipment
Lack of muscular coordination
Inability to read
Daydreaming
Dilated pupils, nodding, craving for sweets, weight loss,
  cramps, nervous agitation
Body odor, dirty face, dirty clothing
Sulking or pouting
Masturbation or exposing one's self
Requests for help when capable
Inability to remain in seat
Refusal to share, hoarding
Giving away possessions
Self deprecating statements
Teasing and taunting others
Loss of appetite, skipping lunch
Noticeable change in behavior or personality

> Certainly we want to be proud of our children. We should have high
> expectations, but it is imperative that parents be realistic and objective
> about their children.

But being realistic does not mean that parents must stop short
of demanding an equal education for their children. They
have rights to transportation to school, adequate books and
supplies in the classroom, equal classroom space, location in a
regular school building (or the least restrictive setting possible), the right to due process hearings, and the right to see the
school records. For these rights, parents may be as emotional
as they like.

Another parent, a frequent contributor to parent and
teacher magazines, wrote to me about her encounter with a
state official:

> The official said "Mrs. _____, you must accept the fact that
> your boy isn't going to play basketball." I retorted, "What I can't
> accept is the fact they he can't even get through the front door!" And I
> mean it. Ramps are just excuses. They symbolize other barriers.
> Anxiety, fear, discomfort. . . .

Type 8: *Double talk.*

When several groups of parents, representing individual disability categories and a coalition of such groups, spoke out
against construction of a special segregated facility for children
with disabilities, they were told by one high level education
planner, "I agree with your philosophy but we have to be
practical." As one parent put it, "Why does being practical
always mean second class services?"

Another common double talk phrase is, "I agree with
you, but I'm not in a position to make the decision." When a
regional school director made that comment in response to
parental demands for establishment of local deaf programs,
one father stood up and remarked within earshot of a local
newspaper reporter, "We used to call that the old Army trick
of buck passing." Double talk is giving way to accountability,
for it does not justify second rate services. The law requires
equal opportunity for disabled children.

Type 9: *"Give to the handicapped. Without your help we cannot provide the necessary programs."*

Charity poses a barrier too. A picture appearing in a local newspaper showed several handicapped children sitting in front of a bucket of pennies — presumably a media gimmick to spur contributions. One week later the annual United Way campaign began, replete with advertisements of three multiply handicapped children whom viewers presumably were expected to pity and therefore help (with monetary contributions). Fortunately, the new right-to-education legislation makes it unnecessary to transform disabled children into objects of pity and symbols of guilt. We will not have to place disabled children in the spotlight or claim, for purposes of charity campaigns, that disabled children represent a major financial burden to their families and society. The most basic service, education, is now a matter of right, not charity.

Type 10: *"You must be so patient."*

Every parent and every teacher who has been asked about their children or their employment in special education has been subjected to the comments, "Oh, you must be so patient. Those kinds of children need special attention, don't they?"

All children need attention, but it is part of the pity image applied to people with disabilities to make parenting and special education into missionary-like pursuits. When someone tells me I must be "so patient," I invariably feel that, underneath the kindness, people are saying, "I'm glad it's you, and not me, who works with children who have disabilities." It seems as if people are saying that children with disabilities are a "burden." In response, I always say, "No, it's not the children who need my patience; my patience is most taxed by society's discrimination and society's low expectations of children who have disabilities." The new federal social policies fortunately make this same assumption — that disabled children need rights, not pity.

In addition to the "types" elaborated above, school officials use numerous other strategies to resist change. Parents, school personnel, and others involved in the disability rights movement have heard the following excuses and many more: "The child is not in our jurisdiction. It is beyond our sphere of influence"; "Sorry, we do not make the rules"; "The Unions will never buy it. They will not take on any extra work"; "We need evidence before we can act"; "We will need more time. You must learn to be patient"; "This child is an exceptional child among exceptional children. She just doesn't fit"; "If we included your child, we would have to cancel an art teacher for typical children"; "We have always sent such children to institutions or to private schools"; "We need at least ten of them with the same disability before we can set up a specialized program"; "The other children will just scapegoat your child. Don't make her a martyr. It's not fair to her. Don't push your values on her."

Bureaucratic resistance to change is not a new phenomenon. But the existence of national social policies and a burgeoning advocacy movement to help identify and overcome such resistance are both unusual and encouraging. The federal disability-rights laws provide parents and advocates with a new legitimacy, while at the same time divesting professionals of unfettered access to bureaucratic behavior. These laws fully support the concept that, for people with disabilities to enjoy equality in their lives, they must have access to basic services, respect and power.

REFERENCES

Alinsky, S. *Deciding to organize* (film). Toronto: Canadian Film Board, 1967.
Mental Health Law Project. *Basic rights of the mentally handicapped.* Washington, DC: Author, 1973.

17

The Principle of Normalization

Wolf Wolfensberger

Until about 1969 the term "normalization" had never been heard by most workers in human services areas in the United States. Today it is a captivating watchword standing for a whole new ideology of human management.

To the best of my knowledge, the concept of normalization (though not the term) owes its first promulgation to Bank-Mikkelsen, head of the Danish Mental Retardation Service, who phrased it as "letting the mentally retarded obtain an existence as close to the normal as possible." Bank-Mikkelsen (1969) was instrumental in having this principle written into the 1959 Danish law governing services to the mentally retarded.

However, it was not until 1969 that the principle was systematically stated and elaborated in the literature by Nirje

---

This chapter originally appeared in a slightly different and more extensive form in Wolf Wolfensberger, *The Principle of Normalization in Human Services*, Toronto, Canada: National Institute on Mental Retardation, 1972.

(1969), in a chapter of the monograph *Changing Patterns in Residential Services for the Mentally Retarded* (Kugel & Wolfensberger, 1969). Before that, in 1967, a new, far-reaching Swedish law governing provisions and services for the mentally retarded was developed from the principle and became effective in 1968 (Swedish Code of Statutes, 1967 (4), dated December 15, 1967).

Nirje's chapter was mostly concerned with implications of the normalization principle to the design and operation of residences for the retarded; however, the relevance of this principle beyond residential aspects, and even beyond mental retardation to deviancy and human management in general, was clearly recognized and stated. In a synthesizing chapter in the same book, Dybwad (1969) pointed to the principle as a major emergent human management concept, while also elaborating on some of its implications for the location, design, staffing, and operation of residential services.

A REFORMULATION OF THE NORMALIZATION PRINCIPLE

For purposes of a North American audience, and for the broadest adaptability to human management in general, I propose that the definition of the normalization principle can be further refined as follows: "Utilization of means which are as culturally normative as possible, in order to establish and/or maintain personal behaviors and characteristics which are as culturally normative as possible."

From the proposed reformulation it is immediately apparent that the normalization principle is culture-specific, because cultures vary in their norms. The term "normative" is intended to have statistical rather than moral connotations and could be equated with "typical" or "conventional."

Since deviancy is, by definition, in the eyes of the beholder, it is only realistic to attend not only to the limitations in a person's repertoire of potential behavior but also to those characteristics which mark a person as deviant in the sight of others. For instance, wearing a hearing aid may be a greater obstacle to finding and keeping a job than being hard of hearing (Kolstoe, 1961).

Thus, the proposed reformulation implies both a process and a goal, although it does not necessarily promise that a person who is being subjected to normalizing measures and processes will become normal. It does imply that in as many aspects of a person's functioning as possible, the human manager will aspire to elicit and maintain[1] behaviors and appearances that come as close to normative as circumstances and the person's limitations permit. Great stress is placed upon the fact that some human management means will be preferable to others. Indeed, sometimes a technique of less immediate potency may be preferable to a more potent one, because the latter may reinforce the perceived deviance of the person and may be more debilitating than normalizing in the long run.

The normalization principle can be viewed as neutral as to whether a specific deviant person or group *should* be normalized. That decision must be based on values independent of the normalization principle. Here it is useful to recall that our society considers it appropriate that normalizing measures be *offered* in some circumstances, and *imposed* in others.

The normalization principle has powerful theoretical force vis-á-vis other human management systems. Despite its late emergence, considerable empirical evidence — primarily from social psychology and related fields — can be marshalled in support of it. The principle differs from a number of other approaches in its simplicity, parsimony, and comprehensiveness. It subsumes many current human management theories and measures but goes beyond them in stipulating other measures that have been neglected so far. Some enlightened

---

[1]The distinction between "elicit" and "maintain" has several implications. For instance, "maintain" underlines the importance of not only supporting normative behavior in a person previously deviant but also assisting some persons never perceived as deviant from coming to be so perceived.

human management systems, such as the "therapeutic milieu," either have been fragmentary in their conceptualization, or have failed to incorporate features which clearly flow from the normalization principle.

Simple and uncomplicated as it is, the normalization principle is the human management principle most consistent with our socio-political ideas and current psycho-social theory and research on deviancy, role performance, and other social processes.

However, the normalization principle as stated is deceptively simple. Many individuals will agree to it wholeheartedly while lacking awareness of even the most immediate implications. Indeed, many human managers endorse the principle readily while engaging in practices opposed to it, without being aware of this discordance until its significance is spelled out. Then a manager may find himself in a painful dilemma.

IMPLICATIONS OF THE NORMALIZATION PRINCIPLE

One can schematize the normalization principle as having implications in two dimensions of proximity to the person and on three levels of societal organization. The two dimensions are: direct social or physical interaction with the person; and the interpretation of the person to others, via labels, forms of address, attitudes, images, symbols, etc. The three levels of societal organization are: the individual person as a system; the larger but still primary or secondary social systems of the person, such as family, peers, immediate service setting, neighborhood, etc.; and the larger societal system such as the entire school system of state (province) or even nation, the laws of the land, and the mores of society.

Of great importance to the way devalued persons are perceived by others are labels, stereotypes, role perceptions, and role expectancies applied to them. Role perceptions and stereotypes are known to exert considerable influence on behavior. For instance, normalizing role expectations have

308

**A Schema of the Expression of the Normalization Principle
on Three Levels of Two Dimensions of Action**

Levels of Action	Dimensions of Action	
	Interaction	Interpretation
Person	Eliciting, shaping, and maintaining socially valued skills and habits in persons by means of direct physical and social interaction with them	Presenting, managing, addressing, labelling, and interpreting individual persons in a manner emphasizing their similarities to rather than differences from others
Primary and intermediate social systems	Eliciting, shaping, and maintaining socially valued skills and habits in persons by working indirectly through their primary and intermediate social systems, such as family, classroom, school, work setting, service agency, and neighborhood	Shaping, presenting, and interpreting intermediate social systems surrounding a person or consisting of target persons so that these systems as well as the persons in them are perceived in a valued fashion
Societal systems	Eliciting, shaping, and maintaining socially valued behavior in persons by appropriate shaping of large societal social systems, and structures such as entire school systems, laws, and government	Shaping cultural values, attitudes, and stereotypes so as to elicit maximal feasible cultural acceptance of differences

been used with great effectiveness in treating members of the armed forces who display mental disorder (Talbot, 1969). However, only through some recent research has the full power of the feedback loop between role expectancy and role performance been brought into sharp focus. In turn, such research is consistent with and explains a number of other research findings, such as the persistent findings that retarded children placed into special classes underachieve grossly when compared with their retarded peers in regular classes who are receiving little or no special attention.

Normalizing Action on the Individual Level

Direct interaction. Much of the programming offered by human management fields and agencies falls into the general category of the individual directly interacting with the devalued person to maximize his behavioral competence. However, we appear to be much more effective in shaping skills to be physically adaptive than in shaping them to be socially normative, or in shaping their *habitual* normative exercise. For example, the normalization principle demands that a person should be taught not merely to walk, but to walk with a normal gait; that he use normal movements and expressive behavior patterns; that he dress like other persons his age; and that his diet be such as to avoid obesity or debility.

The design of a building devoted to human management can have much to do with the shaping of both skills and habits of its users. Life space should be zoned so as to permit individuals to interact in small rather than only in large groups. Some designs discourage almost all interaction. Buildings used even in part by the severely physically handicapped should have both ramps and stairs. Residential facilities should provide residents with access to the controls that adjust room and water temperature, turn lights on and off, flush toilets, open and close windows, blinds, and curtains. To do otherwise deprives residents of culturally normative opportunities, learning opportunities and fosters non-normative dependency.

Shaping the images of individuals. In some situations a person's public image does not depend entirely on what he is or does but on how he is presented. Therefore, the manager should see that such a person is presented to the public in a fashion that lowers the "perceived deviancy threshold" as much as possible. A moderately retarded adult can be taught to dress himself habitually in a normative fashion; a moderately retarded child still must be dressed by others or told what to wear, and the proper selections can be made. A retarded adult living independently in a society may become deviantly obese; but a mildly retarded adult under a supervised arrangement can have his diet regulated to some degree.

When a person's appearance is less determined by himself than by others, it is important to attend carefully to such things as grooming. A young man with Down's syndrome can be given a "soup bowl" haircut, which accentuates his perceived deviancy, or a haircut which minimizes the stigma of Down's syndrome. Cosmetic surgery often can eliminate or reduce a stigma, and can be as effective in enhancing a person's acceptability as teaching him adaptive skills, changing his conduct, or working on his feelings.

Labels can be as powerful as appearances. Public response to the young man with Down's syndrome will depend significantly on whether he is introduced as Mr. Smith or William Smith; somewhat condescendingly as Bill or Billy; perhaps derogatorily as Billy the mongoloid; or contemptuously as a mongolian idiot.

Although a person is already clearly identified as deviant, it is important to reduce his perceived deviancy. There are degrees of deviancy; every additional measure becomes another social handicap, further reducing a person's self-image and increasing the likelihood that he will emit nonnormative maladaptive behavior.

Normalizing Action on the Level of Primary and Intermediate Social Systems

Direct interaction. On the level of primary and intermediate social systems we work through social systems such as family or school which impinge directly upon the person's life. If the systems are maladaptive, all the work done on the individual level can be rendered meaningless. This often has been the case in residential institutions.

In an interesting study (Rubin & Balow, 1971), it was found that of 967 children tested normal in kindergarten by the school system, 41% were classified within three years as having appreciable problems or requiring special services, and 12% had repeated a grade. Phenomena such as this strongly suggest that systems often are in greater need of diagnosis, treatment, and reshaping than the individuals they purportedly serve.

Working through a social system includes counseling the family of an impaired person or helping the family obtain a physically more suitable home for rearing a handicapped child. In the school we might counsel his teacher, help start a class into which the handicapped person might fit, or prevail upon a governing body to replace an agency director who had served the person poorly in the past.

A person identified as deviant is often further dehabilitated by being deprived of normalizing social contacts, or by being cast into social roles in which he is actually expected to act deviantly. For instance, by placing a deviant client among other deviant clients, we may reduce his social contacts with nondeviant persons. Often we compound this problem by permitting a disproportionate number of staff members working with a deviant group to be deviant themselves. Usually human managers defend such juxtaposition on the grounds that the deviant worker can make a contribution by such an arrangement and can be habilitated by it. However, when a person perceived as deviant administers services to others similarly perceived, the public inevitably concludes that the people being served are of low value. The juxtaposition devalues both groups, but particularly the client.

Also, when deviant individuals work for and with other deviant persons or socialize intensively with each other, a climate or subculture of deviancy is created which exaggerates the deviancy of those within this climate. Even adaptive behavior often decreases. Far from being habilitative, the chances of habilitation for either group, especially the much larger client group, are likely to be reduced.

312

Normalization principles thus not only argue against the juxtaposition of deviant workers with deviant clients, but demand that, as much as possible, deviant individuals be surrounded by non-deviant ones. Those who serve a group of deviant clients should meet at least the same standards of qualification applied to persons who work with non-deviant groups.

Buildings should be so designed and located as to be physically integrated into the community, encourage maximal social integration of the persons served in and by them, and provide client-users with a wide range of normalizing experiences. The size of a facility should accommodate no more deviant client-users than can readily be absorbed by the resources of the surrounding area. In most cases, residential units should be small and should not be placed too close together. Smallness of size, in turn, dictates that residential services should be specialized[2] for specific purposes.

Normalizing dispersal of specialized residences generally means that the location, distribution, and concentration of facilities should follow the prevailing population distribution. Thus, service facilities and especially group residences must not only be dispersed across communities within a region, but also within specific communities. One of the first comprehensive community service plans based on the normalization principle (Menolascino, Clark, & Wolfensberger, 1968, 1970) envisioned as many as 50 small, dispersed, specialized residences, hostels, and apartments for mentally retarded persons in Douglas County, Nebraska (an urban area containing the city of Omaha and a total population of about 400,000). By means of such a specialized, dispersed system, it is planned to eliminate entirely the need for traditional institutional residences, even for the most severely impaired.

---

[2]Specialization, or "model coherency" in the context of normalization, refers to more clearly identified management models and suitable client groupings (Wolfensberger & Glenn, 1975).

In regard to size of a facility or client group, it is important not merely to consider the ability of the surrounding social systems to absorb deviant individuals, but also the size of a grouping that tends to create clannishness, exclusiveness, and inward-centeredness. Members of small groups tend to gravitate outward and to interact with other social systems; but as group size increases, this tendency diminishes. The sheer size of the group may create mutual barriers of attitudes; and a person in a large group may find too many of his social needs met too conveniently to motivate him to reach out for normalizing socialization.

In regard to the juxtaposition of children and adults, we must remember that many normative services for children in the mainstream of society are separate from services for adults. Furthermore, deviant adults are only rarely and in limited ways appropriate role models for children. Often this is true because today's adults did not receive the kinds of services we can offer to the children of today and tomorrow. Thus, we do not want the children to acquire some of the less adaptive characteristics of the casualties of yesteryear, but want them to be exposed as much as possible to healthy, normal children or adults who are appropriate models for their development.

Additionally, when a service for children and a service for adults are placed in close context to each other, they are often under the same administrator, who usually will be either adult- or child-oriented. If adult-oriented, the children's program will suffer, as it has in psychiatry generally, which is overwhelmingly adult-centered. If child-oriented, the adults may be cast into children's roles. Similarly, the virtually unavoidable close interaction between the staff of the children's program and the adult clients may denormalize the adults by imposing the eternal-child role upon them.

The optimal physical locations of children's and adult's services often are quite different. By selecting the same site for both, one service often is disadvantaged in regard to the most normalized location for its particular mission.

The underlying principle of all the juxtaposition issues is that any negative aura (identity, role expectancy, etc.) attached to a setting will be transferred to everyone within that setting. It is much more powerful, both in terms of public perception and direct behavior modification, to include a devalued person or minority in a valued majority than to mix devalued groups with each other, or to place a valued minority with a devalued majority. One of the recurring and stronger findings of social psychology is that deviant members of a group are much more likely than non-deviant members to change their behavior to meet groups norms (Berelson & Steiner, 1964).

Shaping the image of groups. Considerable thought must be given to the naming of service facilities. For instance, Outwood (in Kentucky) is an unfortunate name for an institution for the retarded. The name of a facility should promote a role perception of its client-users that minimizes the perceived deviancy. Words such as "retarded," "crippled," and "handicapped" should be avoided in facility names. In fact, some facilities might fare better in being unnamed altogether — perhaps being referred to informally according to location; e.g., the Harney Street Hostel, or the Kennedy Square Workshop.

Similarly, the labels applied to groups of clients are extremely important. Adults should not be referred to as "children," or "inmates"; but as *men, women, clients, citizens, trainees, workers, residents,* or *guests,* as the case may be — all these latter terms lacking stigma and conveying respect. The term "patient" should be used only in contexts which are unequivocally medical and in which the various obligations and privileges of the sick role are appropriate for the persons served (Parsons & Fox, 1958).

Even the symbols surrounding a potentially devalued person or group should be carefully considered. When cattle prods are used to train the retarded, a conscious or unconscious perception of the trainees as "dumb cattle" is apt to be reinforced.

Contrary to common belief, a staff-to-client ratio that is any higher than necessary is undesirable. A high ratio implies that clients are more deviant than they are, and can be denormalizing under certain circumstances. We should group clients so that each group can be served with the minimum feasible number of restrictions and personnel, which is also one of the reasons why service facilities (especially residences) should specialize.

In many instances, a normalizing measure shapes a normative skill and simultaneously creates a normative role perception in an observer. This, in turn, elicits additional normative behavior from the deviant client in a beneficial circularity. For example, the social structure and the building used by adults should produce at least as much mingling of sexes as in a hotel. Only in a few contexts — many of these in adolescence — are activities normally sex-segregated.

Another example concerns work. A physically or mentally handicapped adult should be engaged as much as possible in work that is culturally normative in type, quantity, and setting. Even if conducted in sheltered settings, work should be culturally typical adult work rather than activities commonly associated with children or leisure. Sheltered workshops should resemble industry.

An important aspect of normalization is to apply the same health, safety, and comfort standards to human management programs that are applied to settings for other citizens. This has important implications for publicly operated services, which often operate below the legal standards prescribed for private facilities. Reception and waiting areas also should be as comfortable, attractive, and private as typical citizens might encounter in comparable community services.

Also in regard to physical facilities, thought must be given to the way the physical facility will be perceived by the public. A building that looks like a prison or that was recently used by disturbed individuals is apt to elicit associations not conducive to integration of subsequent client-users. Positive or negative associations affect not only outside observers, but also those who work with the client who is being perceived.

Architecture speaks a powerful language. A drain in the middle of a living room floor says that persons who live in that room are animals who must be "kept" and cleaned as in a zoo. A non-enclosed toilet says that its users have no human feelings of modesty. An isolated location or bars on the windows suggest that the building's inhabitants are a menace to society.

Normalizing Action on the Level of Larger Societal Systems

Direct interaction. Direct interaction on the level of larger societal systems might mean, for example, working to change the entire school system of a state or nation, rather than one class or school. Many authorities have stated that our present school system unconsciously encourages teenagers from disadvantaged backgrounds to drop out. To change this, we may have to change laws, perhaps reform teacher training institutions, revise funding and taxing patterns, and alter our priorities.

Manipulation of deviant people's image in society. Perhaps the major challenge in changing the image of deviant groups on the societal level is to achieve a redefinition of deviancy and to foster greater acceptance of some behaviors considered deviant. Teaching, demonstration, and lifestyle modelling may be necessary to convince the public that deviancy is of our own making and often is harmless. We should work for greater acceptance of differentness in modes of grooming, dressing, speaking; in skin color, race, religious and national origin; in appearance, age, sex, intelligence, and education. We also should encourage greater acceptance of physical and sensory handicap and people with epilepsy and emotional disorder.

SOCIETAL INTEGRATION AS A COROLLARY
OF NORMALIZATION

Maximal integration of the perceived or potential deviant person into the societal mainstream was established, in the preceding section, as one of the major corollaries of the principle of normalization. One major paradigm is to obtain services from generic agencies which serve the general public, rather than from special agencies which serve groups of individuals perceived as deviant. Visually limited children were once educated almost entirely by special schools or special classes; today, they are increasingly educated in the regular classroom by regular teachers who receive orientation and support from resource rooms, resource teachers, and so on.

In the past, generic services often were denied to special groups on the basis of two arguments. One was that since the generic agency did not possess the necessary skills and resources, the person with a special condition would be better served by a special service. The second argument was that certain deviant individuals should be segregated from the mainstream of society and served apart, even if not always expertly; people who were different should remain "with their own kind" — to use the popular expression. The first argument was primarily an empirical-technical one, but the second was largely value-based.

Today, we can marshal powerful empirical and programmatic arguments that segregated services, almost by their nature, are inferior services. This principle was most forcefully promulgated by the courts in regard to racial segregation; it also holds true for segregation of other minority-deviancy groups.

Programmatically, segregation is self-defeating in any context that claims to be habilitational, which includes special education. If we are serious about preparing a person toward independence and normative functioning, we must prepare him to function in the context of the ordinary societal contacts which he is expected to handle adaptively in the future. Much of our rehabilitation human management, and especially traditional special education and rehabilitation, has been weak in preparing persons for normative functioning. Training often took place in an artificial, segregated, and non-normative context; at the end of the training period came a precipitous transfer into realistic normative societal settings. The fact that our failure rates have not been higher is due more to the resilience of man than to the merit of our practices. Programs that fail to incorporate a relatively demanding pace of carrying clients stepwise and increasingly into culturally normative contexts and activities are, by their very nature, not genuinely habilitational.

The arguments involving primarily issues of values have also changed. One of these arguments is that unless a person is a proven menace, he cannot be separated from society by fiat, merely because his presence is inconvenient or unpleasant. Our society is becoming more pluralistic; even the armed forces have had to accept a soldier's right to wear sideburns and peace medals. That a deviancy is harmful and warrants denial of societal participation must now be proven painstakingly, individual by individual; such a judgment no longer can be imposed upon a class of persons. Admission, and even commitment, to an institution no longer can be equated with loss of citizenship rights, as was almost universally the case in the past, especially in the field of mental retardation. Even the fact that parents are no longer held responsible for the support of handicapped offspring who have attained adulthood bespeaks subtly of a new legal interpretation of the handicapped adult; he is an adult rather than an eternally dependent child, even if he should require legal guardianship throughout his life.

The Two Integrations: Physical and Social

If integration is one of the major means for achieving and acknowledging societal acceptance, as well as for accomplishing adaptive behavior change, we must examine it closely.

First, let us define integration as those practices and measures which maximize a person's participation in the mainstream of his culture.

Ultimately, integration is meaningful only if it is social; i.e., if it involves interaction and acceptance, not merely physical presence. However, social integration can be attained only if certain preconditions exist — among these, physical integration.

Physical integration. Physical integration refers to aspects of client grouping and physical (environmental) arrangements which lay favorable groundwork for the transaction of social integration. The physical integration of a service facility is determined primarily by four factors: location, physical context, access, and group size (or dispersal).

Location — The location of services should be at the community level at which the persons are to be served, so as to facilitate the likelihood of the persons remaining in or being absorbed into the prevailing social systems. Physical isolation of settings should be avoided unless it is part of an appropriate human management model or rationale, such as a retreat camp.

Physical Context — The type of area in which the program is to be located should be consistent with the type of service to be provided; e.g., industrial park areas for vocational services, residential areas for hostels. Upper lower-class neighborhoods of medium population density with a wide array of resources (post office, stores, restaurants, libraries, churches, playgrounds, movies, etc.) probably will be capable of absorbing deviant persons at a high rate, while thinly populated upper class suburban areas beyond walking distance from community resources would be less suited.

Access — Favorable location in itself does not assume ready access, nor is remote location to be equated with poor access. Convenience of transportation and other specific circumstances must be considered.

Size, or Dispersal — These terms refer to numbers of devalued people grouped together. Every effort should be made not to congregate deviant persons in numbers larger than the surrounding social systems are likely to be able to assimilate. Instead of single large facilities, a number of modestly sized facilities should be established to permit greater normalizing dispersal within, as well as between, population centers, especially in the larger communities. Dispersal is particularly important for the numerically most-needed programs, and especially for residential services.

Social integration. A service can be optimally integrated physically, and yet suffer from extensive social segregation. Such factors as agency policy or service structures still might keep a deviant person out of the cultural mainstream, segregated from normalizing social intercourse. A person needs not only to be *in* but also *of* the community.

It would appear that once physical integration exists, social integration will be determined by at least four factors: program features affecting social interactions, labels given to services and facilities, terms applied to the clients, and the way in which the service building is perceived.

Program Features — A few examples may suffice: Handicapped children should be integrated into generic developmental day care and, as much as possible, into regular classes. Vocational training often can be provided in generic programs rather than special workshops, and in the mainstream of business and industry itself. With special effort, deviant individuals can participate in recreational activities in which they interact with ordinary people. Special support and training will enable many handicapped persons to utilize ordinary community transportation, rather than special car pools or segregated buses. The list of integrating opportunities is virtually endless — limited more by the ideology and the imagination of programmers than the extent of an individual's deviancy.

Labeling and Terminology — Social integration also is affected by the way in which clients and their families, as well as service locations and facilities, are labeled. Names and labels should be carefully considered so as to promote a role perception of the client that is valued, nondeviant, or as minimally deviant as possible.

Building Perception — Some thought also should be given to the way the physical facility is perceived by the public. The external appearance or context of a building can exert a detrimental effect upon citizens' response to the persons associated with it. For instance, a building recently used as a prison or brothel may elicit associations not conducive to integration.

The factors specified above affect not only outside observers, but also those who work with the client.

Contemporary Opportunities for Integration

Educational programs. For a long time, the idea has prevailed that special education is and must be synonymous with segregated education. However, we are finding that segregation often brings with it a lowering rather than an improvement of standards; and that by the very nature of things, integrated education has certain normalizing features which can make it preferable.

In early childhood education for the handicapped, we are used to thinking mostly in terms of day care centers, nurseries, or kindergartens which either serve only the handicapped or have special sections for them. But integration at this level is relatively easy. Very young children are less perturbed by individual differences; early education programs in general have groups of mixed ages and sizes; and the programs themselves are oriented to be more individualized. Among the major benefits of early integration are the breaking down of social barriers and stereotypes for the students, as well as their parents.

Already one can note many early education programs which have included small numbers of handicapped children — although sometimes more by oversight than by design. In almost every instance I have encountered, I have been impressed with the smoothness of the integration process and the progress made by the handicapped children. At this age level, normal peers seem to be non-threatening models from which the handicapped (especially the retarded) children learn more than from their impaired peers.

In the regular grades most of the mildly impaired, and many severely impaired such as deaf and blind children, can function if additional services (e.g., resource rooms, resource teachers) are provided. Other severely impaired children, such as the severely retarded, can function in special classes integrated into regular schools. Secondary work-study programs, which often use only in-school or sheltered workshop assignments for their work training, need to emphasize assignment in business and industry instead.

Legislation along with attitudinal changes presently are opening up new integrative vistas in vocational education. The option now exists to incorporate within the mainstream of the rapidly expanding vocational education field much of what was previously done in the stigma-attached field of rehabilitation or in secondary special education.

It is gratifying to note that in the future, integrated special education will become better and easier to accomplish if all education becomes "special," as we move more and more from lockstep teaching to individualization of the learning-teaching process. Vast improvements in the educational manpower structure already have taken place, and such improvements can make for better and more individualized education. Other developments will be the increased availability of new and better educational aids, the use of computer assisted and managed instruction, and new administrative methods of structuring the educational process. As all education becomes special, grade leveling and grouping of children, as we now know it, should disappear. Integration no longer will present the problems it does today.

Industry-integrated work stations. For many years we have aspired to the establishment of more vocational service centers ("workshops") which would offer vocational evaluation, training, long-term employment, and possibly other vocation-related services, either to the handicapped in general or to special handicapped groups. The need for workshop places for the retarded sometimes was estimated to be as high as 1.4 for every 1,000 population (e.g., Goodwill Industries of America, 1961). The concept of "integration" was used mostly to refer to integration of one handicapped group with other groups perceived as deviant, as in a generic (Goodwill-type) workshop.

Actually, from a normalization (though not always economic) viewpoint, little can be gained by favoring a generic over a specialty workshop. In the generic center a deviant person would still be grouped with others similarly perceived (e.g., the retarded, blind, emotionally disturbed). On the other hand, integration of a deviant worker with typical workers in business and industry would constitute a major normalizing advance.

The time has come to establish the functions of the "sheltered workshop" within the confines of specific firms, right on the work floor. Service systems can rent floor space from factories, often for nominal sums. "Segregated" work space can serve for initial placement of trainees or workers, with integration restricted to space and functions associated with the time clock, the toilets, and the cafeteria and/or canteen area. After a period of transition, some handicapped workers can be integrated directly onto the work floor. Many eventually will achieve a normative level of production and will become eligible to be hired in the regular job market.

Establishment of work stations in industry can reduce the need for special and segregated services considerably. In 1968 the plan for comprehensive mental retardation services in Douglas County, Nebraska, called for five vocational service centers with a total of about 340 places (Menolascino, Clark, & Wolfensberger, 1968). Later, the staff of this service system concluded that with the establishment of a number of industrial work stations, only one or two vocational service centers for the retarded may suffice.

Integrating residences for special-need groups. Utilization of adoptive, foster, and boarding placement for handicapped children (even the profoundly retarded) is most desirable. In addition, much community integration of the handicapped can be achieved by small, homelike group residences and highly dispersed special apartments.

Even where community-integrated group residences are established, the possibility is seldom considered that integration can also be achieved within the residence itself. For instance, two or three mature college students might share an apartment with two or three retarded persons working in competitive industry or in sheltered situations. A college might lease some rooms to be used by handicapped young adults on a temporary basis while they are training in a vocational center. Group homes might serve both handicapped and homeless non-handicapped children, instead of only the handicapped. Public housing might be designed from the very beginning to accommodate both the impaired and the unimpaired (e.g., Klein & Abrams, 1971).

The objection is sometimes heard that the handicapped do not want to be integrated. Often, this is a defensive claim, advanced to avoid having to pursue such integration. One survey of 658 handicapped persons (Columbus & Fogel, 1971) certainly suggests that lack of opportunity is a greater factor than lack of desire.

Miscellaneous areas ready for integration. It is absurd to build expensive dental suites and surgical operating theaters specifically for the retarded or disturbed, as is done in so many institutions. Today, we conduct special camps for the handicapped and reserve bowling alleys and swimming pools for them. Often, such segregation is practiced from failure to pursue a strategy of integration consciously and systematically. Why not reserve a few bowling lanes dispersed among the others? Why not go swimming in small groups so as not to reserve an entire pool? With a few extra counselors, a modest number of handicapped persons can be integrated into regular camping activities. In the early 1970s, about 25 social clubs for young people in Stockholm, Sweden, had memberships which were balanced evenly between the retarded and the non-retarded, and in which the retarded acquired a vast range of normative skills by imitation.

Nowhere is integration more appropriate than in an atmosphere where the emphasis is on the essence rather than the accidents of man's nature, as in religious worship and instruction. Here, much integration can be accomplished by thoughtful planning. Of course, no community has enough churches to integrate the thousands of retarded or disordered persons who may be congregated in a nearby institution. In religion, as elsewhere, integration is feasible only if the persons who are perceived as deviant are dispersed.

REFERENCES

Bank-Mikkelsen, N.E. A metropolitan area in Denmark: Copenhagen. In R. Kugel & W. Wolfensberger (Eds.), *Changing patterns in residential services for the mentally retarded.* Washington, DC: President's Committee on Mental Retardation, 1969, pp. 227-254.

Berelson, B., & Steiner, G. *Human behavior: An inventory of scientific findings.* New York: Harcourt, Brace, & World, 1964.

Columbus, D., & Fogel, M.L. Survey of disabled persons reveals housing choices. *Journal of Rehabilitation,* 1971, *37*(2), 26-28.

Dybwad, G. Action implications, U.S.A. today. In R. Kugel & W. Wolfensberger (Eds.), *Changing patterns in residential services for the mentally retarded.* Washington, DC: President's Committee on Mental Retardation, 1969, pp. 383-428.

Goodwill Industries of America. *A report on the institute on sheltered workshop services for the mentally retarded.* Washington, DC: GIA, 1961.

Klein, S.D., & Abrams, S.L. Public housing for handicapped persons? *Journal of Rehabilitation,* 1971, *37* (2), 20-21.

Kolstoe, O.P. An examination of some characteristics which discriminate between employed and non-employed mentally retarded males. *American Journal of Mental Deficiency,* 1961, *66,* 472-482.

Kugel, R., & Wolfensberger, W. (Eds.). *Changing patterns in residential services for the mentally retarded.* Washington, DC: President's Committee on Mental Retardation, 1969.

Menolascino, F., Clark, R.L., & Wolfensberger, W. (Eds.). *The initiation and development of a comprehensive, county-wide system of services for the mentally retarded of Douglas County* (2nd ed.). Omaha, NE: Greater Omaha Association for Retarded Children, 1968 (Vol. 1) & 1970 (Vol. 2).

Nirje, B. The normalization principle and its human management implications. In R. Kugel & W. Wolfensberger (Eds.), *Changing patterns in residential services for the mentally retarded.* Washington, DC: President's Committee on Mental Retardation, 1969, pp. 179-195.

Parsons, T., & Fox, R. Illness, therapy, and the modern urban American family. In E. G. Jaco (Ed.), *Patients, physicians and illness.* Glencoe, IL: Free Press, 1958, pp. 234-245.

Rubin, R., & Balow, B. Learning and behavior disorders: A longitudinal study. *Exceptional Children,* 1971, *38,* 293-299.

Talbot, J.A. Community psychiatry in the army: History, practice, and applications to civilian psychiatry. *Journal of the American Medical Association,* 1969, *210,* 1233-1237.

Wolfensberger, W., & Glenn, L. *Program Analysis of Service Systems (PASS): A method for the quantitative assessment of human services,* Vol. I. Washington, DC: Institute on Mental Retardation, 1975.

18

Normalizing Activation for the Profoundly Retarded and/or Multiply Handicapped

Wolf Wolfensberger

To many readers, it may come as a surprise to hear that mental retardation was a dynamic and change-oriented field between about 1850 and 1920, because after that time it lay dormant for almost 40 years. This stagnation was due to the dissipation of dynamism during the frenzy of the "genetic alarm period" (circa 1890-1920), when it was thought that mental retardation was the mother of all social ills and could destroy our society. In the early 1950's, dynamism slowly began to return to the field, and bold leaders began to stake

This chapter, in somewhat modified and more extensive form, was originally published in Wolf Wolfensberger, *The Principle of Normalization in Human Services*, Toronto: Canada National Institute on Mental Retardation, 1972. The author acknowledges Rosemary and Gunnar Dybwad, Karl Grunewald, Una Haynes, Elsie Helsel, Robert Kugel, and Robert Perske for substantial critiques of earlier drafts of this work.

out new frontiers for action, such as special education for the mildly retarded.

A more recent frontier has been educational services for the severely impaired — the subject of this chapter. Although the decisive battle for inclusion in educational programs has been won, sizeable mop-up operations remain. One of the newest areas of activity is the reform of residential services. Scandinavians refer to their approach of intensive programming for the severely impaired as "activation." The term refers not only to the involvement of persons in meaningful, and hopefully normalizing, activities but also, to a significant degree, motor involvement and ambulation, or at least mobility.

THE TRAGEDY OF THE UNACTIVATED

Today, in many of our traditional mental retardation institutions and even in some newer residential centers, we still see acres of beds occupied by individuals who are not ambulatory, who spend virtually their entire time in bed, and who — for the most part — are profoundly retarded. Sometimes a superintendent may challenge his staff to "get them out of bed," but the staff may be so little attuned to the growth potential of the retarded or nonambulatory that little more may be done than to transfer the resident from the bed to the floor. When the next challenge to "get them off the floors" is issued, the nonambulatory residents may be placed on raised, table-like platforms. But neither on the floor nor on the platform may the residents be activated any more than in their beds. Even placement in wheelchairs may lose most of its meaning if this is not accompanied by additional measures.

Some interesting data have been provided by a number of studies. In a survey of 22 Western state institutions (Payne, Johnson, & Abelson, 1969), 24% of the 24,257 residents (an astounding total of 5,943) were found to be nonambulatory. Also remarkable was the fact that the nonambulatory population was reported to be as low as about 2% in one institution, and as high as 96% in another.

In a survey of 26,000 residents of New York State institutions for the retarded (Rosenberg, 1969), 46% were judged to require "substantial medical or nursing care," 24% had to be bathed or dressed, and 14% could not ambulate independently.

A rather detailed survey (conducted by Craig Affleck, and reported in Governor's Citizens' Committee, 1968) of 1,908 residents at Nebraska's only, and rather typical, state institution for the retarded revealed a startling degree of behavioral inadequacy (see following table), especially if one considers that at least 77% of the residents were classified as above the profound level of retardation, and that less than 5% were below five years of age.

Percentage of Residents Needing Help at a Typical Midwestern State Institution

| Behavior | Total | Help Needed | | | |
		Consid-erable	Some	Little	None
Grooming	32%	6%	7%	14%	42%
Dressing	30%	8%	10%	13%	39%
Eating	13%	2%	3%	9%	73%
Bath-Shower	41%	6%	8%	8%	37%

The report also revealed that 4% of the residents included in the survey could not even sit up, 7% could sit up but not stand, and 3% could stand but not walk. Only 72% could negotiate stairs unsupported. Most tragically, perhaps, was the finding that 48% of the residents never left the ward, and only 30% left it regularly for at least four hours a day. These percentages assume special meaning when one considers the number of individuals involved, and the congregation of these large numbers of individuals into large groups. For instance, most of the individuals who could not sit up (4%, or 78 persons) were found in two living units.

There has been relatively little or diminishing controversy that much could be accomplished with the mildly, moderately, and even severely retarded residents of our institutions. There also has been growing awareness, especially in recent years, that a much larger percentage of the ambulatory severely and profoundly retarded could be toilet trained. (For purely historical reasons, toilet training has become somewhat of a fixation of behavior shaping approaches.) However, when it comes to the nonambulatory retarded, especially the nonambulatory profoundly retarded, widespread acquiescence still prevails to the inevitability of their helplessness. Also, one encounters the attitude that the normalization principle loses its applicability as one deals with more severely impaired individuals.

Indeed, some well-meaning analyses in recent years have even contributed to this fatalism. For instance, several writers in recent years have documented that institutional admissions have tended toward younger and more seriously impaired individuals.[1] However, rather than sounding a call for extra measures of activation to meet this challenge, most of these projections implied a need to prepare hospital-like wards and nursing homes for permanently invalid and helpless individuals, many of whom were expected to spend their lives hovering near death.

To many, death has come swiftly and — under the circumstances — mercifully. The magnitude of the death rate after admission, though incredibly high, has received little attention in the field, perhaps because the reality was too unpleasant to contemplate. One review (Kurtz & Wolfensberger, 1969) found that children's mortality in the first year of institutional residence was sometimes near 50%.

---

[1]There is reason to believe that this trend has stabilized (Wolfensberger, 1971).

However, a time trend study (Tarjan, Brooke, Eyman, Suyeyasu, & Miller, 1968; Tarjan, Eyman, & Miller, 1969) suggested that even when younger and more handicapped persons are admitted, first-year mortality can be reduced sharply, apparently as a result of a more aggressive medical treatment policy. Thus, high death rates do not have to be accepted as inevitable concomitants of resident characteristics.

THE CHALLENGE OF THE SCANDINAVIAN EXPERIENCE

We have had so much to learn from Scandinavian services to the retarded that an irrational defensive backlash sometimes can be noted. At some professional and even parent meetings, one merely has to make a reference to the Scandinavian model to feel a wave of resentment, or to note members of the group tuning out.

On my visit to Scandinavia in 1969, I experienced some new and profound insights, even though I had seen literally dozens of slide presentations on Scandinavian services, heard Scandinavian leaders talk, and had interacted intensively with them on a personal and collaborative basis (see Bank-Mikkelsen, 1969; Grunewald, 1969; Nirje, 1969a, 1969b). I saw both activation and normalization carried to degrees I had not believed possible, and I can only conclude that for the vast majority of persons professionally "reared" in North America, no amount of verbal and pictorial communication can equal the learning (almost conversion) impact of a visit to Scandinavia. Some critics who hasten to point to weaknesses in the Scandinavian systems — and I believe some rather obvious weaknesses do exist — fail to recognize the overwhelming reality of the pervasiveness of activation. Thus, the pictures one sees at the Scandinavian travelogue lectures are not isolated examples and showcases; they are rather typical and actually quite inadequate documentations of the scenes one encounters again and again throughout these service systems.

Activation is merely one of many expressions of the ideology of normalization. But to see the normalization principle implemented, especially via activation, demonstrates that the Scandinavians do not merely have ideas and ideals — they have proven on a broad scale that this state of mind can be converted into concrete external realities.

The fact that profound retardation need not be so extensively equated with immobility was poignantly brought home to me by observing a particular living unit in a Scandinavian institution which was actually rather backward by Scandinavian standards. In this unit, 60 of 68 adult residents were not toilet trained, but only one was chronically bedfast, and only about 12 were wheelchair-bound; the rest were ambulatory. A situation such as this would not be particularly remarkable in Canada or the United States, except that in this institution of 650, these were the most retarded and impaired persons to be found!

When visiting Scandinavian institutions, I made a special point to seek out the living units for the most problematic and retarded persons — the kind of living units every administrator feels a bit uneasy about. In one modern institution for over 350 residents, visited in mid-afternoon, I searched high and low but found only three persons lying in bed. Even in a larger and more traditional institution of approximately 1,000, only about 20 residents were in bed, and most of these were sick that day. Many more were nonambulatory, but they were up and about in wheelchairs, walkers, sitters, standers, and what have you, doing things and going places. In some living units it was hard to get around because of all the wheelchairs and special devices — acres of full beds replaced by acres of activation equipment!

Also of interest was a policy in some institutions of distributing nonambulatory residents around the various buildings instead of concentrating them into one unit. The rationale is twofold: Concentration of the most helpless residents into one area creates an attitude of defeatism and apathy in the staff, as we so well know; and dispersal among ambulatory residents brings the nonambulatory person into a more normalizing atmosphere in which he is both expected

334

and apt to participate more, move more, and perhaps become ambulatory or at least mobile, without necessarily affecting the normalization of less handicapped residents.

Another result of both normalization and activation in Scandinavia is noteworthy: One will no longer see the enlarged heads resulting from hydrocephaly. Today, operations are performed in apparently all instances before the head enlarges. What a contrast that is with our attitudes which, to this day, devalue such operations for retarded or presumed retarded persons. We live with the results of these attitudes: Even in 1976, we still can find rows of beds with helpless persons, grotesquely enlarged heads, grievous bed sores, and progressive deterioration — all this leading to the creation of major and expensive nursing problems, lack of learning in the child, and deprivation of social acceptance, potential mobility, and even of life itself.

A NORTH AMERICAN COUNTER-CHALLENGE

I found it remarkable that the Scandinavians could achieve so much ambulation, mobility, and normalization even without the application of operant conditioning which we have come to look upon as our only or major tool in improving the competence of the severely retarded. Furthermore, while much work is done with children, the Scandinavians, like ourselves, have only begun to exploit the plasticity of early childhood for developmental purposes.

These observations have led me to conclude that even the Scandinavians are nowhere near the limit of what can be achieved. Therefore, I have formulated a bold — perhaps foolhardy — challenge to ourselves: to perceive and embrace a concept of activation which includes as a major goal the *virtually total abolition of immobility and, to a large extent, nonambulation of the profoundly retarded and multiply handicapped.*

I feel that the facts justify the conclusion that the service system which will combine operant shaping techniques, activation, normalization, and intensive emphasis upon the

335

young (age 0-6) impaired child will see successes of a degree beyond our power to conceptualize at this time. Among these successes will also be the prevention of intellectual retardation in many severely cerebral palsied children, and the raising of intellectual functioning of many young retarded children by one, two, and perhaps even more levels (a level having a range of about 15-16 IQ points).

Is this an unreasonable prediction? The Scandinavians with whom I discussed it did not think so, and on the abstract level, most North American workers would probably agree, too. I was amused by the fact that some of my Scandinavian friends, basking in the glory of their programs, seem to be looking over their shoulders with some unease. As one of them put it: "Once the Americans discover what can be done, and put their energy and money to it, they will not merely catch up with us, but overtake us, and even finally leave us far behind."

I believe this view has much validity, and that we can bring about this state. However, all of us, and Americans in particular, must divest ourselves of the widespread delusion that money is the solution to all problems. With all the money in the world, we shall achieve nothing unless our ideology tells us what to do. I have seen one attendant sit and stare from behind a glass wall at a vast day room with 50 children milling purposelessly, and I have seen the same scene with seven attendants sitting and staring. Money for 50 attendants would have yielded no additional benefits, because there would have been no ideology to convert the money or the manpower into beneficial action and tangible results.

Perhaps for the first time, we now have some comparative data to support objectively some of the impressions gained by visiting Swedish mental retardation services. The mental retardation office of the Swedish National Board of Health and Welfare conducted a national survey of movement-impaired retarded persons in 161 residences for the retarded all over Sweden (Wallner, 1970), accommodating a total of 12,338 persons. Only 382 persons were defined as "bed-lyers." Even among these, 34% got out of bed at least 6 hours a day, 24% got out 7 hours, and 17% got out up to 8 hours. Only 126 (33%) never left the bed. Furthermore, 117 (31%) were below age 10, and only 37 (10%) were above age 60, bearing testimony to the effects of activating programs earlier in their lives.[2]

When these figures for a population of 8 million compare with figures available on Nebraska (population of 1.5 million), we find that Nebraska has a rate of approximately 0.00024 bedfast or nearly bedfast retarded persons, versus 0.000048 for Sweden; i.e., *five times as many* at a comparable point in time. I would not be surprised if more precise comparisons should reveal an even larger difference.

It seems fairly evident that Scandinavians have virtually solved the problem of non-mobility. Why do we have so many people who see no alternatives to our current practices? More than money, we need an ideology, an attitude, a conviction, a determination!

HOW IS ACTIVATION TO BE ACHIEVED?

Some approaches to activation have been mentioned above, and, obviously, intensive environmental enrichment and systematic developmental programming are the general means of activation. However, seven specific vehicles will be elaborated upon: physical therapeutics, a movement-oriented curriculum, emphasis on younger children, operant shaping, developmental materials, special developmental environments, and developmental role perceptions.

Physical Therapeutics

In the last decade, our institutions usually have laid claim to a medical model without being able to deliver either the

---

[2]Higher mortality in Sweden can almost certainly be ruled out as an explanation for the low number of inactive aged.

needed quantity or quality of medical services. An example (if any is really needed) has already been cited: the almost incredibly high mortality rates of those persons newly admitted to institutions, especially of those admitted at an early age (see review by Kurtz & Wolfensberger, 1969). To give another example: In 1962, George A. Andrews conducted a survey determining the availability of various therapies to the multihandicapped residents of our institutions. He concluded that two-thirds of the institutions were providing mainly custodial care for such persons (cited in Stimson, 1967).

Paradoxically, now that we are moving away from medical models and toward adoption of developmental models, we may be able to include in them a medical component of adequate quantity and high quality. Within this medical component, outstanding glory can be earned by what I will loosely call "physical therapeutics." By this, I mean primarily orthopedics and physiatry, and related areas such as orthotics and physical therapy.

Orthopedic surgery has been widely withheld from the retarded because of judgments that such surgery was "wasted," particularly for the severely and profoundly retarded. In part, this was a dehumanizing value judgment; but in part, it was also an accurate empirical judgment because of the lack of appropriate therapeutic follow-up without which surgery is largely meaningless.

One major element of such follow-up consists of the design and supervised use of devices which enable, support, enhance, or encourage sitting, standing, walking, mobility, and other adaptive behaviors. Turning frames prepare for standing and can enhance educational participation of the totally nonambulatory. Corsets, braces, and orthopedic shoes help develop erect posture, sitting, and standing, as do various types of chairs such as "relaxation chairs." Cutout, stand-in, and standing tables, as well as standing stabilizers, support or develop sustained standing behavior and thereby prepare for walking. Walking aids include suspension devices, skid walkers, infant walkers, C.P. walkers, walkerettes, and diverse types of gliders and crutches. A multitude of wheeled equipment, such as specially designed "belly-boards," velocipedes, tricycles, and trainer bicycles provide playful mobility, as well as excellent activating experiences to children. The ways in which wheelchairs for adults can be modified appear to be limitless.

The list could go on. There is nothing new about any of these devices — except that one sees them used only moderately in retardation, and even less so with the young and/or severely damaged retarded person. It is time to introduce to the field of mental retardation the ingenuity practiced in the mainstream of orthopedics, orthotics, and physiatry, and to correlate, even integrate, these aspects closely with other medical and behavioral measures.

Another element of follow-up is physical therapy. Here, we not only need *more* — we need a new model. Because of manpower shortage, the physical therapy needs of the retarded may be neither met nor meetable via traditional methods of practice. What is probably needed are large numbers of technicians working under the direction of qualified therapists who themselves rarely engage in direct therapy, except for teaching and demonstration purposes. Also, physical therapists must begin to become effective consultants to educational programs and thus "multiply" themselves indirectly.

Young children and the multiply handicapped have the most urgent needs of physical therapy. An early investment here will repay itself manifold.

A Movement-Oriented Educational Curriculum

Our educational programs must be revised. We should introduce more movement and rhythmics and modify our methods so that content now taught with little utilization of perceptual-motor processes is taught in more extensive association with them. Many such methods, and even entire systems, exist. However, such methods often have been developed and described in isolation rather than in a systematic context, and the systems themselves often have been idiosyncratic or dogmatic, thereby scaring away many potential users.

For instance, many creative methods have been developed within the Doman-Delacato system, but its quite unnecessary theoretical framework, the dogmatic isolation of the system, and its advocacy of certain (actually, a very small number of) techniques generally held to be ineffective or possibly even harmful has driven away many potential users. The materials and methods developed within the Kephart system have suffered from unnecessarily close association with the concepts of brain injury. One of the more promising approaches appears to be that of Barsch (1967), whose term "movigenics" I am tempted to apply broadly to what I have called a "movement-oriented curriculum." Another term and concept I find useful is Asher's (1969) "total physical response technique."

One of the major ways of fusing traditional content with physical activation is via the introduction of music, song, and eurhythmics. Musical rhythmics has the advantage of being not only exceedingly activating, but also very enjoyable. However, it would have to consist of more than the undisciplined movements our teachers tend to accept uncritically in the typical musical action exercises observed in our classrooms. Increased and more systematized use of music is one of the latent, undiscovered giants of North American education.

Emphasis on Younger Children

The younger the person, the more effective are activating measures likely to be. Virtually everybody agrees to this, but far too little is done about it. We still exclude severely retarded children from programs because they are not toilet trained, or for the supreme absurdity: because they are not old enough. The myth still lingers that formal programming should wait for some type of "natural" maturation process to have run its course; and somehow, the largely coincidental legal school entry age of ordinary children is still widely perceived as the minimum age for initiating formal programming for the severely impaired.

Activating programming must begin as early as developmental retardation or impairment is recognized. For many types of learning, sensitive or even critical periods exist, and a year's intensive activation at age two or three may be worth two or three years at age eight, or a lifetime at age twelve.

Here is where the rapidly developing early childhood education movement in North America could out-perform the Scandinavians, who provide relatively little early programming to retarded children outside of institutions. Within institutions, early programming focuses more on social and physical development; it is not yet deliberately and consciously oriented to the actual shaping of intellect.

However, in order to institute intensive early activation, we shall need either better early case findings or universal early education, or both. Early case findings will require much reeducation of pediatricians and general practitioners. Fortunately, the prospects for universal early childhood education are favorable, and we probably shall see gradual lowering of public education entry ages down to age three, and perhaps even two.

Operant Shaping

While operant and related principles usually have been present in inarticulated form in all good programming, they only recently have been formally recognized in Scandinavian services. Yet, with its pragmatic ideology and methods, operant shaping — and especially the "precision teaching" version elaborated by O. R. Lindsley — is an approach of vast potential. We now have adequate foundations in this approach so that it could be massively injected into our service systems. However, we must address ourselves consciously to using operant principles in a way which minimizes dehumanizing and artificial elements and features, and which are not only normalizing but also normalized.

Furthermore, we must be aware of the danger inherent in a merely superficial faddish and ritualistic application of operant principles. Today, many programs pay lip service to operant principles and purport to apply them, but the staff may lack understanding of and training in such principles, or commitment to them. Thus, their work can only be described as constituting desultory and cavalier dabbling in operant shaping, and can be harmful to the entire system, which may be judged and condemned because of the failure of its unskilled and mindless application. Also, proponents of operant shaping systems must recognize the limitations as well as the strengths of these techniques and the need to employ additional means, even if these are not yet (or ever will be) as operationally specifiable as the parameters which have prominence in operant conditioning.

Developmental Materials

Many new and good developmental materials have been introduced in just the last few years, but more are needed. Also, their existence and use must be communicated better. Educational material centers in the United States must give up their roles as relatively ineffective and passive depositors and exhibitors of materials, and assume the role for which they were largely created — namely, that of evaluators and experimenters. Indeed, considering the vast sums of money expended on them, they have the responsibility of becoming innovators!

Special Developmental Environments

Examples of special developmental environments are the prototype playground for the retarded designed by a Canadian (Hayden, 1969) under the auspices of the Kennedy

Foundation; the "model recreational park" depicted in the 1968 report of the President's Committee on Mental Retardation; and Heather's (1970) playground garden. Another example is an experimental residential and learning environment designed by the British architect Kenneth Bayes, as presented at the 1969 convention of the National Association for Retarded Children. Also, a number of operant living (e.g., Roberts & Perry, 1970) and workshop environments (e.g., Gardner, 1971)[3] have been designed and described in the literature. Such experimental models need to be extended, made routinely functional, and applied to even the most severely impaired (e.g., Ricke et al., 1967).

On the horizon are automated environments which conjoin the potentials of operant shaping, environmental engineering, and computer technology. The "responsive autotelic environment" ("talking typewriter") developed by O. K. Moore has been an example of a step in this direction, as is the PLAYTEST system developed by B. Friedlander, which automates the shaping of infants' behavior right in their own cribs.

Developmental Role Perceptions

One of the major facts established by social psychologists is that people generally will play the social role that is assigned to them. Social roles can be demanding, and can motivate individuals to virtually "rise above themselves"; or they can be degrading or indulgent, and elicit only a fraction of the behavioral potential of a person. Indeed, role expectancies can even reduce a person so that he will function far below a previous level.

In the past we have imposed extremes of role expectations upon retarded (and often other handicapped) persons. We either demanded normal role performance in all or most aspects of functioning, or we imposed dehumanizing (or at

---

[3]This book contains a chapter on an operant workshop.

least very undemanding) expectations, as when we viewed a retarded person as an "eternal child." To this day, the vast majority of child development and special education programs for the younger retarded are merely advanced babysitting, compared to what could and should be done.

To change the unrealistic developmental role perceptions that have been common in our service systems during the last 40 years will be most difficult unless we take radical measures. To do this, we must distinguish between *higher* expectancies, and *normal* ones; we must distinguish between various areas of functioning; and then we must impose *realistically high* and *occasionally normal* expectancies on *selected* areas and *selected* individuals. We must work, with the aid of our services, toward the handicapped attaining their potential, and we must formulate roles for them that discourage dependency and encourage growth.

Perhaps one of the major ways of achieving this goal is to integrate the physically handicapped with the physically sound, and the mentally retarded with those of higher functioning. Instead of putting all the nonambulatory together into one sea of beds, we should experiment with dispersal of the nonambulatory among the ambulatory, and bestow mobility upon the nonambulatory even if this sometimes means no more than wheelchair mobility. As expectations rise, so will performance, growth, and independence.

We are rather apt to view Scandinavian socialism as leading to pampering, and as imposing low expectations in regard to work and initiative. Yet when it comes to making the retarded ambulatory, the Danes and Swedes become almost fierce in their determination. Their successes prove that their high expectancies for mobility and ambulation have not been unrealistic.

INTERRELATIONSHIPS AMONG ACTIVATING MEASURES

An element which is implicit in virtually all of the mechanisms of activation is *individualization of approach*. Thus, gadgetry and therapeutic appliances may have to be individually designed, fitted, and used; some activities and exercises will have to be planned on an individual basis; schedules of activities will have to vary greatly for different persons; and so forth. This need for individualization has certain secondary implications to our residential centers, where the majority of the severely multiply handicapped retarded live. One of these implications is the need for small living units in order to prevent the otherwise virtually unavoidable — almost "natural" — tendency to regiment large groups, and to manage them according to their lowest common denominator.

Of major importance is the intermeshing of all aspects of activation. These various aspects are not merely additive, but often profoundly interdependent. Orthopedic surgery without physical therapy is largely wasted; physical therapy without orthopedic surgery cannot attain its potential; failure to combine both of these approaches with general environmental enrichment, especially via education (in the broad sense), is grossly inefficient; and so on.

One issue of particular timeliness is the integrated use of physical therapy. Physical therapy practices are still heavily influenced by the polio era, when a major challenge was the strengthening of muscles in individuals who were generally of sound mind. With the passing of this challenge, a new major one today is posed by individuals of severely impaired mentality and with brain injury, who must develop control and coordination of movement, and not merely muscular strength. It is not enough to provide physical therapy for them in the typical isolated settings, in special rooms, and at special times. Having a limb "pumped" or "cranked" sporadically by a therapist is of little avail. If physical therapy is to be fully relevant to them, it must become a part of daily living, and therefore must be practiced by all those who work with the handicapped person, particularly teachers. A commitment to such a conceptualization would imply a profound change in the functioning of many of our physical therapists and other workers.

345

By incorporating a heavier movement element and emphasis into our other educational approaches, we are not merely adding content, and not merely adding economy by combining the learning of motor and other elements; we also are reaping the benefits of growth in those perceptual-motor processes which underlie or even constitute what we call intelligence. Many of these processes, though both essential and shapable, have been neglected in our traditional approaches.

Another by-product that can be expected from activation is strengthening of the body image. In turn, this should result in increased self-confidence and better emotional adjustment.

After reaching its limits, physical therapeutics may still leave the person without having attained full and independent mobility. In such cases, we must strive not merely to maintain the highest level of mobility, but to maximize other kinds of activation and development. For instance, in Scandinavia I saw many severely retarded nonambulatory children attending school on special beds, in wheelchairs, and in standing tables. In some cases these devices were intended not so much to be physically therapeutic but to permit *other* developmental activities to take place. One device (now seen occasionally in North America) was a hoist that could be rolled about, and that could be used to hoist a nonambulatory person from his bed by means of a variety of special-purpose slings, roll him over a bathtub or toilet, and thereby permit him to perform his own bathing or toileting. In North America we would see most such persons in bed with a bedpan, washed with a sponge, or — if "fortunate" — washed on a slab like a corpse. The hoist and its accessories permit the person to gain the dignity of learning to perform these highly personal functions independently and in private.

Just as physical therapeutics can be a means for shaping mentality to enable a multiply handicapped child to attain his full intellectual potential, so can lack of physical maintenance produce tragic mental debilitation.

ACTIVATION ACTION

Fortunately, there are stirrings on the frontier of activation. There is increasing concern with physical fitness of the retarded. An entire new movement originated in Canada, especially with Hayden (1964). This movement was taken up by the Kennedy Foundation in the United States and the Harry E. Foster Foundation in Canada, and has resulted in many developments, including the Special Olympics movement. This emphasis also has stimulated the American and Canadian Associations for Health, Physical Education, and Recreation to become involved in the area, and to issue a series of highly useful publications which are concerned with activating procedures and methods.

There also has been a relatively sudden increase in the number of publications concerned with the movement-mediated development of retarded or otherwise handicapped persons. In Europe, perceptual-motor and movement-related approaches to education have been part of the educational mainstream for over a century. These approaches typically involve a great deal of rhythmics and gymnastics, not only to a degree unknown in North America, but also tied to a large number of developmental theories and sub-theories. We are beginning to rediscover the importance of these approaches which previously had probably their most effective proponent in Seguin (e.g., Talbot, 1969).

Attention to the physical therapy and orthopedic needs of the young and profoundly retarded has increased. Unfortunately, advances along these lines often occur in an imbalanced fashion, underlining the lack in understanding of the interplay among developmental areas. Thus, I have seen institutional programs in which outstanding work was done in corrective and orthopedic surgery, but in the virtual absence of a physical therapy and environmental enrichment program which would have brought to fruition the orthopedic investment. Nevertheless, the many fledgling trends on all horizons are encouraging harbingers of a whole new vista.

REFERENCES

Asher, J.J. The total physical response technique of learning. *Journal of Special Education*, 1969, 3, 253-262.

Bank-Mikkelsen, N.E. A metropolitan area in Denmark: Copenhagen. In R. Kugel & W. Wolfensberger (Eds.), *Changing patterns in residential services for the mentally retarded*. Washington, DC: President's Committee on Mental Retardation, 1969, pp. 227-254.

Barsch, R.H. *Achieving perceptual-motor efficiency: A space-oriented approach to learning*. Seattle: Special Child Publications, 1967.

Gardner, W.I. *Behavior modification in mental retardation: The education and rehabilitation of the mentally retarded adolescent and adult*. Chicago: Aldine-Atherton, 1971.

Governor's Citizens' Committee on Mental Retardation. *The report of the Nebraska Citizens' Study Committee on Mental Retardation*, Vol. 2. Lincoln, NE: State Department of Public Institutions, 1968.

Grunewald, K. A rural county in Sweden: Malmohus County. In R. Kugel & W. Wolfensberger (Eds.), *Changing patterns in residential services for the mentally retarded*. Washington, DC: President's Committee on Mental Retardation, 1969, pp. 255-287.

Hayden, F.J. *Physical fitness for the mentally retarded: A manual for teachers and parents*. Toronto: Metropolitan Toronto Association for Retarded Children, 1964.

Hayden, F.J. *Learn to play center*. Washington, DC: The Joseph P. Kennedy, Jr. Foundation, 1969.

Heather, D. Design for play. *Teaching and Training*, 1970, 8, 6-10.

Kurtz, R.A., & Wolfensberger, W. Separation experiences of residents in an institution for the mentally retarded: 1910-1959. *American Journal of Mental Deficiency*, 1969, 74, 389-396.

Nirje, B. A Scandinavian visitor looks at U.S. institutions. In R. Kugel & W. Wolfensberger (Eds.), *Changing patterns in residential services for the mentally retarded*. Washington, DC: President's Committee on Mental Retardation, 1969, pp. 51-57(a).

Nirje, B. The normalization principle and its human management implications. In R. Kugel & W. Wolfensberger (Eds.), *Changing patterns in residential services for the mentally retarded*. Washington, DC: President's Committee on Mental Retardation, 1969, pp. 179-195(b).

Payne, D., Johnson, R., & Abelson, R. *A comprehensive description of institutionalized retardates in the western United States*. Boulder, CO: Western Interstate Commission for Higher Education, 1969.

President's Committee on Mental Retardation. *MR68: The edge of change*. Washington, DC: U.S. Government Printing Office, 1968.

Ricke, H.K., McDaniel, M. W., Stalling, V.D., & Gatz, M.J. Operant behavior in vegetative patients II. *Psychological Record*, 1967, 17, 449-460.

Roberts, C.D., & Perry, R.M. A total token economy. *Mental Retardation* 1970, 8(1), 15-18.

Rosenberg, A.D. *Appropriateness of the continued institutionalization of the state school population in New York state.* Buffalo: New York Department of Mental Hygiene, 1969.

Stimson, C.W. Physiatry in state institutions for the mentally retarded. *Archives of Physical Medicine and Rehabilitation,* 1967, *48,* 227-228.

Talbot, J.A. Community psychiatry in the Army: History, practice, and applications to civilian psychiatry. *Journal of the American Medical Association,* 1969, *210,* 1233-1237.

Tarjan, G., Brooke, C.E., Eyman, R.K.; Suyeyasu, A., & Miller, C.R. Mortality and cause of death in a hospital for the mentally retarded. *American Journal of Public Health,* 1968, *58,* 1891-1900.

Tarjan, G., Eyman, R.K., & Miller, C.R. Natural history of mental retardation in a state hospital, revisited: Releases and deaths in two admission groups, ten years apart. *American Journal of Diseases of Children,* 1969, *117,* 609-620.

Wallner, T. *Sängliggande utvecklingsstörda: Resultat av en enkät.* Unpublished manuscript, Stockholm, Sweden, 1970.

Wolfensberger, W. Will there always be an institution? I: The impact of epidemiological trends. *Mental Retardation,* 1971, *9*(5), 14-20.

19

Legal Change
for the Handicapped
Through Litigation

Alan Abeson

During the past few years the nation's courts have been flooded with lawsuits relating to government's responsibilities to the handicapped. The suits have focused primarily on the right of handicapped children to obtain an appropriate publicly supported education; the right to treatment, including education for institutionalized handicapped children and adults; and changing improper classification and placement practices which restrict children's opportunities to obtain an appropriate education.

The use of litigation as an avenue to achieve positive change for the handicapped stimulated a need for information about the legal issues and processes which formed the basis of

The work presented herein was performed pursuant to Grant No. DEC 0-182013-3541 (032) from the Bureau of Education, U.S. Department of Health, Education and Welfare. Points of view or opinions stated herein do not necessarily represent official Office of Education policy or position. The present version is an adaptation of the original publication by the Council for Exceptional Children in 1973.

the movement. The information in this chapter was developed to familiarize observers and participants in litigation with ways of achieving legal change for the handicapped. In no way is this material intended to represent training or preparation for legal counsel. Rather, it emphasizes the highly complex nature of procedures and strategies involved in a lawsuit.

In describing the litigation process and explaining legal terminology, this work attempts to be as thorough as possible without undue detail. Many complex areas of the law have been only lightly touched upon.

Two points about litigation must serve as introduction. Changes sought through litigation may be similar to directions the party named as "defendant" has tried to pursue but whose ability to achieve these objectives has been frustrated because of barriers such as inadequate agency commitment or financial support. In this sense, litigation (or the threat of it) may be used as a lever to bring about the action desired by both the potential defendant and plaintiff. In this regard, litigation (or the threat) may be used by potential defendants to motivate their respective agencies and policy makers to initiate the desired change.

The second major point is that litigation is not necessarily a personal attack upon parties named as defendants. Frequently, complaining parties are aware that the party named as defendant has tried to produce desired change. In some of the cases referred to, named defendants have spent days preparing defenses for the suit, and nights assisting the plaintiffs prepare their arguments. It is in the best interests of the handicapped to prevent litigation or the threat of litigation from becoming personal because, regardless of the decision, it is likely that the named defendants will retain a major role in implementing the desired change.

The status of cases referred to is subject to revision and change as the cases progress through the court system. If readers are interested in using the facts and/or outcome of a particular case as examples in other situations, attempts should be made to determine their current status.

WHEN IS LITIGATION APPROPRIATE?

Litigation (only one avenue of legal change) becomes appropriate for exceptional children when their "constitutional or statutory rights" are abridged and when administrative remedies for redress have proven either ineffective or inefficient in protecting those rights.

Because litigation is both costly and lengthy, it is usually in the best interest of all parties to first attempt other means for producing change — such as enacting legislation, changing administrative practices, and/or exhausting all administrative remedies. Not infrequently, a court will require that all administrative avenues be exhausted before legal intervention can begin.

Even when a suit is brought, it is not uncommon that many of the important issues are resolved outside of court, negotiated between the administrative agency and the complaining party. Often, to achieve a solution prior to litigation, attorneys will enter into negotiations with the responsible administrative agency to use its authority to remedy the existing situation. If the negotiations are unsuccessful, then a lawsuit to compel enforcement could follow.

WHEN IS LITIGATION USEFUL?

There are several situations in which litigation might be useful. For example: Many children identified generally or specifically as handicapped are unlawfully prevented from receiving an appropriate public education. Many children, often from low socioeconomic or minority cultures are, in violation of the due process provisions of the Constitution, classified as handicapped for the purpose of assigning them inappropriately to special education programs. Many mentally retarded persons involuntarily committed to institutions are either denied any program or provided with inadequate treatment programs, and are often subjected to conditions which may endanger their psychological and physical well-being.

An example of successful litigation to produce change concerning the rights of handicapped children is the case of *Mills* v. *Board of Education of District of Columbia* (1972). A class action suit was filed in 1971 in the District of Columbia to compel the school board to provide appropriate education for retarded, physically handicapped, emotionally disturbed, hyperactive, and all other handicapped children.

The plaintiffs charged that the city provided insufficient funds for children needing special education. Relatively small numbers of exceptional children were provided with tuition grants enabling them to obtain private instruction; others were placed in public school classes; and hundreds were forced to remain at home receiving no formal education. The suit sought to establish the constitutional right of all children to an education commensurate with their ability to learn. It was charged that although these children could profit from an education, either in regular classrooms with supportive services or in special classes adapted to their needs, they were denied admission to the public schools or excluded after admission, with no provision for alternative educational opportunities or periodic review, and with no procedural safeguards and due process of law.

In August, 1972, Federal Judge Joseph Waddy declared that exceptional children have a constitutional right to a public education, and ordered the District of Columbia to offer all children in the plaintiff class appropriate education placement within 30 days of the decision. The judge also directed the District school system to create hearing procedures under which no pupil could be suspended from school for disciplinary reasons for more than two days or placed in, denied, or transferred to and from a special education class without a hearing. This ruling has had national impact as the first court decision explicitly stating that handicapped children have a constitutional right to a public education.

The lack of funding is frequently cited by public officials as the primary reason for the absence of adequate education programs for exceptional children. In their *Mills* defense, the district school system and the school board stated that it would be impossible to provide special education for the handicapped unless Congress would appropriate millions of dollars for the purpose. The judge responded by saying, "The inadequacies of the District of Columbia public school system, whether occasioned by insufficient funding or administrative inefficiency, certainly cannot be permitted to bear more heavily on the exceptional or handicapped than on the normal child."

Another example of successful litigation concerning the rights of institutionalized handicapped adults and children is the case of *Wyatt* v. *Hardin* (1971).[1] In this case, which was unsuccessfully appealed by the State to the Fifth Circuit U.S. Appeals Court, concrete judicially enforceable standards were developed through litigation for the adequate treatment of the mentally ill and mentally retarded in two of Alabama's state institutions. It was alleged that the two state mental hospitals and a home for the mentally retarded were grossly understaffed and that the programs afforded the residents were extremely inadequate. In March 1971, a federal district court judge ruled that involuntarily committed residents in one of the mental hospitals have a constitutional right to adequate treatment and that the treatment provided in the hospital was inadequate.

Since that time, a number of expert witnesses were assembled by *amici* (friends of the court) and formulated detailed standards of adequate treatment and habilitation for the mentally ill and mentally retarded. After a series of conferences, the defendants in the case agreed to accept and implement many of these standards. To immediately bring the institution for the mentally retarded to a condition which would at least protect the physical safety of the residents, the court ordered that changes be implemented to make the buildings firesafe,

---

[1]Known as *Wyatt* v. *Stickney* prior to appeal, subsequently has been renamed as *Wyatt* v. *Aderholt* and *Wyatt* v. *Hardin*. Stickney, Aderholt and Hardin have been successive Alabama Commissioners of Mental Health.

to control the distribution of drugs, and for the state to hire 300 new employees within 30 days.

This is the first case in which a court held that the institutionalized mentally retarded have a constitutional right to adequate treatment, and the first to objectively set measurable and judicially enforceable standards for adequate treatment. The "minimum constitutional and medical" standards included establishment of individual treatment plans, minimum educational standards including teacher-student ratios and length of school days, a provision against institutional peonage (residents working for the hospital without pay), a number of protections to ensure a humane psychological environment, minimum staffing standards, and a requirement that every mentally retarded person has a right to the least restrictive setting necessary for habilitation. (This case is again in court regarding compliance with the previously established standards.)

Of course, not all litigation attempts are successful. Even with the most conscientious of attorneys, and what seems the most "noble" of causes, cases are lost. Aside from legal considerations, factors such as the judge's familiarity with and disposition toward an issue, the degree of public support for the issue, and the social and political timing for bringing the suit may all have bearing on the outcome. Even when a case is won, it may only signal the beginning of much more work to translate the victory decree into improved programs.

In other circumstances, the negative formal outcome of a lawsuit may produce a positive result. While a judge may rule against the plaintiff on the legal issue, the lawsuit may be the catalyst for initiation of fruitful negotiations and may have served to crystalize the issues in a way that stimulates public interest and, more important, public policy.

PRELIMINARY CONSIDERATIONS

Among the basic prerequisites is that the plaintiffs themselves have been injured or wronged, or those to whom they have direct relationships have been injured or wronged, so that the plaintiffs have standing to sue. Under some conditions, being a taxpayer is sufficient to establish standing for the purpose of a lawsuit. In *Rainey* v. *Watkins,* Chancery Court of Shelby County, Tennessee (March, 1973), a right-to-education case, two of the plaintiffs were taxpayers who bear the tax burden resulting from welfare assistance and institutional care for all handicapped persons who did not receive an education.

The plaintiffs initially must determine what type of relief or remedy they want the court to grant. This decision also will affect who will be named by the plaintiffs as defendants in the lawsuit.

Depending on the type of injury which the plaintiffs have suffered and the number of people who have suffered the injury, a decision must be made whether to bring an individual action or a class action lawsuit.

The plaintiffs must give extensive consideration to selection of an attorney. The defendants, if government, will be represented by attorneys employed by the state or respective local agencies. Another key step for both sides is the collection of all facts relevant to the case, and for the plaintiffs alone to establish the facts of the alleged violation.

What is a "Cause of Action"?

A lawsuit is made up of one or more issues or causes of action based on a violation of some legally protected interest. In *Mills* v. *District of Columbia,* one cause of action was the denial of an appropriate, publicly supported education to school-age handicapped children. Without an established cause of action, courts lack jurisdiction.

What is a Legally Protected Interest or Right?

Citizens and residents of the United States are guaranteed certain rights under federal and state constitutions, federal and state statutes, and state common law. In seeking to vindicate the rights of the emotionally disturbed, mentally retarded, or other handicapped persons, certain provisions of the United States Constitution and many state constitutions are relied upon, such as the right to equal protection of the law. A legally protected right is essential to the court's jurisdiction.

The Fourteenth Amendment of the United States Constitution provides: "nor shall any state . . . deny to any person within its jurisdiction the equal protection of the law." This has been interpreted to mean that it is unlawful to discriminate against a class of persons for an arbitrary or unjustifiable reason.

This is a particularly important right for exceptional children seeking appropriate education opportunities. In *Brown* v. *Board of Education* (1954), the famous desegregation case, the court said:

> In these days, it is doubtful that any child may reasonably be expected to succeed in life if he is denied the opportunity of an education. Such an opportunity, where the state has undertaken to provide it, is a right which must be made available to all on equal terms.

In the *Mills* case described earlier, this reasoning was applied directly to "exceptional children."

Another important right is that of due process of law, which is also provided by the Fourteenth Amendment of the United States Constitution. It declares that "no state may deprive any person of life, liberty, or property, without due process of law." This right encompasses both substantive and procedural due process, although the cases regarding the handicapped have involved primarily the latter area. From a procedural viewpoint, due process refers to the right to have laws applied with adequate safeguards so that a person will not be subject to arbitrary and unreasonable actions.

In *Pennsylvania Association for Retarded Children (PARC)* v. *Commonwealth of Pennsylvania* (1971 and 1972), a case similar to *Mills* regarding the right to an education for the mentally retarded, the courts ordered extensive due process procedures which provide in part that before a child can be expelled, transferred, or excluded from a public education program, that child or his parents or guardian has a right to have a fair hearing, to receive notice about the hearing, and to have counsel present at the hearing.

Forty-nine states presently have compulsory school attendance laws which define both the children who must attend school and the children who may be excluded from school. Although the statutory language differs from state to state, state laws in the past generally have allowed for the exclusion from public education of children who did not meet intellectual, social, behavioral, or physical requirements for existing education programs.

As a result of these exclusion clauses, substantial numbers of handicapped children have been denied an education. Proponents of right to education are seeking to prove such statutes illegal. For example, in *Lori Case* v. *State of California* (1972), involving the termination of the school placement (from a multihandicapped unit of the California School for the Deaf at Riverside, California) of a child diagnosed as autistic, deaf, and possibly mentally retarded, the plaintiff's attorney argued:

> *Meyer* v. *Nebraska* . . . (1923) makes clear that the Fourteenth Amendment obligates the states to guarantee to their citizens the right to learn — to "acquire useful knowledge." Since such a right necessarily requires training in the minimal skills required to acquire knowledge, it follows that the due process also requires the states to discharge the obligation of providing a minimum education to its citizens.

The *Pennsylvania* case and the *Mills* case illustrate the Court's recognition that exceptional children have a right to a publicly supported education, and to adequate procedures to ensure that proper consideration is given before any child is suspended or excluded from a public education program.

Related to that right is the right to appropriate classification; i.e., the right to be protected from inappropriate labels

359

such as "mentally retarded," "emotionally disturbed," "behavior problem," or any other term denoting education difference calling for "special" treatment.

Evidence is increasingly being collected indicating that many of children placed in special education classes, or suspended, expelled or transferred from regular public school classes are from minority and non-English speaking cultural backgrounds. Critics charge that many of these children have been classified on the basis of culturally biased tests which do not accurately indicate their learning ability.

For example, in *Diana* v. *State Board of Education* (1970), in California, 9 Mexican-American public school students from age 8 through 13, alleged that they had been inappropriately placed in classes for the mentally retarded on the basis of biased standardized intelligence tests. The plaintiffs came from home environments in which Spanish was the only or predominant language spoken. When the case was decided in 1970, the defendant school districts agreed to several procedures to ensure better placement, including testing in the children's primary language, the use of nonverbal tests, and the collection and use of extensive supporting data.

The right to treatment and the right of civilly committed persons to receive adequate and effective individualized care when placed in an institution for the mentally ill or retarded are increasingly being addressed by the courts. A case decided in the District of Columbia, *Rouse* v. *Cameron* (1966), was the first in which a court recognized that persons involuntarily hospitalized might have a constitutional right to treatment. The decision was actually based on a statutory right, guaranteed under laws of the District of Columbia.

Wyatt v. *Hardin*,[2] discussed earlier, was the first case in which a court held that institutionalized mentally ill and mentally retarded persons have a constitutional right to

---

[2]This case is discussed in detail in *Basic Rights of the Mentally Handicapped*, Mental Health Law Project (1973).

adequate treatment, and the first case to set objectively measurable and judicially enforceable standards for adequate treatment. The right to refuse treatment is now being articulated, especially in the area of behavior modification and psychosurgery.

The right to treatment has certain corollaries, some of which may appear to be in conflict. Experts who have testified in the cases to date have indicated that the right to treatment includes the right to be treated in the least restrictive setting. Evidence exists that institutionalization itself, even in a relatively good facility, can lead to deterioration and thus make it more difficult for the committed person to be released. The right to be treated in the least restrictive setting makes sense from therapeutic and fiscal viewpoints and also is consistent with an important constitutional principle: Wherever a government restricts a person's liberty against his will in order to accomplish a legitimate governmental objective, it must impose the least drastic restriction.

In *Wyatt*, the Court said:

> No person shall be admitted to the institution unless a prior determination shall have been made unless that residence in that institution is the least restrictive habilitation setting feasible for that person. No mentally retarded person shall be admitted to the institution if services in the community can afford adequate habilitation to such person.

> Residents shall have a right to the least restrictive conditions necessary to achieve the purposes of habilitation. To this end, the institution shall make every attempt to move residents from (1) more to less structured living; (2) larger to smaller facilities; (3) larger to smaller living units; (4) group to individual residence; (5) segregated from the community to integrated into the community living; (6) dependent to independent living.

The right to be free from involuntary servitude is established by the Thirteenth Amendment of the U.S. Constitution and, in the context of the handicapped, refers to deprivation of the rights of institutionalized residents who are forced to perform non-therapeutic labor without compensation. It is alleged that workers also have a statutory right under the U.S.

Fair Labor Standards Act (P.L.89-601) to payment for work which is necessary to operate the facility. This right was upheld in *Sonder* v. *Brennan* (1973). The Court ruled that:

> Economic reality is the test of employment and the reality is that many of the patient-workers perform work for which they are in no way handicapped and from which the institution derives full economic benefit. So long as the institution derives any consequential economic benefits, the economic reality test would indicate an employment relationship rather than mere therapeutic exercise. To hold otherwise would be to make therapy the sole justification for thousands of positions as dishwashers, kitchen helpers, messengers and the like.

Decisions by the United States Supreme Court have established that all constitutional rights are present rights; they must be promptly vindicated unless there is an overwhelmingly compelling reason to justify delay. For example, in *Mills*, the Court required program delivery for the affected children within 30 days.

What are the Basic Legal Approaches for a Lawsuit?

If a person's constitutional rights are violated by anyone acting under color of state law (under the authority of the state), he may bring a case. Thus, officials of government may be sued for not performing statutory obligations.

In addition to gaining recognition of specific rights for exceptional children and handicapped adults, a party might bring a common law tort action.[3] Acts constituting tort under the common law are generally of two types — intentional and negligent. Examples of the former are assault and battery, in which the defendant intended to commit the act that harmed the plaintiff. Negligent torts result from the breach of one individual's duty of ordinary care to another, and do not

---

[3]Common law is the body of law built through case decisions. A tort is a civil wrong for which a private citizen may recover money damages.

require intent. The defendant will be liable if he owes the plaintiff a duty, and his breach of that duty was the proximate cause of plaintiff's injury.

Who Can Bring a Suit?

All plaintiffs must have standing and capacity to sue. Standing means that the plaintiff himself be the one who suffered or is in immediate danger of suffering injury, or that he has a substantial interest. Parents or guardians have standing to sue in the names of their children or wards.

An individual may be outraged at conditions at a training school for the mentally retarded, but if he is not the one suffering from the conditions there, he must have the suit brought in the names of the injured children because it is their rights which are violated by the inadequate care and facilities. This rule is based upon a policy of economy and judicial resources, as well as the fact that a person directly injured will be most likely to prosecute his case with energy and diligence. In some instances, however, an organization can sue on behalf of its members, as is being done by several state associations for retarded children.

A plaintiff also must have the capacity to sue or be sued. Capacity is determined according to the laws of the area where a person resides. Infants (minors) or incompetents must have a representative sue on their behalf. The court is authorized to appoint such a representative — a "next friend" or guardian *ad litem* ("for the litigation") — if no suitable family members or friends are available to protect their interests in the litigation.

For example, *Mills* was brought on behalf of Peter Mills and six other named children of school age by their "next friends." The next friends included the children's parents or guardians, and, in their absence, the District of Columbia Welfare Rights Organization; U.S. Representative Ronald Dellums, a member of the House Committee on the District of Columbia; the Reverend Fred Taylor; and the Director of

FLOC (For Love of Children, Inc.), an organization seeking to alleviate the plight of homeless and dependent children in the District of Columbia.

How Else May One Participate in a Case if he is not Personally Injured?

It is possible to participate in a case as *amicus curiae,* or "friend of the court." The courts often will allow a party to present supporting arguments for one side of the case. This involves submitting a written brief; under extraordinary circumstances, the right to participate orally can be granted. This means that "friends" of both sides can be presented and are subject to cross-examination. Such participation was allowed in *Wyatt,* where *amici* for plaintiffs included the United States of America (the Federal Government), the American Psychological Association, the American Orthopsychiatric Association, the American Civil Liberties Union, and the American Association on Mental Deficiency, The National Association for Retarded Children, and the National Association for Mental Health.

Persons not named as plaintiffs can provide significant assistance by conducting research and fund raising.

What Kinds of Relief Will the Court Grant?[4]

In suits designed to produce social change, the following types of relief are often sought: declaratory relief, injunctive relief, stays, writs of mandamus, writs of habeas corpus, and damages. Plaintiffs seeking *declaratory relief* ask the court to state clearly to defendants that plaintiffs have certain rights.

---

[4]The focus of this chapter is *civil* litigation, in which private individuals are seeking redress of personal grievances; *criminal* litigation is where the State or the Federal Government seeks to prosecute commission of acts which have been defined as "criminal" by statute.

Injunctive relief includes temporary restraining orders and preliminary and permanent injunctions. These are all court orders requiring or forbidding certain actions. They differ in that they are issued for varying lengths of times, at various stages of the litigation process, and on the basis of varying degrees of proof.

A request for injunctive relief often accompanies a request for declaratory relief. For example, in *Harrison* v. *Michigan* (1972), brought on behalf of all handicapped children in Michigan who were denied a publicly supported education, plaintiffs asked the court to declare that the defendants' acts denied the plaintiffs' Due Process of Law and Equal Protection under the Fourteenth Amendment, and to enjoin the defendants from excluding plaintiffs and the class they represented from a regular public school placement without providing (a) adequate and immediate alternatives, including but not limited to special education, and (b) a constitutionally adequate prior hearing and periodic review of their status, progress, and the adequacy of any educational alternative.

In *Wyatt*, the court issued a temporary restraining order before the case was finally decided, requiring Alabama state officials to immediately hire 300 employees to care for institutionalized residents, because the court was convinced that the patients' lives were endangered by the existing substandard conditions of the institution.

Injunctive relief also may include appointment of a master who is given authority to take over the challenged institution or system and supervise implementation of the court's decision. Two masters were appointed by the court in PARC to oversee the implementation of the consent agreement established in this case. The appointing of a master to take over the administration of an institution is unusual.

Stays are orders delaying enforcement of judicial orders until some further step can be taken, such as appealing the decision to the next highest judicial level. In *Wyatt*, after the plaintiffs won in the district court, the defendants attempted to obtain an order staying enforcement of the district court's decision which, if implemented, would have required massive changes in the state's institutions, until the 5th Circuit Court of Appeals had reviewed the case.

Another kind of suit more infrequently used seeks a *writ of mandamus* requiring public officials to perform their legal responsibilities. *Writs of mandamus* have been sought in some states where local districts ignored statutory requirements to develop plans for the education of handicapped children. Plaintiffs may also seek a *writ of habeas corpus*, which is used to obtain release from unlawful confinement. The institutionalized petitioner in *Rouse* v. *Cameron* sought such a writ. *Habeas corpus* also can be used to protest conditions of confinement, as well as to challenge the confinement itself.

Money *damages* may also be sought. For example, in *LeBanks* v. *Spears* (1973), a class action brought on behalf of eight black children and all others similarly situated in the Parish of Orleans, Louisiana, who were allegedly labeled "mentally retarded" without valid reason or ascertainable standards and then denied a public education, each plaintiff was seeking $20,000 for the damage suffered.

The various kinds of damages include *nominal damages* awarded to a plaintiff as a token of the injury, *compensatory damages*, awarded to repay the plaintiff for the injury actually incurred, such as medical expenses and/or pain and suffering, and *punitive damages* awarded when the injury is committed maliciously or in wanton disregard of the plaintiff's interests.

In requests for relief, *court costs* and *attorneys fees* also may be sought. While court costs usually are granted to the prevailing or winning side as a matter of course, attorneys fees in the past rarely have been recoverable and usually occurred only when a statute provided for their recovery or when the court exercised its discretion to transfer the fees. Recently, however, there has been a trend on the part of the courts to award attorneys fees to lawyers representing poor clients on the theory that encouraging such private law enforcement of constitutional rights is for the good of all society and that such lawyers actually are acting as "private attorney generals." Attorneys fees were awarded by the district court in *Wyatt.*

What are a Plaintiff's Considerations in Determining Whom to Sue?

Only one defendant may be involved in a case, or several people may be responsible for alleged legal injuries. In suing a state or local government, as in *Mills,* the plaintiffs name specific persons with administrative responsibilities, and to join or include all the necessary parties having the authority to make desired changes. For example, the defendants in *Mills* included the Board of Education of the District of Columbia and its members, the Superintendent of Schools for the District and subordinate school officials, the Director of Human Resources in the District of Columbia, certain subordinate officials, and the Mayor of the District of Columbia.

The doctrine of *sovereign immunity* often is raised by state or local government units to argue that suit cannot be brought against them. This immunity, however, often is waived by statutes so that suits are possible. However, even if sovereign immunity is not waived, it usually does not affect the right to sue individual officials rather than the state itself, on the theory that officials do not have the authority to act or are acting beyond their authority. Most state and federal officials have immunity from tort actions for money damages, for negligent or wrongful acts, for omissions committed within the scope of their employment, or for failure to use due care in enforcing a statute, although such immunity does not extend to actions seeking injunctive relief. Injunctive relief, however, can be obtained if the issue involves violation of a constitutional right.

What is a Private Action?

A *private action* is a legal action on behalf of one or more individuals or on behalf of an organization. Therefore, whatever the outcome of the case, it will directly affect only the individuals specifically named as plaintiffs in the case, although the indirect effects can be widespread.

What is a Class Action?

In a *class action* a named plaintiff(s) brings an action both for himself and on behalf of all persons similarly situated. In the *Mills* case, the suit was undertaken not just on behalf of Peter Mills and other named plaintiffs, but significantly also on behalf of a *class* of plaintiffs — all "exceptional" children who resided in the District of Columbia. In the *Wyatt* case, the named plaintiff represented all residents of the state of Alabama involuntarily confined to the state's hospitals.

Plaintiffs must satisfy many complex procedural requirements in order to maintain a class action in most jurisdictions. The Federal Courts are considered to have one of the most lenient sets of standards for class actions; many states have more restrictive rules.

In a federal suit pursuant to Federal Rule of Civil Procedure No. 23, one or more members of a class may sue as representatives of all other members of the class if the following basic conditions obtain:

1. The class is so large that it would be impractical to make all members plaintiffs.
2. There are questions of law or fact common to the members of the entire class.
3. Claims of the representatives are typical of claims of the entire class.
4. The representative parties will fairly and adequately protect the interests of the entire class.

Additional qualifications apply to a federal class action. This is a complicated area in which legal counsel is essential.

When Are Class Actions More Desirable than Private Actions?

In a private action, if Peter Mills had been admitted to public school classes during the litigation procedure, the case would have become moot because he would no longer have been denied an education. In a class action, however, the case could have continued, since other children would be directly affected by the outcome.

In a class action, if a temporary restraining order is issued prior to a full hearing, the order applies to the class. In a private action, the order applies to the individual plaintiff. The same distinction applies to final relief granted by the court.

Any member of the class can initiate contempt proceedings if the order of the court is not implemented with respect to him individually. In *Mills,* if the order is not implemented with respect to any handicapped child, a representative of the child can return to court to have the relief enforced, and possibly, to have authorities fined or jailed for failing to obey the court order.

While class actions often are desirable, the risks are also higher. If a suit is lost, it will be more difficult for others in the class to bring another suit on the same issues involving the same circumstances. Also, if the named plaintiffs are not fully representative, have not suffered all the injuries of other members of the class, all relevant causes of action may not be brought out in court, and thus, the relief granted may not be sufficient to provide all members of the class with adequate remedies.

Once Litigation is Begun, Must it be Completed?

At any point in the process, a plaintiff or defendant can reach a settlement. Negotiations held during the course of the litigation may resolve certain issues and remove them from consideration by the court. If an out-of-court settlement is achieved, the opposing party may agree to stop the action at issue. In a class action, however, the court must approve any settlement.

If settlement is made, the court's enforcement powers will not be behind the agreement unless a judicially approved *consent agreement* is obtained, which means *court ratification,* or approval, of settlement. In *Pennsylvania Association of Retarded Children* (PARC) v. *Pennsylvania* (1971 and 1972), a federal court ordered that all mentally retarded children in Pennsylvania be given access to a free public program of education appropriate to their learning capabilities, pursuant to a consent agreement between the parties. Obtaining a consent agreement probably saved lengthy litigation, obviated the possibility of an unfavorable decision for the plaintiffs, and enhanced the prospect of the desired action to occur.

Willingness of parties to settle depends on the objectives sought by the lawsuit. If it is a test case to try to establish a certain right as well as to vindicate the rights of plaintiffs, one purpose may be to have the court recognize that right and articulate its reasons, so the decision will have value as a precedent. If these objectives are sought, settlement may not be possible.

In some situations the threat of a lawsuit alone can accomplish all that is desired by a suit. Approximately two-thirds of all litigation is settled out of court. Settlement is less expensive and time-consuming than litigation and may lead to a more satisfactory conclusion than would result from a court decision. Out-of-court negotiated settlements may be sought at any stage in litigation proceedings, even when the case has reached the appellate level.

What Factors Should be Taken into Account in Choosing an Attorney?

Perhaps the most significant consideration in choosing an attorney is that the attorney must have a positive reputation as being competent. Equally important is that his past must include trial experience which reflects commitment to the

370

position taken by the parties he represents. This does not require commitment to the issues in question, but commitment to do the best possible for his clients. The attorney selected also must be one in whom the client has confidence. Because litigation on behalf of handicapped persons is a fairly new area of the law, the attorney must be willing to draw on already established programs for information and technical assistance. A partial listing of these organizations is included at the conclusion of this chapter.

SELECTING THE APPROPRIATE COURT

Initially in the litigation process, the plaintiff's attorney must select the appropriate court to hear the case. State courts generally become involved with issues of state law or practices. Federal courts hear cases involving parties who live in two or more states and cases involving the U.S. Constitution or other federal law. In some areas of law, courts in both the state and federal systems may have the authority to hear a case.

The Federal Court System

The federal court system consists primarily of 93 Federal District Courts, 11 U.S. Circuit Courts of Appeal, and the Supreme Court of the United States. The District Courts are the *trial-level* courts in the federal system, where suits are actually heard. Each state has at least one District Court. The number of judges in each court varies, depending on the size of the District and the number of cases it hears. Usually a single judge will try a case and hand down a decision. However, in some cases a *three-judge* court is required, consisting of district court judges and appeals court judges. (There are other federal courts not relevant to this discussion.)

The U.S. Circuit Courts of Appeal review decisions of the District Courts. Each circuit includes from three to ten states and the territories and has its own court. Usually, three judges are assigned to each case.

The Courts of Appeal have jurisdiction to review decisions of the District Courts, as well as to review orders of many administrative agencies and, in some cases, to issue original decisions. The appeals process is explained later.

The Supreme Court is the highest court in the country and consists of a Chief Justice and eight Associate Justices. The Justices are appointed by the President with the approval of the Senate, as are all federal judges. The court has the power to review all matters of law relating to the U.S. Constitution and has the final appellate power on all other matters of law.

The State Court Systems

Most states have the same general court structures, even though the courts may have different names and each may have different limitations of power upon the cases it can hear. There are usually several trial-level courts called superior courts or courts of general jurisdiction. Each has certain areas of responsibility designated by state law.

The larger states have two levels of appeals courts, usually referred to as the State Court of Appeals and the State Supreme Court. Many smaller states have only one appeals level court, usually called the Supreme Court. State courts as well as federal courts can construe and apply federal constitutional rights.

The *Lori Case* action, involving the alleged denial of education to a multiply handicapped child, was brought in a California Superior Court. (Because the case involves federal constitutional rights questions, it also could have been brought in a federal district court.) If the case is lost, the losing side may appeal the decision to the California Court of Appeals, then to the California Supreme Court. The last recourse for the losing side is review by the U.S. Supreme Court.

The Abstention Doctrine

In cases involving both state and federal law, federal court judges may decline to hear certain cases for various reasons.

For example, in *Reid* v. *Board of Education of the City of New York* (1971), a class action brought on behalf of New York City parents who alleged that their brain-injured children were not receiving special education in the public school system, the plaintiffs sought a declaratory judgment and preliminary and permanent injunctions to prevent a deprivation under color of state law of their rights protected by the Fourteenth Amendment. In June, 1971, the Judge for the U.S. District Court for the Southern District of New York granted the defendant's motion to dismiss. The court applied the abstention doctrine, reasoning that since there was no charge of deliberate discrimination, and since the City was as concerned as the defendants about the situation, the state court could provide an adequate remedy; resort to the federal courts was unnecessary.

Considerations in Choosing Between State and Federal Systems

If the educative effect of the litigation is important, the plaintiffs may wish to select a court with the greater promise of visibility. Selection also should consider local feelings that would work to the advantage or disadvantage of either side. Another factor to be considered is the previous decisions of the respective judges in both the federal and the state courts at both the trial and appeal levels. Practices of the respective courts on freedom of discovery and the awarding of attorneys fees may be another indicator to be considered. The length of time required to try cases or come to trial in the alternative courts also should be considered.

PREPARATION FOR TRIAL

Assuming a civil suit in a federal court (state procedures are generally similar), several preparatory steps involving the procedures and documentation must be considered prior to formal initiation of the suit.

Potential plaintiffs must inform the court and the defendants, by means of a document called a *complaint,* that they have a lawsuit for which they are seeking the court's intervention. The *pleadings* set forth their issue or causes of action and the relief being requested. A suit may be brought under several different and even conflicting theories, hoping to find one or more which the court will recognize and upon which it will grant relief. The term *pleading* also is used more generally to encompass all the preliminary steps of complaint-answer-replies used to narrow a case down to the basic issues of law and fact.

An *answer* is the defendant's response to the complaint. The defendant will raise *defenses* stating why the complaint is without merit or why he is not guilty of the charges claimed. *Procedural defenses* include basic inadequacies in following the rules of the court, such as lack of subject-matter jurisdiction of the person and improper venue, insufficiency of process, insufficiency of services of process, failure to state a claim upon which relief can be granted, failure to join a necessary part (someone who is also responsible for the alleged violation). Defendants can attempt to have a case dismissed for any of these reasons.

Affirmative defenses are also reasons why the defendant should not be held responsible, and may include such defenses as contributory negligence and duress.

Replies, amendments, and *motions* are further steps that can be taken in refining the pleadings and responding to allegations or defenses raised by both sides. For the purposes of this discussion, it probably is sufficient to understand that parties are not restricted to their *first pleadings* and may make changes even after the trial begins (depending on how the case develops, how the defendants respond, and what the plaintiffs are seeking from the court).

Discovery is the process by which parties learn about the other side's case, including available evidence and the identity of witnesses to be called. In a civil case, parties can "discover" the majority of information relevant to the subject matter of their case, except for privileged material such as that relating to a doctor-patient relationship. The purpose of discovery in civil actions is to remove the element of surprise and allow both sides to prepare themselves adequately for the trial.

Several devices can be used as part of discovery:

1. A *deposition* consists of asking a potential witness to answer oral or written questions under oath in the presence of a court reporter. Attorneys for both sides can be present and can cross-examine the witness or raise objections to the questions or testimony.
2. An *interrogatory* is a means of obtaining written answers to questions from any of the *parties* (plaintiffs or defendants). The questions are sent to the party, to be answered under oath and returned within a specified time. The attorney can assist the party with answers, but because no representatives of the opposing side are present, there can be no cross-examination.
3. *Production of documents or material objects.* Either party may obtain documents and physical objects relevant to the case which are within the control of the other side; e.g., a psychological evaluation completed on a child, used to deny admittance to a program. *The Freedom of Information Act* (P.L.89-487) requires federal officials to make available most public documents upon request.
4. Physical and mental examinations may be required, with a showing of *good cause,* of a person under custody or legal control of the court. The examining

professional may then testify about the results. The examinations must be related to the matter in controversy.

5. *A request for admissions* is a request that opposing parties admit the truth of certain statements so that time will not have to be spent proving these particular facts. For example, the defendants in the *Wyatt* case stipulated to a number of objective facts concerning the status of Alabama's mental institutions.

Many considerations are taken into account in determining which discovery devices to use. For example, depositions are more expensive than interrogations because the party requesting them must pay for the time of all the attorneys, the witness, and the court reporter but, on the other hand, depositions may be of more value because there is opportunity to freely question witnesses, which is not possible with interrogatories.

An *expert witness* is a person with recognized competence in the area in which he is testifying. At trial the expert will be asked to state his background before providing substantive testimony. The judge and opposing attorney will question him as to his competence, and the opposing attorney may try to discredit his testimony, either directly or indirectly. Both sides may call expert witnesses.

Experts are vital at two stages of litigation. With regard to actions involving the handicapped, experts may be needed to review programs and tour the facilities which are the subject of the suit. Expert testimony in the *Wyatt* case was a necessary prelude to the court's findings that conditions in Alabama's institutions were inadequate by any known scientific and medical minimum standards.

If the court finds that plaintiff's rights are being violated, experts again have a vital role to play in informing the court of generally accepted program or treatment standards. In the *Pennsylvania* case, for example, a number of experts provided a new definition of education for the court, stressing that all persons can learn and that learning involves not just academics but the acquisition of skills enabling individuals to better cope with their environment. This concept was regarded as a key success of the litigation. Implementation of the concept means that for severely mentally retarded children, education also may mean the acquisition of basic self-help skills, including feeding and toileting. In the *Wyatt* case, plaintiffs, defendants, and amici agreed to a large number of specific standards for adequate treatment, and experts offered testimony explaining to the court why certain specific standards were necessary to insure adequate treatment. Based upon the experts' endorsement, the court ordered the recommended standards to be implemented as constitutionally required minimums.

THE TRIAL

Parties have a right to a trial by jury except when they are seeking injunctive relief. Even with the right to a jury, their attorneys must demand a jury trial or the judge will automatically decide the case. A jury can only determine questions of fact, such as who was telling the truth, while the judge always determines questions of law, such as what must be proved to indicate that someone's right to an education has been violated. If there is no jury, the judge determines questions of both law and fact.

Usually, the plaintiff's attorney will present his evidence first. The defendant's attorney can cross-examine the plaintiff's witness. Both sides may object to any evidence or testimony if they do not believe it should be admitted. The judge will rule on whether the evidence in question is admissible, based upon such factors as its relevance, trustworthiness, prejudice, and prior appellate decisions on the issue.

When the plaintiff's attorney has presented all of his evidence, he will rest his case. At that time, the defendant's attorney may make a *motion for a directed verdict* or a *motion for summary judgment,* which means he is asking the court to

377

decide that as a matter of law the plaintiff has failed to prove the facts necessary to establish the case, or that based upon the facts established by the plaintiffs, the defendants must win as a matter of law. The court can then grant the motion ending the trial or continue with the defendant's attorney presenting his evidence, followed by the plaintiff's attorney cross-examination and the raising of appropriate objections.

When the defense rests, either side may move for a directed verdict. If the judge denies the motion, he may then weigh the evidence of each side and immediately decide the case, or he may delay his decision until after he has had time to study the issues involved. He may ask each side for *trial briefs* stating each side's position on disputed points of law which are areas where courts have disagreed or have not actually decided on a particular point under these circumstances.

Usually, attorneys for each side will present oral arguments emphasizing why the case should be decided in their favor and explaining what relief they are seeking.

After the verdict is reached, the "winner" will make a motion for a judgment on the verdict, and the "loser" will make a motion for a judgment notwithstanding the verdict, such as asking the court to decide for the losing side even though it lost the jury verdict. The judge will issue a judgment which sets out the relief to be granted to the winning side. For the loser, other steps are still possible, such as filing a motion for a new trial and, if this is refused, a motion for appeal.

The losing side can appeal if it believes the decision was decided incorrectly as a matter of law or that the judge made procedural errors during the trial, such as improperly admitting or excluding evidence. The losing party must have raised objections to such errors at the time they occurred or an appeal will not be permitted.

An appeal is not another trial, since there will not be another chance to call additional witnesses or to present additional evidence. Pursuit to an appeals court asks the court to review the record of the trial court proceedings, which consists of all the written materials from the trial. In addition, both sides will submit a brief which sets out the errors allegedly made by the trial judge, with appropriate supporting legal arguments and cases. Counsels for each side will usually also present *oral arguments* before the judges, summarizing their cases as well as answering questions.

The appeals court judges review actions of the trial judge and may also review fact determinations by the jury. If the appeals judges find an error, they will reverse the trial judge and either grant some or all of the relief being sought, or remand (send back) the case to the trial court for a retrial on some or all of the issues. A judgment will not be set aside unless the error affected substantial or material rights of the parties.

The loser of the first appeal may be able to appeal again to the next higher court. In states with two appeals levels, the highest court may have great discretion in deciding which cases it will review and may not have to review every case, except those involving constitutional questions. After the highest state court or the appropriate U.S. Court of Appeals, if it is a federal case, it may be possible to obtain review by the U.S. Supreme Court; but again, the Supreme Court need accept only a limited number of cases *by appeal*. Most of the cases which it hears occur through the granting of a *writ of certiorari*, which is a request that the Court use its discretionary powers to hear the case. It also may hear a case *by certification* if a court of appeals requests instructions on a question of law.

Even though a party believes he has a case that was decided incorrectly, the Supreme Court is not required to review it and usually will choose to hear only those cases involving issues it deems important. Four of the nine Justices must decide to hear a *cert (writ of certiorari)* case before it is brought before the entire court.

A *precedent* is a rule to guide or support other judges in deciding future cases seeking similar or analogous decisions. For example, in the *Mills* case, the judge based his decision that handicapped children have a constitutional right to public education on due process and equal protection of the laws. In support of his decision, the judge cited several famous educational decisions as *precedents*, including *Brown* v. *Board of Education*, the 1954 Supreme Court decision outlawing segregated schools, and the *Hobson* v. *Hansen* (1967), decision by Judge J. Skelly Wright outlawing the so-called "track system" in the District of Columbia. As a precedent, a decision will have most value in the jurisdiction where it is handed down. For example, courts in Alabama are more likely to follow prior Alabama decisions than prior New York decisions on the same issue. Courts in one area of the country are more likely to follow decisions by other courts in their region, so some decisions are said to have regional impact.

Decisions in certain state courts, certain federal district courts, or certain appeals courts are considered more influential than others and may be weighed more heavily by some judges because of the recognized competence or reputations of the judges who made the decisions.

A decision from a circuit court of appeals is of even greater value than one from a district court. A decision by the U.S. Supreme Court establishes the greatest possible precedent because the decisions of the Supreme Court are binding across the country. Usually all state courts, when hearing cases involving federal law, conform their decisions to Supreme Court rulings.

A word of caution should be interjected, however, because in interpreting and applying Supreme Court decisions to different facts, lower courts still may resolve similar cases differently until other Supreme Court rulings clarify or strengthen the position. Little absolute or "apolitical" law remains immutable, as public policies change and interests of society shift.

The importance of a decision depends on the level of the court that issued it, on whether the decision is published and available, on whether it is being appealed, and on the quality of its reasoning.

A decision also may have spillover value and contribute to change. For example, the decision in a private action in theory directly affects only the plaintiff, and the defendants are legally bound to change their actions in relation only to him. However, the defendants may be influenced by the decision to change their actions towards all persons in similar situations. Similarly, a class action may join only the residents at one hospital, and the defendants are legally bound to improve conditions at that single facility. However, the defendants and other persons with statewide responsibilities who become aware of the court's decision might decide, on the basis of the ruling, to improve the situation in all state institutions, knowing that similar suits could arise. Spillover affects practices in locales other than the one directly affected by the decision.

LITIGATION EXPENSES

Three main costs are involved in bringing a suit: attorneys fees, litigation expenses, and court costs.

Different attorneys charge different fees, depending upon the nature of the case, the time expended in preparation and trial, the attorney's experience and reputation, and the ability of a client to pay. Attorneys fees also may vary considerably from one geographic region to another. Generally, however, attorneys fees are high. Average hourly costs may range from $20 to $100, and $50 an hour is not uncommon. If plaintiffs win the case, there is a chance they will be awarded court costs, but it is more difficult to recover attorneys fees, except where a statute provides for their recovery or where the court uses its discretion to award the fees.

Recovering attorneys fees is an area of expanding law, however, particularly in cases which are won by public interest groups and which demonstrate benefits that extend to members of society beyond the plaintiffs. For example, in the *Wyatt* case, the Court found that by successfully prosecuting the suit, plaintiffs benefited not only the present residents of the two state hospitals and school for the mentally retarded, but all others who might in the future be confined to those institutions. As the Court stated, "Veritably, it is no over-statement to assert that all of Alabama's citizens have profited and will continue to profit from this litigation. So prevalent are mental disorders in our society that no family is immune from their perilous incursion. Consequently, the availability of institutions capable of dealing successfully with such disorders is essential, and, of course, in the best interest of all Alabamians." The Court ordered that the defendant Alabama Mental Health Board pay the expenses and plaintiff's attorneys fees.

In attempting to determine a reasonable fee under the circumstances, the Court referred to the Criminal Justice Act, which provides compensation to attorneys appointed to represent indigent defendants. The Act's legislative history makes it clear that although the amount provided ($20 per out-of-court hour and $30 per in-court hour) is below normal levels of compensation in legal practice, it nevertheless is considered a reasonable basis upon which lawyers can carry out their professional responsibility without either personal profiteering or undue financial sacrifice. The Court applied the $20 and $30 fee schedule in *Wyatt,* and reasoned that the attorneys embarked upon the case with knowledge that their named clients were unable to pay them and were motivated not by desire for profit, but public spirit and a sense of duty. A total of $36,754 was awarded by the Court to cover attorneys' fees and expenses.

It also may be possible to involve a public interest law firm in the types of cases described here, or the Public Defender Service or attorneys from a local Legal Aid office. Profit-making "public interest" firms usually charge very low fees. In addition, many regular law firms also devote a portion of their time to work in the public interest without compensation.

While most attorneys' fees are computed on an hourly basis as indicated above, some attorneys will charge a flat fee for conducting that suit through one or more levels. Those bringing a tort action frequently can acquire an attorney who will handle the suit on a contingency-fee basis. If the case is won, the attorney will receive as his fee a percentage of the amount awarded by the court.

Litigation expenses include payment for such items as necessary discovery devices (e.g., costs of taking depositions and giving physical examinations, travel expenses for lawyers and expert witnesses, filing fees, and duplicating expenses).

Court costs are fees and charges required by laws of the various jurisdictions for the time of the courts and some of the officers of the court. Court costs normally are awarded as a matter of course to the prevailing (winning) party and paid by the losers.

Litigation should not be pursued on the assumption of no financial responsibility in bringing the suit. Neither, however, should litigation be rejected because it appears financially out of the question. If an individual or organization becomes a party in a suit involving exceptional children or handicapped adults, the resource groups listed at the end of the chapter could be of assistance.

AFTER LITIGATION

Declaration by a court that handicapped persons have a right to education, treatment, or proper classification merely signals that the hard work of implementation still lies ahead. It also may conclude only the first round of litigation since, if required implementation does not occur, the parties could once again be in court.

Complicating the implementation of a court order is the basic fact that in the types of litigation discussed here, victories for handicapped persons, and particularly if class actions, often require action on the part of the public agencies and employees who have been publicly defeated. Although litigation is not necessarily a personal attack, some lawyers say there is no such thing as a friendly lawsuit.

Establishment by the court that certain individual rights are protected by the constitution or that specific actions must be undertaken to observe those rights does not in any way guarantee that the needed corrective action will occur. To bring about action requires, at a minimum, changes in established human behavior patterns at possibly a number of governmental levels and agencies. The consent agreement achieved in *PARC* involved the education agencies at the state, intermediate, and local levels, as well as the state agency administering state institutions and other non-school programs for the mentally retarded. Thus, to implement the order, behavior had to be changed in state and local policy-making bodies such as boards of education, administrators including school and institution superintendents as well as individual building principals and, finally, the whole range of staff.

Implementation of victorious class actions of the nature described here likely will require additional resources. In *Wyatt,* the court required the immediate hiring of 300 ward attendants to insure the physical well-being of institutionalized persons. Data collected in one intermediate district in Pennsylvania after the implementation of the *PARC* decree indicated that costs for the total program of special education have increased 40 percent (Sheer, 1973).

Another problem concerning implementation is that after conclusion of the litigation, few people — often only those in the highest levels of responsibility — become familiar with the decision and its meaning. The majority of persons involved in implementation learn about the decision by rumor or are provided with the "pieces" of the order that are particularly relevant to their job responsibilities. Equally significant is that in some situations where government is required to alter its practices, officials at the highest levels never publicly acknowledge past injustices or approval of the decision, or even announce the commitment of their offices and administrators to implementation. However, Governor Schapp of Pennsylvania put the entire state on notice that implementation of the *PARC* consent agreement was to occur.

Often, two extremes of response by the victorious side occur in the aftermath of a decision. One response is based on the misperception that total victory has been achieved. The other extreme focuses on vindictively monitoring every movement of the defeated side for the purpose of reporting to the court, the public, and the victorious constituency. While monitoring is clearly required, it must not be done with malice, nor must the victorious stand aside and offer no assistance to those now involved in making changes. Clearly, positive change requires the wedding of both sides of the litigation.

Discussion of these problems points the way for identification of solutions. To achieve effective implementation, the public must be educated on the issues leading to the litigation, the results, and the requirements to bring about change. If handicapped children who previously were excluded from school are to profit from their newly won right to enroll in a school where there may be non-handicapped children, the quality of their experiences may well depend on the information related to and the attitudes of parents of the non-handicapped children.

Public education must involve the use of mass media. In *Mills,* the court required the insertion of quarterly advertisements in Washington's three major daily newspapers announcing that all District of Columbia children have a right to a free, publicly supported education.

Change from past behavior to new behavior requires the infusion of new ideas and extensive work. Many of the new ideas can result from a merging of the resources of previous adversaries. Persons outside government can work effectively in an advisory role in committees with agency representatives. Often the non-governmental resource people are involved with private agencies such as national parent groups, which can be of great assistance in disseminating information as well as other tasks.

Involvement by the winner of the suit with the loser also builds the base for effective monitoring of the steps being taken for implementation. In addition, monitoring in this fashion will make clear, to those outside, the needs that exist within to facilitate the implementation process, and will allow for development of exterior strategies and activities to meet those needs.

The implementation process will not always occur in smooth fashion, and old issues and differences of opinion will not necessarily disappear. This is the reality. The resolve of these disputes should occur, if possible, without court intervention. This function can be effectively discharged by masters, if appointed by the court. In many judicial orders, requirements for reporting to the court on progress made may serve as a means of resolving these issues.

The point cannot be made strongly enough that a judicial decision may not be worth the paper on which it is written if it is not implemented. Delay in integrating schools for some 20 years after the *Brown* v. *Board of Education* decision in 1954 serves as an example of the difficulties in implementing a decree, even when it is issued by the highest court in the land.

Rouse v. *Cameron*, a 1966 case which was hailed as a landmark in the right-to-treatment area, provides another example of the unfortunate lack of implementation. Seven years after *Rouse*, judicial recognition of the right to treatment has occurred in only a few jurisdictions, with little implementation of the right where it has been recognized. The needed changes of behavior and dialogue between mental health professionals and lawyers have yet to take place.

Ultimately, the remedy of injustice toward the handicapped will occur because increased public awareness will lead to a change in the attitudes and fiscal priorities required to establish needed programs and services. The right-to-education movement for handicapped children that has been occurring for the past few years has produced a climate in

which high-level government officials have publicly committed their resources to remedy the injustice.

In the legislative area, a number of bills introduced during
the 92nd and 93rd Congress regarded education of the handicapped. Some of these (e.g., S. 6 and H.R. 70) focused
specifically on providing the states with financial assistance to
improve and expand their education programs for handicapped children. This effort was concluded in November, 1975,
with passage of P.L. 94-142, The Education of All Handicapped Children Act. Since the beginning of the litigation effort,
numerous[5] bills have been introduced and passed in the
states. Totally new and comprehensive legislation providing
for education of the handicapped recently has been passed in
many states, with the basic policy that all children are entitled
to a free public education.

Other effects have been seen in attorney generals' rulings.
In Delaware (1973), the attorney general issued an opinion
which declared, on the basis of *PARC* and *Mills*, that statutory
limitations on the growth of some special education programs
are unconstitutional.

Because the right-to-treatment movement has not pro-
gressed at the same rate as the right-to-education movement,
change is less evident. Yet, it is known that administrative
practices have changed and that fiscal alterations can be expected in the future.

While it must be emphasized again that litigation alone is
not a solution, it can clarify the problem and establish multiple
bases for instituting change. All avenues of public policy must
be brought to bear on altering the present status of the
handicapped. In a society characterized by a good deal of
commotion over numerous causes, only a few "successes"
ever really stand out; these are the situations in which the

---

[5]In 1971, 899 bills were introduced (U.S. Office of Education Commissioner,
1972).

plaintiffs and their supporters never stop asking, "Now have we won?"

RESOURCE ORGANIZATIONS

Following are some of the groups which in the past have been involved in efforts related to the areas discussed, to improve practices on behalf of handicapped children and adults, as well as bringing about change in the legal base upon which such services are delivered.

The Council for Exceptional Children, 1920 Association Dr., Reston, VA 22091.

National Center for Law and the Handicapped, 1235 No. Eddy St., South Bend, IN 46617.

Mental Health Law Project, 1751 N Street, NW, Washington, DC 20036.

American Association on Mental Deficiency, 5201 Connecticut Ave., NW, Washington, DC 20015.

National Association for Retarded Citizens, 2709 Avenue E East, Arlington, TX 76010.

National Legal Aid and Defenders Association, 1601 Connecticut Ave., NW, Washington, DC 20009.

American Civil Liberties Union, 84 Fifth Avenue, New York, NY 10011.

Harvard University Center for Law and Education, 38 Kirkland St., Cambridge, MA 02138.

United Cerebral Palsy Associations, Inc., 66 East 34th St., New York, NY 10016.

National Center for Law and the Deaf, Gallaudet College, 7th and Florida Ave., NE, Washington, DC 20002.

REFERENCES

Brown v. *Board of Education,* 347 U.S. 283, 74 S. Ct. 686, 98 L. Ed. 873 (1954).

Case (Lori) v. *California,* Civil No. 101679 (S. Ct. Riverside County, CA, filed Jan. 7, 1972).

Delaware Attorney General's Opinion, Dover, DE, March 26, 1973.

Diana v. *State Board of Education,* C. 70, 37 RFR (1970).

Harrison v. *Michigan,* 350 F. Supp. 846 (E.D. Mich. 1972).

Hobson v. *Hansen,* 269 F. Supp. 401 (D.D.C. 1967).

LeBanks v. *Spears,* Civil No. 71-2897 (E.D. La. N.O. Div., April 24, 1973).

Mental Health Law Project. *Basic rights of the mentally handicapped,* 1751 N Street, NW, Washington, DC 20036 (1973).

Meyer v. *Nebraska,* 262 U.S. 390, 43 S. Ct. 625, 67 L. Ed. 1042 (1923).

Mills v. *Board of Education of District of Columbia,* 348 F. Supp. 866 (D.D.C. 1972).

Pennsylvania Association for Retarded Children (PARC) v. *Pennsylvania,* C.A. 71-41, 334 F. Supp. 1257 (E.D. Pa. 1971) and 343 F. Supp. 279 (E.D. Pa. 1972).

Rainey v. *Watkins,* C.A. No. 77620-2, Chancery Court of Shelby County, TN (April 1973).

Reid v. *Board of Education of City of New York,* 453 F. 2d 328 (2d Cir. 1971) (pending Admin. Proc. before Commissioner of Education, argued Jan. 16, 1973).

Rouse v. *Cameron,* 125 U.S. App. D.C. 366, 373 F. 2d 451 (1966).

Sheer, Richard. Oral presentation, Dover, DE, March 23, 1973.

Sonder v. *Brennan,* C.A. No. 482-73, U.S. Dist. Ct., Washington, DC, 1973.

U.S. Office of Education Commissioner. Oral presentation, Washington, DC, March 1972

Wyatt v. *Hardin,* 334 F. Supp. 1341 (M.D. Alabama, 1971), 325 F., Supp. 781 (M.D. Alabama 1971) (originally *Wyatt* v. *Stickney* & *Wyatt* v. *Aderholt*).

ADDITIONAL REFERENCES

Abeson, A. *A continuing summary of pending and completed litigation regarding the education of handicapped children.* Arlington, VA: The Council for Exceptional Children, 1972.

Abeson, A. Appropriate education for all handicapped children — Now is the time. *Mental Hygiene,* Spring 1973, *57*(2).

Burnham v. *Department of Public Health of the State of Georgia,* 349 F. Supp. 1335 (N.D. Ga. 1972); appeal docketed, No. 72-3110, 5th Cir., Aug. 1972; argument heard Dec. 6, 1972.

Casey, P. J. The Supreme Court and the suspect class. *Exceptional Children,* October 1973, *40*(2).

Diamond, P.R., & Reed, J. Rodriguez and retarded children. *Journal of Law and Education,* July 1973, *2*(3).

Gilhool, T. Education: An inalienable right. *Exceptional Children,* May 1973.

Marland, S.P. (former U.S. Office of Education Commissioner). Oral presentation, Washington, DC, March 31, 1972.

Syracuse Law Review, 1972. 23(4). Syracuse, NY: Syracuse University College of Law.

Trudeau, E. *Digest of state and federal laws: Education of handicapped children.* Arlington, VA: The Council for Exceptional Children, 1972.

Weintraub, F., et al. *State law and the education of handicapped children: Issues and recommendations.* Arlington, VA: The Council for Exceptional Children, 1971.

20

Advocacy Comes of Age

Douglas Biklen

Advocacy has come of age. In 1970, 64 advocacy projects were funded by the Office of Child Development (OCD), the National Institute of Mental Health (NIMH), the Bureau for the Education of the Handicapped (BEH), and the Division of Developmental Disabilities (DDD). The Department of Health, Education, and Welfare (HEW) as yet offers no future mandate for advocacy, but there can be no turning back.

In the wake of the now famous *Pennsylvania Association for Retarded Children (PARC)* v. *Pennsylvania* case (1971), which established the principle that all children can benefit from educational programming, similar right to education and right to treatment suits have sprung up throughout the country. These cases create precedents that will stand for years to come. Numerous national organizations, including action research groups such as the Children's Defense Fund and The

Originally published in *Exceptional Children*, March 1976, 42(6), 308-313.
Reprinted with permission.

Center on Human Policy, as well as major professional associations such as the American Association on Mental Deficiency and The Council for Exceptional Children, have sponsored and/or formally supported advocacy litigation, training, and policy research. Yet the spread of advocacy has not been without confusion, inconsistencies, setbacks, and uncertainty.

AUTONOMY TO ADVOCATE

Because many people call themselves advocates, the term advocacy often generates confusion. Is "advocacy" simply a faddish word which has caught the fancy of people who work with or for children? Is it a term which (like so many others) has been chosen to mean almost anything? When Kahn, Kamerman, and McGowan wrote their baseline study on child advocacy (1972), they described an HEW Regional Director who suggested that advocacy may be found in agencies that provide virtually any kind of human service, whether drug and alcohol related treatment, maternal and infant care, early childhood development, or job training (Kahn et al., 1972).

Kahn et al. found four advocacy programs in operation in Nashville, Tennessee. Here the confusion emerged in microcosm. The programs included the following:

1. A BEH/NIMH project targeted to the needs of 1,000 families;
2. A Youth Development and Delinquency Prevention Administration program for crisis intervention with "troubled" youth;
3. A Family Advocacy Program to lobby for progressive social legislation;
4. A Citizen Advocacy Project designed to assist institutionalized persons in their return to the community.

As one Nashville advocate described it, the roles of advocacy staff for these various projects ranged from semisocial worker to semilegal. Some were tied to traditional service agencies; others were more or less autonomous. The confusion centered on whether advocates were also providers of service, or whether they were exclusively engaged in monitoring services.

Autonomy is crucial for advocates (Wolfensberger, 1972a). Wolfensberger proposed a firm rule that advocates must always operate independently of service delivery. Logically, it would be difficult to refute Wolfensberger's warning that advocates must remain independent of the service provider role. That was a lesson of Watergate — separate the monitor from the monitored. One would not, for example, ask Ralph Nader to serve on the Board of Directors at General Motors. Similarly, superintendents of school districts cannot act as the chief advocates for children — yet this has been suggested in New York State (1973). In response to a similar phenomenon in which an institution's monitoring of itself becomes mere window-dressing, Seymour Sarason has suggested a simple truism:

> Like the rest of humanity, the professional person, especially if he is in an important administrative position, needs to be controlled against himself for his sake as well as for those in his overall care (Blatt, 1970, p. xiii).

Advocacy resembles other consumer protection movements in its need for safeguards against conflicts of interest. Yet, essential to advocacy is not only the independence it requires, but the far reaching and radical shift in orientation that advocacy brings to "helping" children.

HELPING RELATIONSHIPS

There are many ways of helping people, not all of them equally valuable. The pitfalls of the "expert knows best" approach, in which clients receive available services on a take it or leave it basis, have been amply described (*Children's Defense Fund*, 1974; *Task Force*, 1972). People with disabilities often have had no options, either within human services or within the broader society (Kriegel, 1969). One might call this kind of help "assistance without dialogue" or "service without accountability."

Another way of "helping" people is through the charitable model. Many of the national voluntary associations for children with disabilities depend on charity as their life blood. Human services that have been notably absent in the public sector have been provided by charitable organizations. Yet, for all it has done to relieve immediate human suffering, charity has its problems and limitations:

1. Charity often communicates pity toward the recipient;
2. Charity can romanticize children with special needs as "holy innocents," "angels," or "poor souls," rather than treating all children as equals and as multifaceted;
3. Charity keeps the recipient in a dependent situation;
4. Charity may relieve human suffering of a few or even many individuals without altering the root causes of the suffering (e.g., societal prejudice);
5. Whenever charity is called upon to provide basic human services to fill a void created by unresponsive public agencies, it has the inadvertent effect of allowing service fragmentation and public irresponsibility.

Every citizen should possess a sense of social responsibility to be charitable with others. But charity must not become a palliative for social injustice. Charity cannot solve societal problems; it can only delay or temper their impact.

ADVOCACY DEFINED

Still another way of helping people is to become an advocate. Advocacy perhaps can be defined best as an independent movement of consumers (e.g., parents, people with disabilities, and children) and their allies to monitor and change human service agencies. The following are principles by which advocates attempt to promote quality human services:

1. Advocates attempt to identify those conditions that make a person dependent. Ideally, the advocate works with the person who has disabilities so that he becomes more independent, self reliant, and free from dependence on charity and privileges. The advocate helps the person to achieve human services as a right.

2. Advocates try to understand the person's feelings, experiences, and needs through his own words and accounts. Advocates try to treat others as equals, as allies, as people who are strong and capable, as people who do not want to be falsely glorified, but who want to participate in the normal mainstream.

3. Advocates do not express pity, but rather anger about the conditions and attitudes in this society which dehumanize those who have disabilities. Institutions cause human abuse; social attitudes create discrimination; prejudicial school policies explain the current figures that 2,000,000 children have been excluded from school (*Children's Defense Fund,* 1974). Advocates work consciously, with the purpose of making change possible. Desire for change, not a feeling of pity or guilt, motivates the advocate.

4. Advocates sometimes must be willing to accept the disdain and criticism of those agencies and people whom they question. The advocate must be ready to adopt an active stance, even when colleagues are of opposite persuasions.

Quite understandably, this set of principles makes advocacy sound like an idealistic, if not impossible, enterprise. Fortunately, however, experiences of recent years now afford an accounting of specific advocacy methods. Consequently, one can envision a practical, assertive, advocacy role.

METHODS OF ADVOCACY

In the world of advocacy, one cannot help thinking that lawyers are better prepared than other professionals or laypersons to break down barriers that exclude and impede people who have disabilities. The Constitution serves as a powerful tool for change. Yet, legal victories have not, by themselves, necessarily altered the shape of day to day policy and programs. For this reason, it is helpful to review books about community organizing (Alinsky, 1972; O. M. Collective, 1971; Ross, 1973; & Sharp, 1972) and to talk with parent and professional advocates throughout the country. From all these sources, it has been possible to assemble a modest list of useful techniques for advocacy (Biklen, 1974). The following headings reflect that list, without the step-by-step suggestions for implementation.

Demonstrations

Demonstrations are a form of public expression or "community presence" that has been used by the women's suffrage movement, the civil rights movement, and other human rights struggles. Formats for demonstrations include: marches, vigils, sit-ins, phone-ins, overloading administrative systems, jam-ins, sing-ins, leafleting, and picketing (Sharp, 1972). Demonstrations publicize issues and, perhaps more importantly, serve as an easy, successful, short-term action that often has the added effect of creating a sense of group purpose and accomplishment.

Demands

Making demands has become a familiar tactic for community organizers and consumer groups. Demands can take the form of a bill of rights, a list of grievances, consumer needs, strike terms, and contracts. Aside from winning concessions, demands serve as effective community education tools. People often do not expect traditionally powerless groups such as parents of disabled children to make demands.

Letter Writing

Letter writing can include many effective forms — carbon copies to attorneys, public letters, leaflets, letters to editors, skywriting, newsletters, letter bulletins, letters of support, letters of complaint, letters to create a record, and open letters.

Fact Finding Forums

Forums include citizen investigation panels, town meetings, community polls, seminars by expert panels, and television question and answer programs. Any citizen can give testimony (usually five to ten minutes worth) before legislative panels, town councils, county legislatures, and school boards. If these formats do not adequately meet the advocates' objectives, alternative forums may be arranged.

Communications

Communications are the heart of any advocacy effort. In addition to newsletters and town meetings, organizers may use a variety of communication networks and media. Among them are booklets, pamphlets, seminars, workshops, slide shows, movies, resource guides, press conferences, television debates, radio shows, exposés, phoning campaigns, advertisements, public service announcements, press releases, and posters. In order to change policies and practices, one first must change attitudes. Communications help to educate the community. They serve as the symbol that advocacy is alive and will influence the future.

Symbolic Acts

Perhaps the most fun of all the organizing tactics is the symbolic act — usually a mock event or a theatrical rendition of an actual problem. The symbolic act calls attention, often sarcastically, to a policy or practice or need that deserves exposure. The refusal of an award, for example, can focus attention on the event and an issue. Because it appears shocking or unusual, the symbolic act is talked about long after the action has occurred. For that reason, the symbolic act must be chosen with utmost caution.

Negotiations

In every type of organizing effort, there will be times when confrontation is not needed, when negotiations such as fair hearings, meetings with bureaucracies, individual negotiations, and contract bargaining achieve the same concessions. Negotiation always should be a first step in a series of actions, if only to find out where the policymakers stand.

Education

Workshops, teach-ins, consciousness raising groups, consumer meetings, speakers bureaus, speeches, posters, and newspapers fall into the category of education. Workshops or teach-ins help to build skills among consumer groups. A workshop or teach-in is a good way to bring together various groups; workshops also highlight community needs. When hundreds of parents attend a workshop on legal rights, for example, the community at large will realize that legal rights are an issue to be reckoned with.

Boycotts

Boycotts, (strikes, noncooperation, slow compliance, stalling, refusal to pay for services, and work-ins) are a familiar organizing tactic — but a difficult tool for advocates of children. In order to boycott, one must have something to boycott. Economic boycotts work, for example, because businesses need consumers to buy their products. But schools do not *need* disabled children in order to survive. In fact, schools and other human services sometimes are content to serve only typical children (*Children's Defense Fund,* 1974). Furthermore, a boycott with children as the prized commodity may victimize the children by keeping them out of much needed services.

Despite these warnings, a brief boycott (one week, perhaps) sometimes can prove so embarrassing to policymakers that it will provoke change.

Lobbying

Advocacy for legislative change or administrative policy change involving a variety of tactics — phone calls, petitions, alternative budgets and alternative plans, telegram campaigns, and public statements — may be described as lobbying. The purpose of lobbying is, obviously, to change laws and policies so they more closely reflect one's interests. While lobbying often has been regarded as the key strategy for change, legislative or policy change always must be accompanied by change at the local day-to-day level where children actually live their lives. Advocacy has no single track solution.

Model Programs

Group homes, integrated day care, vocational training, information and referral, physical therapy, and special education may be considered as model programs. The creation of alternative social institutions often forces existing institutions to change. However, if there is a need for new service agencies in the community, these should be organized separately from advocacy programs so as not to confuse advocacy with providing direct services. Again, the advocate monitors human services but does not provide them.

Legal Advocacy

Law has been a favorite strategy of nearly every social change movement in America. It is an indispensable tool for advocates. Legal advocacy includes lawsuits, legal memoranda, legal rights booklets for lay citizens, civil rights statements, legal representation in fair hearings and other negotiations, and legal advice.

Demystifying

Demystifying is the final strategy on the list, and one of the most important of all. Professionals can empower their allies, consumers of services, by translating research findings, diagnostic terms, testing procedures, and all other elements of education and service into everyday language. Too often, pseudo-scientific jargon becomes a method for professionals to intimidate and control consumers rather than to assist communication and development. For professionals seeking a role in advocacy, demystifying the profession may be a most valuable contribution.

THE FUTURE OF ADVOCACY

Anyone who has engaged in advocacy probably has heard the various warnings: "Don't push too fast," "Don't use children for your test case," and "Don't be so negative." Ironically, advocates rarely do any of these things. But perhaps the warnings actually reflect another concern — that social change is inconvenient and sometimes even painful. Most advocacy groups seek the enforcement of longstanding rights which, whether purposely or inadvertently, have been ignored. As for advocates *using* children, that is always a real question for people involved in human service for children, at least whenever children do not participate in the decision making themselves. Finally, advocates may be perceived at times as "negative" for all their tradition breaking, demystifying, and irreverence; but they are not pessimistic. In fact, a precondition for advocacy is optimism. People do not work for social change unless they believe change is possible.

Fortunately, advocates do not have to take optimism as an act of faith. Despite all of the cynicism surrounding any effort to create change, whether through deinstitutionalization, mainstreaming, or normalization, concrete successes exist to sustain feelings of optimism. These include:

— Legislative, legal, and policy changes (Abeson, 1974) that have enabled more children with disabilities to attend public schools.
— Concise analytic reports of the important issues, including school exclusion *(Task Force on Children,* 1971; *Children's Defense Fund,* 1974) and institutional abuse (Blatt, 1973; Rivera, 1972).
— New ways of thinking about human services (Sarason, 1970; Wolfensberger, 1972b). One can witness changes in our language: Instead of privileges, we speak of rights (Gilhool, 1973). It is now more appropriate and acceptable than ever to look at society as a cause of handicap as much as one might look to a person's fate by birth. And, most importantly, an awareness is emerging that no parent or person with a disability need feel alone and isolated in his or her struggle for change.

If all these developments seem modest when measured against continued labeling, dehumanization, and nonservice, then what better reason to call for an expanded advocacy movement?

REFERENCES

Abeson, A. Movement and momentum: Government and the education of handicapped children, II. *Exceptional Children,* 1974, *41,* 109-115.
Alinsky, S. *Rules for radicals.* New York: Vintage Books, 1972.

Biklen, D. *Let our children go: An organizing manual for parents and advocates.* Syracuse, NY: Human Policy Press, 1974.

Blatt, B. *Exodus from pandemonium.* Boston: Allyn & Bacon, 1970.

Blatt, B. (Ed.). *Souls in extremis.* Boston: Allyn & Bacon, 1973.

Children's Defense Fund. *Children out of school in America.* Cambridge, MA: Author, 1974.

Gilhool, T. K. Education: An inalienable right. *Exceptional Children,* 1973, *39,* 597-609.

Kahn, A., Kamerman, S., & McGowan, B. *Child advocacy: Report of a national baseline study.* Washington, DC: U.S. Department of Health, Education & Welfare, 1972.

Kriegel, L. Uncle Tom and Tiny Tim: Some reflections on the cripple as Negro. *The American Scholar,* 1969, 38(3), 412-430.

New York State Board of Regents, *Position paper, #20.* Albany: New York State Education Department, 1973.

O. M. Collective. *The organizer's manual.* New York: Bantam, 1971.

Pennsylvania Association for Retarded Children v. *Commonwealth of Pennsylvania.* Civil Action No. 71-42, Order, Injunction, and Consent Agreement, October 7, 1971.

Rivera G. *Willowbrook: A report on how it is and why it doesn't have to be that way.* New York: Vintage, 1972.

Ross, D. *A public citizen's action manual.* New York: Grossman, 1973.

Sarason, S. B. *The culture of the school and the problem of change.* Boston: Allyn & Bacon, 1970.

Sharp, G. *The politics of nonviolent action.* Boston: Porter Sargent, 1972.

Task Force on Children Out of School. *The exclusion of children in Boston.* Boston: Beacon Press, 1971.

Task Force on Children Out of School. *Suffer the children: The politics of mental health.* Boston: The Task Force, 1972.

Wolfensberger, W. *Citizen advocacy.* Toronto: National Institute of Mental Retardation, 1972. (a)

Wolfensberger, W. *The principle of normalization in human services.* Toronto: National Institute of Mental Retardation, 1972. (b).